D1617544

States and Markets

States and Markets

Comparing Japan and Russia

Guoli Liu

Westview Press

BOULDER • SAN FRANCISCO • OXFORD

Copyright © 1994 by Westview Press, Inc.

Published in 1994 in the United States of America by Westview Press Inc., 5500 Central Avenue, Boulder, Colorado 80301-2877, and in the United Kingdom by Westview Press, 36 Lonsdale Road, Summertown, Oxford OX2 7EW

Library of Congress Cataloging-in-Publication Data
States and markets : comparing Japan and Russia / by Guoli Liu.
    p. cm.
  Includes bibliographical references and index.
  ISBN 0-8133-8799-X
  1. Industry and state—Japan.   2. Industry and state—Russia.
3. Industry and state—Soviet Union.   4. Industry and state—Russia
(Federation)   5. Japan—Politics and government—1968–   6. Russia
(Federation)—Politics and government.   7. Japan—Economic
policy—1989–   8. Russia (Federation)—Economic policy—1991–
I. Title.
HD3616.J32L58   1994
338.947—dc20
                                                                                                          93-34543
                                                                                                          CIP

Printed and bound in the United States of America

The paper used in this publication meets the requirements
of the American National Standard for Permanence of Paper
for Printed Library Materials Z39.48-1984.

10   9   8   7   6   5   4   3   2   1

Contents

Interaction of Internal and External Factors, 131
Re-examining Key Lessons from Japan, 133
Learning from Comparative Analysis, 136
Questions and Prospects, 140
Notes, 144

Foreword

Initial excitement in the West over the reform of Soviet communism under Gorbachev and then euphoria over the disintegration of the USSR have now been replaced by concern, controversy, and sometimes despair over prospects for democracy and a market economy in the countries of the former Soviet Union. Despair is reflected in the popular joke that the transition from a communist centrally planned economy to a capitalist market economy is like the transition from fish soup to an aquarium. Only time will tell if the aquarium analogy holds water. Meanwhile, as policy makers in Russia and elsewhere in the former Soviet Union grapple with strategies, tactics, and details, scholars and policy advisors continue to debate questions of sequence, timing, and appropriate models.

With regard to sequence, some assert that economic reform is primarily a political process; others focus more exclusively on economic institutions in the process of economic reform. Aspects of this debate are holdovers from the Gorbachev era when pundits argued over whether political reform should precede economic reform, or economic reform should precede political reform, or both should occur simultaneously.

With regard to timing, some argue in favor of "shock therapy" for rapid economic change as embodied in the 1990 Shatalin 500-day plan (Jeffrey Sachs and Anders Aslund); others argue for a more gradual approach because of the necessity to build political consensus (Padma Desai) or because "shock therapy" goes against the grain of 1,000 years of Russian history and, therefore, condemns to failure progress toward democracy (Stephen F. Cohen).

There also is divergence of opinion concerning appropriate models both for Russia's transition to a market economy and the type of market economy it should seek to establish. Given the success of "shock therapy" in creating economic stabilization and market economies in Bolivia and Poland, Jeffrey Sachs holds them up as models for Russia. But skeptics could argue that current conditions and enduring historical factors (of both near and distant origin) are so different that neither country is a relevant model for Russia. Although China may serve as a "laboratory experiment" should Russia choose to implement reforms similar to China's privatization of agriculture, China won't do as a model for Russian economic reform because the Stalinist model has a longer history and is more deeply ingrained in the Russian/Soviet experience than anywhere else (Marshall I. Goldman) and the Russian state sector is much larger than China's (Sachs) with the result that Russia has a stronger and more resistant bureaucracy, a qualitatively different level of economic development, and greater "distortions" in its society (Aslund). Nor can China serve as a model for gradualism because of Russia's much larger state sector that is the very source of bureaucracy, inertia, and inefficiency. Neither is Hungary an appropriate model (Aslund), since a good degree of state intervention will be required and that can happen successfully only in a country with an orderly society and state administration (i.e., Hungary, but not Russia).

Economists such as Aslund prefer the analytical-structural approach; political scientists such as Cohen prefer the historical-cultural approach. As a result, Cohen stresses that Russia will have to "find its own way"; it simply cannot do it the American or any other way. Again, one has to take account of 1,000 years of Russian history and (one must add) the fear of at least some Russian citizens, managers, and officials that the United States and other capitalist countries want privatization/marketization in Russia in order to reduce it to the status of a Third World country whose main contribution to the world economy is the export of raw materials.

Despite these differences, there is some agreement concerning the role of the state, not only in the transition to a market economy in Russia but also in its practice. Although there have been reforms in the direction of privatization and marketization, a large state sector will remain a fixture of the post-command economy, says Cohen, because it is a Russian tradition. Aslund agrees that the state is the most crucial economic institution, although he feels its capacity is limited because both Russian society and its state administration are "less orderly."

This leads us to the question of an appropriate balance between states and markets, and that is precisely the question addressed by Guoli Liu in his exploration of the relevance of the Japanese experience for contemporary Russia in this important and timely book.

Building on Robert Gilpin's seminal study of "the mutual interactions of very different means for ordering and organizing human activities: the state and the market" (*The Political Economy of International Relations*, 1987), Dr. Liu has produced a worthy successor to the first detailed attempt to compare the political economies of Japan and Russia: *The Modernization of Japan and Russia: A Comparative Analysis* (1975) by Cyril E. Black and his colleagues. After comparing the role of the state and the market in Russian and Japanese economic and political development in the pre-Soviet and Soviet periods, Dr. Liu then inquires into the synergistic relationships between marketization and democratization during the period of *perestroika* in the USSR. His analysis and conclusions will help us all understand much better the dynamics of Russian economic reform in the post-Soviet era.

There are, to be sure, great differences between the cultures, the political systems, and the historical development of the two countries relating to the state and the market. Among other issues, the Japanese state relied on cooperation with the market, while the Soviet state relied on an administrative command system to implement its plans. Nevertheless, as the author points out, the two countries share the important tradition of a strong state and a weak market. It is perhaps for this reason that there are signs that first Mikhail Gorbachev, and then Boris Yeltsin, have looked to Japan as a potentially appropriate model for the USSR and now Russia to "find its own way." As Russians move toward capitalism there is another important reason for them to look to Japan. Lester Thurow reminds us in *Head to Head* (1992) that there are two quite different forms of capitalism in the world today: one based on individualistic values, as in the United States and Great Britain; another based on communitarian values, as in Germany and Japan. Communitarian capitalism seems more suited to Russian culture, in which a tradition of communalism has been deeply embedded for centuries.

There were clear signs that by the late 1980s the Soviet leadership was increasingly aware of the necessity to move away from its traditional administrative command system as the result of both internal and external pressures. Among the external pressures were the growth of global interdependence and the internationalization of markets. Autarky was out; interdependence was in. A major problem now facing Russia is that it is trying to become an economic superpower at a time when the nature of international competition is itself undergoing a radical transformation from what Thurow calls niche competition to head-to-head competition: "Niche competition is win-win. Everyone has a place where they can excel; no one is going to be driven out of business. Head-to-head competition is win-lose. Not everyone will get those seven key industries. Some will win; some will lose" [*Head to Head: The Coming Economic Battle Among Japan, Europe, and America* (New York: William Morrow, 1992), 30]. Hence, not only must Russia shift its priorities from military to economic competition, it must position itself to compete in a head-to-head fashion. If Russia positions itself to compete in niche competition, it will repeat an error the Soviet Union made at the end of World War II when it rebuilt its damaged economy on the basis of 1930s technology at a time when most advanced countries were undergoing a technological revolution. The result of that error was to put the Soviet Union decades behind the United States, Japan, and Western Europe. Russia and the other successor states of the USSR cannot afford to repeat this type of blunder. How Russia will respond to these challenges and what the Soviets learned and the Russians can learn from the Japanese experience in economic and political development are the focus of this book.

Frederic J. Fleron, Jr.

Acknowledgments

During several years of research and writing of this book, Professor Frederic J. Fleron, Jr., provided guidance and intellectual stimulation. He made valuable comments on the drafts, and helped make the connections between social science theories and area studies. Professors Gary Hoskin and Claude E. Welch, Jr., offered advice and helpful comments. I would like to thank all of them for enlightening me on significant political and socioeconomic questions. I appreciate the strong support provided by the Department of Political Science at the State University of New York at Buffalo.

The contribution of many scholars are acknowledged in the notes and bibliography. By building on their findings, I hope that this book adds new insights on the changing patterns of state-market relations in Japan and Russia.

I am grateful to Susan McEachern for her support and encouragement. Jeanne Saraceni and Karla Merrifield provided assistance with enthusiasm and superb skills.

Guoli Liu

1

Introduction

> *LEVIATHAN hath the use of*
> *so much Power and Strength*
> ---- Thomas Hobbes

Japan and Russia are different in many respects, but they share a tradition of a strong state and a weak market. Traditionally, the states of the two countries were leviathans dominating their societies and economies. The leviathans harnessed or suppressed market forces to serve state interests as perceived and defined by the political elites. The Japanese leviathan was defeated and reformed by the Americans as a result of World War II. With a fundamentally restructured but more effective state, the Japanese economy gained unprecedented vitality and strength. The tsarist state was destroyed by the Bolshevik revolution in 1917 and replaced by a new leviathan with even greater totalitarian and authoritarian features. The market was not allowed much space to operate, except in the informal sectors. Mikhail Gorbachev and his successor, Boris Yeltsin, have been trying to tame the Russian leviathan, but they face greater difficulties than the Japanese, because they are dismantling their leviathan without a war.

Social scientists and policy makers are facing two extraordinary cases of state-market relations: First, the collapse of the Soviet party-state and centrally planned economy and the emergence of multi-party politics and a market economy in newly independent Russian and other post-Soviet republics;[1] and second, the dramatic growth of the Japanese "plan-oriented market economy" in which the state plays an active role.

While Russia and other newly independent states are moving from communist totalitarian rule to representative democracy, and from a centrally planned economy to a market-oriented economy, it is important to examine the possible lessons from Japan. We shall explain in detail later about why we compare and

1

contrast state-market relations in Japan and Russia/USSR. One significant factor is that Japan is one of the few countries that has made the transition from authoritarian rule to democracy and from a militaristic state economy to market-oriented economy. In analyzing what the post-Soviet states can learn from Japan, the central theoretical concern of this study is the dynamics of the transition from command to market economies, and from totalitarian and authoritarian dictatorship to democracy.

The debate on state-market relations is not a purely intellectual exercise. It has great practical implications, e.g., countries following different lines of argument in the debate have taken sharply contrasting roads of political and economic development. At their early stage of modernization, Japan and Russia followed the road of state capitalism. Modernizing reforms in the two countries stressed the role of the state in economic development.

After several decades of the development of state capitalism, the two countries experienced dramatically different transformation in their state-market relations. Following the 1917 revolution, the Bolsheviks attempted to limit and eliminate the market. Stalin's revolution from above in the late 1920s and early 1930s created the foundation of the centrally planned economy which lasted until the late 1980s. In Japan, state capitalism deteriorated into a *zaibatsu-* (big family-controlled financial cliques) dominated economy. The rise of the militarists and fascists in the 1930s and early 1940s resulted in an extremely authoritarian regime and highly centralized economy in Japan. Russia/USSR and prewar Japan did not have a tradition of free market economics.

The more contrasting cases are Japan and the USSR in the postwar era. The last half-century witnessed the decline of the military and the rise of the trading state in Japan on the one hand and the expansion of Soviet military power and stagnation of the Soviet economy and society on the other hand. The defeat in World War II and the American occupation facilitated the rise of the trading state in Japan. In the postwar era, the Soviet Union continued its military and political expansion but went through economic stagnation and decline.[2] In the late 1980s, the USSR entered deep political and socioeconomic crisis while Japan emerged as an economic superpower.

Soviet reformers realized that the old Stalinist system did not work. They also recognized the danger of further economic crisis and political instability in the absence of fundamental systemwide reform. However, there has been no consensus on reform strategy and agenda. The Soviet leaders did not have a "theory of simultaneous transitions from a totalitarian/authoritarian to a liberal/socialist or social democratic government and from a planned to a mixed or market economy."[3]

This study will contribute to the search for such a theory by comparative analysis of state-market relations in Japan and Russia/USSR from 1861 to 1991. Although there is a large body of literature on Japan and Russia/USSR respectively, there are few explicitly comparative analyses of the two countries except the excellent work by Cyril Black and his colleagues.[4] With dramatic changes in both countries in the last two decades and with the advantages of new materials made available by *glasnost,* now is the time for more efforts at comparative analysis of Japan and Russia/USSR in general and in their state-market relations in particular.

Jerry Hough suggested that Mikhail Gorbachev was looking at Japan for a model of development.[5] Gorbachev made it clear during his visit to Tokyo in 1991 that the Soviet Union could learn much from Japan. Boris Yeltsin and some of his advisers also realized that Japan can be a model to build a competitive economy based on high technology and active participation in the world market.[6] However, there has been no serious academic analysis of the lessons from Japan for the Soviet Union comparable to the research on Japan and the United States, Japan and Great Britain, or Japan and the newly industrialized economies.[7]

By focusing on state-market relations, we can better understand the changing nature of the Japanese and Russian/Soviet states. As Andrew Janos recently pointed out, many scholars studying industrialization and/or modernization of the Soviet Union missed the militaristic nature of the Soviet state as described by Herbert Spencer.[8] Thus, they have had enormous difficulty in understanding the "genuine shift from the principles of militancy to true industrialism" taking place in the former Soviet Union.[9] A similar weakness existed in many works on Japanese modernization. Most analysts saw big differences between prewar and postwar Japanese society in terms of level of economic development and the degree of democratic participation. However, many of them missed the dramatic transformation in state-market relations and the changed nature of the state. Of course, there are exceptions to this general statement. For instance, Richard Rosecrance insightfully pointed out the dramatic shift from the military-territorial state to the trading state in postwar Japan.[10] According to Paul Kennedy, the history of the rise and fall of the "Great Powers" in the last five centuries "shows a very significant correlation *over the longer term* between productive and revenue-raising capacities on the one hand and military strength on the other."[11] This study can strengthen Janos', Rosecrance's, and Kennedy's theses of transition from militancy to industrialism and from the military state to the trading state by comparing the transition process in Japan and Russia/USSR.

The long-term comparative historical analysis taken by this study contributes to discovering the underlying patterns of state-market relations in Japan and Russia/USSR. Facing an information explosion regarding the two countries, we find that a large proportion of the literature is about short-term policy problems rather than long-term historical macro-trends. Experience suggests that research focusing on short-term, on-going events is not necessarily useful for theoretical construction. We believe that studying the key turning points in state-market relations in Japan and Russia/USSR between 1861 and 1991 will help us reveal the historical patterns of development and avoid being deceived by short-term ups and downs.

Furthermore, this study provides not only theoretical analysis but also policy suggestions on the lessons from Japan for the new Russia and other post-Soviet states. There are key lessons from Japan that can be very instructive for the post-Soviet states in their historical transition from a command economy to a market-oriented economy. Lessons from Japan can be especially relevant for Russia because they shared the common experience of highly militaristic state control of the economy and society.[12] Japan is a potentially influential model for post-Soviet development because many post-Soviet elites have expressed appreciation of the Japanese competitiveness in the world market. Considering the historical and contemporary differences between Japan and the post-Soviet states, are the lessons from Japan repeatable in Russia and other republics? We shall demonstrate below that the answer is affirmative. Differences among nations do not preclude mutual learning. In fact, Japan was/is quite different from the West in many aspects. Nevertheless, Japan has succeeded in learning from the advanced Western nations in important political and economic fields.

Ideal Types and Models of State-Market Relations

State-market relations is a topic of long-standing controversy in the social sciences. Two of the earliest theorists on this subject, Adam Smith and Karl Marx, had profound impacts on the development of the market economy and the planned economy respectively. As the leading advocate of the free market system, Smith viewed the market as an alternative to government control of economic life. Smith saw the state as a necessary evil whose functions should be limited to some clearly defined fields. Marx, on the other hand, was antagonistic toward the capitalist market. He stressed the role of the state as a tool of the ruling class. In his original design, contrary to the highly centralized state in the Soviet Union, the state would wither away following the proletarian revolution.

Marx's theory was once held as official ideology by the Soviet Union and its allies. However, most believers of the theory found it was impossible to put the classic Marxist theory into practice because it was too utopian. Lenin revised Marxism; Stalin created his own version of Marxism-Leninism. All other former communist countries had to make revisions of Marxism in order to adjust it to their specific conditions. The 1989 revolution in Eastern Europe and dramatic changes in the Soviet Union since then have totally discredited the official ideology.

From a different perspective, Max Weber analyzed the two ideal types of market economy and planned economy; his theoretical formulation provided insights into the current debates on the state and the market. Weber pointed out the essential difference between a market and a planned economy: In a "market economy" economic action is oriented to advantages in exchange on the basis of self-interest. In a "planned economy," in contrast, economic action is oriented systematically to an established substantive order, whether agreed or imposed, which is valid within an organization.[13]

Weber agreed with Smith that free and rational pursuit of self-interest is the essence of the market economy: "The market economy is by far the most important case of typical widespread social action predominantly oriented to 'self-interest.'"[14] But Weber pointed out an ideal type of planned economy, unimagined by Smith, in which authority rather than exchange was the norm. Weber clearly warned of the danger of economic bureaucratization without the market. "The abolition of private capitalism would simply mean that also the top management of the nationalized or socialized enterprises would become bureaucratic. ... State bureaucracy would rule alone if private capitalism were eliminated."[15]

The relationship between politics and the economy has been discussed by scholars from different perspectives and with different approaches. Charles Lindblom proposes "exchange" and "authority" as the central concepts of political economy. Charles Kindleberger prefers "power" and "money"; Richard Rosecrance contrasts "market" and "territoriality."[16]

Following the Weberian tradition, Robert Gilpin conceptualized two ideal types of state-market relations, i.e., a purely political world and a purely market world.

In a purely political world in which the market did not exist, the state would allocate available resources on the basis of its social and political objectives; such state allocative decisions would take the form of the state's budget. In a purely "market" world in which state intervention did not occur, the market would allocate and operate on the basis of relative prices of goods and services; decisions would take the form of the individual pursuit of self-interest.[17]

There are inherent tensions between the state and the market because they follow different logic. "The logic of the market is to locate economic activities where they are most productive and profitable; the logic of the state is to capture and control the process of economic growth and capital accumulation."[18] Due to its internal tensions and conflicts, a market economy has its cycles of expansion and stagnation, boom and recession or even depression. There is always the danger of market failure, e.g., the rise of unemployment and negligence of public welfare. The resulting tendency, therefore, is "for states to intervene in economic activities in order to advance the effects of markets beneficial to themselves and to counter those that are detrimental."[19]

In short, markets constitute a powerful source of sociopolitical change and produce equally powerful responses as societies attempt to protect themselves against negative impacts of market forces. No state permits the full and unregulated development of market forces. A market is not politically neutral; its existence creates economic power which one actor can use against another.[20] Similarly, a state is not neutral either. A state can play a critical role by making authoritative decisions regarding the production and distribution of goods and by influencing supply and demand. However, a "strong and interventionist state does not guarantee economic development; indeed, it might retard it."[21]

In *Fundamentals of the Economic Role of Government*, Warren J. Samuels critically scrutinized diverse approaches to the economic role of the state and pointed out that the "market-plus-framework approach is probably the dominant paradigm" in the social sciences. "It maintains that the market exists within a framework of legal and nonlegal institutions that both form and work through the market."[22]

States with different structures and ideological orientations can play various roles in economic development. There are fundamental differences between the centrally planned Soviet economy and the plan-oriented Japanese market economy. The Soviet government defined its economy as a "centrally planned economy." However, the Soviet model did not fit the ideal-type planned economy because of the existence of the informal adjustment mechanisms, including the second economy, and "rampant particularism and irrationality."[23] Although described as a "plan-oriented market economy," the Japanese model does not fit the ideal type market economy well. The role of the Japanese state in economic planning and development is so significant that scholars tend to view it as a "developmental state."[24]

In short, the Weberian ideal types of planned economy and market economy and Gilpin's conceptualization of the purely political world and purely market world are the basic starting point of this research. We view Japan and Russia/USSR as traditionally closer to the planned economy. Japan made a fundamental transition toward the market economy following World War II and American Occupation reforms. In spite of such dramatic change, contemporary Japan is still substantially different from more market-oriented countries like Great Britain and the United States. The Japanese state plays a more active role than many of its Western counterparts.

Nevertheless, fundamentally speaking, Japan today is closer to the market economy than the planned economy. Russia and other post-Soviet states are making the transition from a centrally planned economy to a market-oriented economy. The changing role of the state in this critical transition is the focus of our analysis. In addition to the Weberian ideal types and Gilpin's analysis, we will explore later the relevance of other theoretical models.[25]

Expansion and Decline of the Militaristic States

Both Russia and Japan carried out defensive modernization. As a result, Russia developed the largest standing army in the world. Japan's Meiji Restoration reflected the determination of its elite to avoid being dominated and colonized by the West. Japan had to be modernized not simply because individual entrepreneurs wished it, but because the "state" needed it. For Russians and Japanese striving to modernize their countries, economic power and military power went hand in hand. That was true for most great powers in the pre-World War II era.

The historian Paul Kennedy pointed out the strong statist tradition was combined with militaristic samurai spirit in Japan:

> It seems indisputable that the strong Japanese sense of cultural uniqueness, the traditions of emperor worship and veneration of the state, the samurai ethos of military honor and valor, the emphasis upon discipline and fortitude, produced a political culture at once fiercely patriotic and unlikely to be deterred by sacrifices and reinforced the Japanese impulses to expand into "Greater East Asia," for strategic security as well as markets and raw materials.[26]

With their victory in the 1895 war with China and the 1905 war with Russia, Japan's armed forces were glorified and admired. The military and fervent nationalists gained increasing influence in Japan as a consequence of the economic depression in the late 1920s, which deepened the sociopolitical crisis in Japan. They assassinated civilian leaders who opposed their aggressive policy. The military's share of government spending rose from 31 percent in 1931-1932 to 47 percent in 1936-1937. After the assassination of finance minister Takahashi, the armed services took 70 percent of government expenditure in 1937-1938.[27] Johnson described the rise of the "economic general staff:" The advent of rationing raised new demands that an "economic general staff" be empowered to plan for the whole economy. This economic general staff, in the form of the Cabinet Planning Board, came into being on October 23, 1937, under the added impetus of the China Incident.[28]

In addition to taking the lion's share of government expenditure, the Japanese military had ready access to manpower because of conscription. Pursuing a military expansionist policy, the Japanese army invaded Northeast China in 1931, following it with a large-scale invasion in 1937. The war on the Chinese mainland increasingly became a big burden for the Japanese economy. When Japanese military expansion came into conflict with the U.S. open door policy, the United States used economic sanctions against Japan. In order to build its dream of the Great East Asian Co-prosperity Sphere and achieve economic autarky, Japan finally initiated the surprise attack on Pearl Harbor and started the Pacific War.[29] Japan moved toward total failure because it over-stretched itself by fighting wars simultaneously on the East Asian continent and in the Pacific.

The failure of Japan's militaristic expansion and its defeat in World War II were followed by a thorough de-militarization during the American occupation. The occupation reforms fundamentally changed the nature of the Japanese state and helped to form the basic characteristics of postwar state-market relations in Japan. Article 9 of the Japanese constitution, written by the Americans, states: "the Japanese people forever renounce war as a sovereign right of the nation and the threat or use of force as means of settling international disputes. ... Land, sea and air forces, as well as other war potential, will never be maintained."[30] This new constitution laid down the legal foundation for building a trading state.

Foreign expansion was a deeply rooted tradition in Russia, which grew from a small state into a multi-national continental empire. Russian industrialization was very closely related to military needs--railways, iron and steel, armaments, and so on. Russia's socioeconomic backwardness in comparison with the West and its military expansionist policy led the country into a deep sociopolitical crisis at the beginning of the twentieth century. Military failures in World War I resulted in a revolutionary crisis that provided the Bolsheviks a historic opportunity to seize power.

The 1917 revolution transformed the Russian political system. However, the Stalinist revolution from above was more fundamental and far-reaching in its socioeconomic and political impact. Stalin's revolution also dramatically transformed state-market relations. In the 1930s, the foundation of the Soviet centralized party-state and administrative command economy was established.

In spite of dramatic transformation, there was a strong continuity between tsarist Russia and the Soviet Union in the strong militaristic nature of the centralized state. In 1931, for instance, Stalin urged his fellow citizens to close the productive gap with the West. To slacken the tempo would mean falling behind. And those who fall behind get beaten. The Russia of the tsars had suffered "continual beatings" because it had fallen behind in industrial productivity and military strength.[31] Therefore, Soviet industrialization was driven by the need to build a strong base for military power.

As Janos suggested, the Soviet society was a military society and a garrison state as described by Spencer.

> Stalin created a perfect example of Spencer's model of militancy--a powerful military state in which the 'industrial part of society' remained a 'mere commissariat existing solely to supply the needs of governmental-military structures of an externally powerful state.' The term garrison state is therefore not an inappropriate description of the Stalinist political system.[32]

According to Janos, the "post-Stalin period witnessed the decline of charismatic salvationism but not the end of militancy and externally oriented public policy." He argued that the Soviet Union was a military society under Stalin and remained a military society under Stalin's successors. The post-Soviet states are in the throes of devolution from Spencerian militancy to competitive industrialism.[33]

In order to build a strong military on a relative backward socioeconomic basis, both the tsarist and the Stalinist regimes resorted to compulsory service for the Russian/Soviet people. Compulsory service system in Russia became a big obstacle for the development of market capitalism. As Weber pointed out:

A system of provision by compulsory services in kind hinders the development of market capitalism above all through the confiscation of the labor force and the consequent impediments to the development of a free labor market. It is unfavorable to politically oriented capitalism because it removes the typical prospective advantages which enable it to develop.[34]

The centrally planned economy well served the purpose of building a strong army and a heavy industrial base with extensive growth strategy. However, the expansion of Soviet military-industrial complex was achieved by exploiting agriculture and sacrificing other industrial and consumer sectors. At the advanced level of modernization, the Soviet Union was losing a competitive edge to the advanced market economies not only in civilian but also in military technology.[35]

There emerged a paradoxical situation in the Soviet Union. On the one hand, the Soviet Union substantially increased the destructive power of its military. It developed a new class of intermediate-range nuclear missiles, the SS20. Soviet military spending grew steadily throughout the 1970s. On the other hand, the Soviet economy was not able to produce any significant consumer goods that were competitive in the world market. By the 1980s, South Korea was exporting more to the world market than the Soviet Union. What made matters worse was that the Soviet economy was not only losing competitiveness in the world market but also increasingly having difficulty in meeting the daily needs of the Soviet citizens.

The rapid expansion of Soviet military and strategic forces raised serious concerns among other countries. It became clear that the USSR could not escape from the classic security dilemma. The Soviet policy of single-minded expansion of military power did not enhance the level of security but created new tensions between East and West. In the early 1980s, the Soviet Union found that it had stimulated a hostile alliance of nations ringing its borders. Nuclear deterrence limited the possibility of direct Soviet military applications of force. The costly Soviet military build-up had not succeeded in producing political and economic advantages.[36]

By 1987, the Soviet economy was on a downward spiral that could easily become a free fall. Economic growth continued to slow to the point that by 1989 the Soviet economy actually declined. The next three years witnessed a deep crisis of the Soviet economy and a sharp decline of productivity.[37] The Soviet Union was forced to change its expansionist policy. The withdrawal from

Afghanistan, the removal of SS20 missiles from the Western part of the Soviet Union, and the breakup of the East European satellite system all reflected the decline of the Soviet militaristic state. The emergence of new political thinking was not incidental. It reflected Gorbachev and other reformers' realistic diagnosis of the Soviet dilemma and their perception of the changing nature of power in the contemporary world. Gorbachev explained a key reason for his initiative with President Reagan to stop the cold war: the former defeated powers like Japan and Germany were rising high in the world market while the USSR and the U.S. were still trapped in a costly arms race.[38]

Transition to the Trading State:
The Japanese Experience and the Soviet Dilemma

If Janos is right, then the post-Soviet states are in the throes of devolution from Spencerian militancy to competitive industrialism. Translated into Richard Rosecrance's language, the devolution process is the shift from a military-territorial state to a trading state. Some observers are quick to conclude that the collapse of the Soviet Union and the end of the Cold War represented the end of history.[39] But foresighted analysts do see the beginning of a new historic era in which trading states rather than military states are becoming increasingly prominent.

Rosecrance pointed out the fundamental differences between the two kinds of state:

> ...military-political and territorial states are homogeneous competing countries. Each seeks to secure hegemony or at a minimum to gain independence and self-sufficiency from foreign control. They do not generally cooperate except when the balance of power requires opposition to a hegemonic aspirant. Trading states, in contrast, are interdependent nations which accept equality of status on the basis of differentiation of function. Their objectives--to improve national welfare and the allocation of resources through internal development and trade--do not require preventing other states from achieving similar goals.[40]

If war is costly, difficult, and uncertain; if trading strategies hold out the prospects of rapid new growth, the latter will likely be selected as the primary means of national advancement. Many nations, and Japan first among them, have accepted heavy dependence on the resources and markets provided by the rest of the world. Japan relies on the trading system for its sustenance and growth. The trading states improve their positions by improving domestic production and promoting international trade. As their industries became more competitive and could sell more effectively in world markets, they would gain a large share of world trade and corresponding advantages in economic growth rates. Trading states like Japan and Germany no longer think of improving their national positions through territorial gain but rather seek to use strategies of economic growth sustained by foreign trade to maintain and increase the standard of welfare enjoyed by the population.[41] Postwar Germany and Japan succeeded economically not because of totalitarian episodes, military expansion, or traditional power politics, but because losses of empire left them with factor endowments that indisputably forced them to trade. Japan emerged as the symbolic leader of the new trading world. Through trade Japan has achieved the world's second largest GNP, surpassing the highest records of the former Soviet Union.

With a population of 123 million, just half that of the United States, Japan produces a gross national product three-fifths the size of that of the U.S. Japanese corporations now dominate the list of the world's largest business enterprises. Most of the world's largest financial firms are Japanese. In 1990, Japanese per capita GNP was $25,430, which compared favorably with that of the U.S. ($21,790) and the United Kingdom ($16,100). Japanese exports grew annually by 11.4 percent between 1965 and 1980 and by 4.2 percent between 1980 and 1990. The comparative data for the U.S. were 6.4 percent and 3.3 percent.[42]

All these factors demonstrated that it is possible for a former militaristic state to be transformed into a successful trading state. The Japanese succeeded in building a trading state not just because of good luck but more importantly because they made correct political and economic choices. External variables also played a critical role. Total failure in World War II forced the Japanese people and their leaders to reorient their policies. Having experienced frustration and defeat in the Cold War, political leaders and citizens in the post-Soviet states are facing equally challenging choices. The task of dismantling the old system has almost been completed. The more complicated work of building a new type of state-market relations has just begun. Decisions to be made during the transition period tend to be decisive for future development.

The Japanese postwar transition initially took place under the American occupation. Having an externally imposed supreme authority allowed Japanese reforms to proceed without much organized domestic resistance. Coming out of the grand failure of World War II, the majority of the Japanese people were sufficiently prepared to bear the burdens of painful reforms. The new pattern of state-market relations established after the reforms contains distinctive features.

In fact, the particular interaction of state and market in Japan is very interesting. As analyzed by John Zysman, Japanese industrial strategy assumes that the market pressures of competition can serve as an instrument of policy. It is not simply that the government makes use of competitive forces that arise naturally in the market, but rather that it often induces the very competition it directs. It induces competition by creating the market for products and the conditions for high returns, thus seemingly assuring a profit and attracting the entry of many competitors. The competition is real, but the government and the private sector also possess the mechanisms to avoid "disruptive" or "excessive" competition.[43] T. J. Pempel puts it directly: "The most central concern of the Japanese state, both prewar and postwar, has been economic development."[44]

Transition to the market is likely to be a more difficult and painful process for the post-Soviet states than it was for Japan. The main reason is that the Soviet Union was under communist rule for more than 70 years. As a result, the centrally planned economy had a deep impact on the whole society. The majority of Soviet people had no personal experience in a modern market economy. Even the reform leaders and economists only have very limited knowledge about how a market system works.

Soviet managers had been protected from outside competition for so long that they were afraid of getting into the world market. Strong protectionism does not show the strength but the weakness of a system. If the protection of the market decreases the level of competitiveness of domestic manufacturers and reduces the quality of goods produced, as the situation in many Soviet factories, then it is clear that protectionist policies lead to the weakening of the state and the economy. Gorbachev realized the failure of the old system but was hesitant to choose a new route of development. Without fundamental economic restructuring, the Soviet economy continued to decline further and further in a morass of half-measures and uncertainties. Even with decisive restructuring, the economy would continue to face serious difficulties in the near future.

In August 1990, the Shatalin workshop under Gorbachev and Yeltsin concluded that: "Mankind has not managed to create anything more efficient than a market economy. It gives strong incentives to materialize a man's abilities, to activate labor and business, and to expedite greatly the progress of science and technology."[45] The Gorbachev plan, a revised version of the Shatalin plan approved by the USSR Supreme Soviet in October 1990, also acknowledged the failure of the state-controlled economy and announced an ambitious effort to adopt a market-based system. "There is no alternative to changing over to a market system. The entire experience of the world has proven the vitality and effectiveness of a market economy."[46]

The collapse of the Soviet Union and the rise of independent states finally provided the republican leaders such as Russian President Yeltsin with the opportunity to move substantially and decisively toward the market. Although many difficulties and uncertainty still remain, the centrally planned economy ceased to function and the necessary but perhaps not sufficient political ground for the emergence of the market economy has been laid out. If they succeed, then the world would be one in which the predominant members are trading states rather than traditional military states. A world largely made of trading states will be a more peaceful and prosperous place for future generations to live.

Notes

1. As a practical solution to problems of terminology, the terms Soviet Union and the USSR will be used throughout to refer to the Union of Soviet Socialist Republics from 1917 to December 1991. Likewise, the term "the Soviets" will be used throughout to refer to people in the USSR. In addition, the term Russia is used herein to refer to either the pre-1917 Russian empire, not simply ethnic Russians, or the post-Soviet Russia according to the context.

2. See Paul Kennedy, *The Rise and Fall of the Great Powers: Economic Change and Military Conflict from 1500 to 2000* (New York: Vintage Books, 1987); and Richard Rosecrance, *The Rise of the Trading State: Commerce and Conquest in the Modern World* (New York: Basic Books, 1986).

3. Frederic J. Fleron, Jr. and Erik P. Hoffmann, "Sovietology and Perestroika: Methodology and Lessons from the Past," *The Harriman Institute Forum*, Vol. 5, No. 1 (1991), p. 8.

4. Cyril E. Black et al., *The Modernization of Japan and Russia: A Comparative Study* (New York: Free Press, 1975).

5. Jerry Hough, *Russia and the West: Gorbachev and the Politics of Reform* (Cambridge: Simon and Schuster, 1988), p. 198.

6. James Clay Moltz, "Commonwealth Economics in Perspective: Lessons from the East Asian Model," *Soviet Economy*, Vol. 7, No. 4 (1991), pp. 342-363.

7. See Ezra Vogel, *Japan as Number One: Lessons for America* (Cambridge: Harvard University Press, 1919); Ronald Dore, *Taking Japan Seriously: A Confucian Perspective on Leading Economic Issues* (London: Athlone, 1987); and Peter L. Berger and Hsin-Huang Michael Hsiao (eds.), *In Search of an East Asian Development Model* (New Brunswick and Oxford: Transactions Books, 1988).

8. Andrew C. Janos, "Social Science, Communism, and the Dynamics of Political Change," *World Politics*, Vol. 44, No. 1 (1991), pp. 81-112.

9. *Ibid.*, p. 100.

10. Rosecrance, *The Rise of the Trading State.*

11. Kennedy, *The Rise and Fall of the Great Powers*, p. xvi.

12. Both the Soviet Union and Japan experienced totalitarian and authoritarian rules. For the classic exposition of the concept of totalitarianism, see Carl J. Friedrich and Zbigniew K. Brezinski, *Totalitarian Dictatorship and Autocracy* (Cambridge: Harvard University Press, 1956). For analysis of the nature of Japanese fascism (domestic repression and foreign expansion), see Barrington Moore, Jr., *Social Origins of Dictatorship and Democracy: Land and Peasant in the Making of the Modern World* (Cambridge: Harvard University Press, 1966), esp. chapter 5.

13. Max Weber, *Economy and Society: An Outline of Interpretative Sociology* ([1922], Berkeley and Los Angeles: University of California Press, 1978), p. 109.

14

14. *Ibid.*, p. 111.

15. *Ibid.*, p. 1402.

16. Charles E. Lindblom, *Politics and Markets: The World's Political-Economic Systems* (New York: Basic Books, 1977); Charles P. Kindleberger, *Power and Money: The Economics of International Politics and the Politics of International Economics* (New York: Basic Books, 1970); and Rosecrance, *The Rise of the Trading State.*

17. Robert Gilpin, *The Political Economy of International Relations* (Princeton: Princeton University Press, 1987), p. 9.

18. Robert L. Heilbroner, *The Nature and Logic of Capitalism* (New York: W. W. Norton, 1985), pp. 94-95.

19. Gilpin, *The Political Economy of International Relations*, p. 25.

20. *Ibid.*, p. 23.

21. *Ibid.*, p. 49.

22. Warren J. Samuels (ed.), *Fundamentals of the Economic Role of Government* (New York: Greenwood, 1989), p. 216.

23. Jerry Hough, *The Soviet Prefect: the Local Party Organs in Industrial Decision-making* (Cambridge: Harvard University Press, 1969).

24. Chalmers Johnson, *MITI and the Japanese Miracle: The Growth of Industrial Policy*, 1925-1975 (Stanford: Stanford University Press, 1982).

25. *Ibid.*; George Breslauer, "On the Adaptability of Soviet Welfare-State Authoritarianism," in Erik P. Hoffmann and Robbin F. Laird (eds.), *The Soviet Polity in the Modern Era* (New York: Aldine de Gruyter, 1984), pp. 219-245; and Rosecrance, *The Rise of the Trading State.*

26. Kennedy, *The Rise and Fall of the Great Powers*, p. 208.

27. *Ibid.*, p. 300.

28. Johnson, *MITI and the Japanese Miracle*, p. 120.

29. Michael A. Barnhart, *Japan Prepares for Total War: The Search for Economic Security, 1919-1941* (Ithaca and London: Cornell University Press, 1987).

30. *The Constitution of Japan* (1947), published by U.S. Department of State, pp. 2, 3.

31. After recalling many cases of historical failures and suffering in Russian history, Stalin claimed: "We are fifty or a hundred years behind the advanced countries. We must make good this lag in ten years. Either we accomplish this or we will be crushed." Cited in Theodore H. Von Laue, *Why Lenin? Why Stalin? A Reappraisal of the Russian Revolution, 1900-1930* (Philadelphia and New York: Lippincott, 1964), p. 212.

32. Janos, "Social Science, Communism, and the Dynamics of Political Change," p. 97.

33. *Ibid.*, pp. 98, 101.

34. Weber, *Economy and Society*, p. 199.

35. Russell Bova, "The Soviet Military and Economic Reform," *Soviet Studies*, Vol. XL, No. 3 (1988), pp. 385-405.

36. Jeffrey T. Bergner, *The New Superpowers: Germany, Japan, the U.S. and the New World Order* (New York: St. Martin's, 1991), p. 16.

37. U.S. Central Intelligence Agency and U.S. Defense Intelligence Agency, *The Soviet Economy Stumbles Badly in 1989*, report to Technology and National Security Subcommittee, Joint Economic Committee of the Congress, 20 April 1990. According to PlanEcon estimates, the Soviet GNP declined 2 percent in 1990 and contracted by 14 percent in 1991. Donald W. Green, "The Soviet Economy Through Nine Months of 1991: Country Falling Apart, Economy Collapsing," *PlanEcon Report* Vol. VII, No. 43-44 (1991), pp. 1-2.

38. See "'There Is No Way We Can Turn Back': Mikhail Gorbachev Discusses Economic Reform, Nuclear Weapons and U.S.-Soviet Cooperation," *U.S. News and World Report*, Vol. 111, No. 23 (December 2, 1991), p. 67.

39. Francis Fukuyama, "The End of History?" *National Interest*, No. 16 (1989), pp. 3-18.

40. Rosecrance, *The Rise of the Trading State*, p. 28.

41. *Ibid.*, pp. 43, 48, 77.

42. Bergner, *The New Superpowers*, pp. 114-115. The World Bank, *World Development Report 1992: Development and the Environment* (New York: Oxford University Press, 1992), pp. 219, 245.

43. John Zysman, *Governments, Markets, and Growth: Financial Systems and the Politics of Industrial Change* (Ithaca and London: Cornell University Press, 1983).

44. T. J. Pempel, "Japanese Foreign Economic Policy," in Peter J. Katzenstein (ed.), *Between Power and Plenty: Foreign Economic Policies of Advanced Industrial States* (Madison: University of Wisconsin Press, 1978), p. 139.

45. A working group formed by a joint decision of M. S. Gorbachev and B. N. Yeltsin, *Transition to the Market: Part I (The Concept and Program)* (Moscow: Cultural Initiative Foundation, 1990), p. 7.

46. *Basic Guidelines for Stabilization of the National Economy and Transition to a Market Economy*, (October 19, 1990, Decree passed by the Supreme Soviet), in Foreign Broadcast Information Service (FBIS), *Daily Report on the Soviet Union*, October 22, 1990.

2

The State's Vital Role in Modernization

This chapter examines the interaction of the state and market in the modernization of Japan and Russia/USSR with an emphasis on the special role played by the state. For Japan and Russia/USSR, the period between the 1860s and the 1940s was a "transitional stage in which the two societies were transformed from a predominantly rural and agrarian to a predominantly urban and industrial way of life."[1] We shall argue that the state played extremely important roles in both countries during the transitional processes.

The Meiji Restoration was led by Japanese reformers in order to enrich the country, and more important, to strengthen the military against foreign pressure. It also was a state-building process through which the Tokugawa feudal regime was transformed into a modern centralized bureaucratic state conducive to capitalist development. The mutually supportive government- business relations were formed during the Japanese industrialization drive. Japanese modernizers selectively borrowed from the West and gradually integrated some aspects of Western civilization into the traditional Japanese culture. Through a process of conversion and adaptation, some traditional aspects of Japanese culture were made compatible with the development of modern state and market systems.

In Russia, the emancipation of serfs in 1861 facilitated the rise of state capitalism and accelerated industrialization. The 1890s was a decade of dramatic economic development. However, the First World War and revolutionary crisis drastically changed the course of Russian political and economic development. Following the 1917 revolution, the Bolsheviks attempted to suppress and eliminate the market. They nationalized the means of production and initiated centralization of economic control. War communism (1918-1921) led to a deep economic and political crisis and was replaced by the New Economic Policy (NEP). NEP allowed limited roles for the market and provided Russian farmers incentives to work. When Stalin defeated his key opponents in the party state in the late 1920s, he rejected NEP and carried out forced agricultural

18

collectivization and centrally planned industrialization. The formulation and implementation of the First Five-Year Plan was the beginning of the highly centralized command economy. Contrary to the anticipated withering away of the state as suggested by Karl Marx, the Soviet state grew into a leviathan--a gigantic, oppressive, and powerful bureaucratic machine.

The State and Modernization: The Meiji Restoration and the "Great Reform"

The decade of the 1860s was a turning point in both Japanese and Russian history. Facing challenges from the more powerful industrial states of Western Europe and North America, the reform-minded elites in Japan and Russia initiated reforms from above in order to achieve industrialization and build strong military forces. With a keen sense of urgency, many Russian and Japanese leaders saw the market as an inadequate mechanism for developing the economic basis of state power. In their view, the state was not just a regulator but also a planner, initiator, financier, and even direct entrepreneur. The Great Reform and the Meiji Restoration are well-known stories and there are excellent accounts for them.[2] Thus, we do not intend to go into historical details. What is fitting and appropriate here is to make a comparative analysis of the role of the state in the modernization of Japan and Russia.

Primary focus on the role of the state during transition can be justified. Comparative history demonstrates that countries beginning industrialization in a setting of relative backwardness require leadership and strong action to get started.[3] An effective modern state is both a means to and an end of political modernization. The state not only provided political guidance but also engaged in economic development in both Japan and Russia. By emphasizing the role of the state during transition, however, we do not mean that one should ascribe all success to government and a minor and inactive role to the private sector. The key point is that in the transitional processes the state performed many tasks of vital importance.

Modernization is not simply industrialization; it is a very complex process which involves a multitude of socioeconomic and political changes.[4] Many such changes would necessarily create tensions and conflicts within the polity and society. The state played a crucial role in conflict resolution. On the one hand, a similarity of Japan and Russia during the transitional period was the ability of government leadership to mobilize people and resources for very considerable efforts. On the other hand, the two countries demonstrated differences in the amount of coercion involved. The imperial regime in Russia from 1860 to 1917, and especially the communist government thereafter, employed far more coercion and terror than did the Japanese government.

Russia and Japan had a tradition of strong political control over society even before modernization. As Cyril E. Black and his colleagues observed: "Both Japan and Russia had known a long historic continuity as independent, integrated states, and by the nineteenth century their governments had developed an impressive capacity to mobilize skills and resources on both a regional and a national scale."[5] For example, government in both countries tended to monopolize, or at least closely regulate, such diverse activities as domestic prices, foreign trade, transportation and communications.

The political history of Japan and Russia from the 1860s to the 1940s is dominated by themes of crisis, revolution, and the conversion of older patterns to meet new needs. Such critical situations further strengthened the argument for strong state powers. Thus, it is not incidental that the first task of Meiji reforms was "political centralization."[6]

Russia's "Great Reforms" were less sweeping and innovative than the Meiji reforms. But the role of the state was also clearly visible in the emancipation of the serfs, introduction of the jury system, reform of military institutions, and new regulations for higher education. However, the "constitutional and parliamentary experimentation that occupied reformist leaders in both countries from the 1890s to the World War assumed an antiregime character in Russia, whereas in Japan it was for the most part supportive of the prevailing system."[7] Russian intelligentsia were much more critical of the regime than their Japanese counterparts.

One significant role of the state in the Japanese and Russian modernization was planning at the national level. Both governments performed unusual feats of social engineering in forecasting and planning for socioeconomic changes. It is reasonable to argue that the Japanese and Russian governments were forerunners of modern national planning. The two modernizing governments formulated development strategies and worked hard to bring about desirable changes.

In some efforts the national governments themselves assumed the central and often dominant role. The early Meiji state established industries such as cement, glass, and machine-tool factories; it also extended credit, subsidies, and technical aid to the private sector, and in 1884 adopted a ten-year plan for expansion of industry. The Russian state grew very active in industrialization. After the Bolshevik revolution and especially through the First Five-Year Plan, the Soviet state fundamentally transformed the ownership of the means of production and the ways of managing the economy and society. As a result, the party state became the single most powerful instrument of political change and economic development.

During the entire transformation period the direct role of the state was more crucial in Russia than it was in Japan. Yet, the role of government in Japanese growth was by no means unimportant. The Japanese government directly invested in the industrial sector. Until about World War I, these investments generally exceeded those of the private sector. Black and his colleagues pointed out:

> Government was also active in improving the quantity and quality of social overheads and of course it took full responsibility for raising Japan's military capability. Indeed, during the Meiji era a large part of central government capital formation can be accounted for by summing up expenditures on public works, particularly railroads, and military investments.[8]

The Japanese government provided a favorable environment for economic growth by removing feudal restrictions on trade within the country and on individual activities, by assuring internal stability, and by providing sound currency, adequate banking facilities, a reasonable tax system, and efficient government services. It pioneered many industrial fields and sponsored the development of others. The Japanese leaders were particularly interested in developing the strategic industries on which modern military power depended. The government also took the lead in developing modern communications, because of the public nature of this undertaking and its great cost.[9]

Japan experienced a unique pattern of direct state entrepreneurship and state disengagement in direct economic management. In the 1860s, the Japanese state spearheaded the industrialization process by pioneering and financing new undertakings over a broad front. The obvious cases are in railway building and operation, the establishment of the telegraph line, and the opening of coal mines. In the early 1880s, however, Japanese government-run business started to lose money and ambitious government development projects created budget deficits. In the face of financial crisis, the government decided on a policy of economic retrenchment.[10] Soon the government began to leave to the private sectors those industrial areas in which Japan had comparative advantages (labor-intensive industries, especially textiles) and in which private firms had a chance of surviving even in the face of foreign competition. Thereafter, the state concerned itself mainly with developmental bottlenecks the private sector could not manage. Most nonstrategic government industries were sold to businessmen closely associated with the political leaders.

Based upon a detailed case study of technology and investment in Japan, Barbara Molony pointed out: "The government, having guided the creation of Japan's economic infrastructure, then shifted course and proceeded to disengage itself from direct production well before the end of the nineteenth century."[11] Most of the state's industrial properties were soon disposed of at prices low enough to attract ready buyers. They went mainly to certain big capitalists enjoying official favor. The result was to endow the leading industrial and financial families with fresh opportunities to extend their activities. It consolidated the pattern of close association between the financial/industrial oligarchy and the government. Thereafter state capitalism in the sense of public ownership played a declining role in Japan until its revival in the war economy of the late 1930s and the early 1940s.

One interesting thing was that the political elite with samurai background played a more important role than other social groups in Japan. In the large samurai class, however, it was only a few rather untypical figures who distinguished themselves as successful businessmen. It was unique that feudal samurai could be turned into successful entrepreneurs and effective bureaucrats. The samurai brought to the economic arena a willingness to learn from advanced countries due to the tradition of Dutch learning. They also had a spirit of risk taking which was helpful for capitalist ventures.

The rapid Japanese industrialization was accompanied and facilitated by the growth of legal-rational authority. Legal renovation was fundamental to technological modernization and was necessitated by the abolition of the old class structure. Concepts of legal rights, as opposed to the traditional emphasis on social obligation, came to permeate the new laws. Most of the legal reforms were instituted piecemeal, and a thorough recodification of the laws proved a difficult and slow task. A complete code, revised largely on the basis of German legal precedent, finally went into effect in 1896. Pragmatism gained strength during the Meiji Restoration. The Meiji leaders found encouragement for their points of view in the growing secularism, nationalism, and materialism of the nineteenth-century West. Although Meiji Japan advanced along the road of the rational-legal system, one traditional feature was too deeply rooted to be reformed: the ultimate power and authority belonged to the emperor rather than to the people.

Two key steps in the achievement of security were Japan's victories over China and Russia at the turn of the century. These two wars proved that Japan had indeed developed the "rich country and strong military" on which security seemed to depend. But they also started Japan on a course of foreign conquest and empire that was to end a half-century later in catastrophe.[12]

In Russia, the role of the state was prominent both in the 1890s and particularly after the late 1920s. In the 1890s, under the vigorous leadership of the minister of finance, Sergei Witte, the Russian government pursued a forceful program of stimulating industrial development. One of the prime elements in this program was the expansion of railroad construction.[13] After 1900 the direct role of the government decreased in importance as an element in the tsarist growth mechanism. Although the role of government increased again when the Communists took power in 1917, it did not reach the heights later associated with the Soviet economic model until the inauguration of the plan era in 1928. At that point the direct control of the government over the economy became, at least in a formal sense, total. In reality the central regime was not able to exercise its control in a totally effective manner. Nevertheless, the plan era can be characterized as one of direct, centralized administration, analogous to military organization. The growth mechanism became one in which the state not only mobilized both human and material resources through enforced high rates of investment and saving, but also directed them into sectors chosen by the political elites.

According to Merle Fainsod, the transcendent role of state power was everywhere manifest after 1861, weakening in the last years of the empire and powerfully reasserting itself in the Soviet period, sometimes seeking to bar social change, at other times manipulating, guiding, and even accelerating it in the regime's interest. Economic policy emerges as a handmaiden of state policy, only incidentally concerned with meeting the welfare needs of the population and focused on overcoming the consequences of retarded economic development. The state looms large, overshadowing the individuals who are its subjects.[14]

The role of the state was one of the most obvious continuing traits of Russian society. As Black pointed out, throughout the transitional period the state had a virtual monopoly of political power, except for brief transitional phases of anarchy. Through the instrumentality of the bureaucracy and of the political police, it kept a close control over all social, intellectual, and spiritual activities that might challenge its position. The Russian state took the primary initiative in economic growth through investment, ownership, supervision, and fiscal policy.[15]

The year 1928 was a dramatic turning point in Stalin's coercive drive to transform Russia. The end of NEP pushed the Soviet economy further away from the market. The inauguration of the First Five-Year Plan, and the use of the vast state power to mobilize the resources of the country in the drive for industrialization, produced social consequences out of all proportion to those of the political revolution in 1917.[16]

In comparison with the Russian case, Japanese political leadership was more steady and consistent in guiding political, economic, and social change throughout the period of transformation. One of the most conspicuous features of the Japanese modernization is the political role of the emperor. The traditional imperial institution was used by Meiji leadership as an effective symbol and instrument of national unity and discipline. In the economic field, the maintenance of small traditionally organized units of production alongside the most modern factories contributed to the rapid and effective economic development of Japan.

At the beginning of the twentieth century, Russia appeared to be moving in a similar direction of state disengagement from direct economic control. But World War I and revolutionary crisis dramatically changed the direction of Russian development. The October Revolution of 1917 fundamentally altered the institutional forms and the social basis of politics in Russia. It opened a deep gulf between subsequent developments in Russia and Japan. Notwithstanding this break, the Japanese as well as the Russian state became preoccupied with the problem of creating new centers of authority in the late 1920s and 1930s. By that time the oligarchy that had dominated Japanese life during the half-century of the Meiji era had died off, leaving a struggle for power among rival interests--a struggle from which the military eventually emerged dominant.

The Stalin Revolution and Japanese Militarization

Modernization is a complex process; it is often full of twists and turns. "There are no four-lane highways through the parks of industrial progress. The road may lead from backwardness to dictatorship and from dictatorship to war."[17] This cool-headed statement is based upon facts. Rapid socioeconomic development may create enormous political pressure on the regime.[18] The interplay of domestic and international conflicts created crises in the Russian and Japanese regimes. Russia went through the 1905 and 1917 revolutions; the destruction of the autocratic tsarist state did not bring about a democracy but rather led to a highly centralized communist system. Democracy did not succeed in prewar Japan either. The Japanese military grew into a dominant position and controlled not only the polity but also the economy.

After Stalin's revolution from above in the late 1920s and early 1930s, the Soviet economy was put under strict central planning and administrative control. In terms of its impact on state-market relations, the Stalin revolution in 1928-29 was no less significant than the 1917 revolution. The Soviet state directly controlled and managed all the major industrial enterprises. The state farms and collective farms also were under strict central regulation. Individual entrepreneurship was viewed as dangerous and thus was suppressed by the state. Furthermore, the state dominated not only production but also distribution of goods and services. The Soviet government fixed prices of most products with little concern for market principles.

During the period of Soviet industrialization, there existed a certain compatibility between the Stalinist economic system and the extensive model of growth, especially because the country had enormous labor and natural resources. As a latecomer to modernization, the Soviet Union for a sustained period was able to borrow heavily from the technological advances of more developed industrial countries. Thus, the Soviet centralized economic system and extensive growth strategy worked well in the early stage of industrialization process. Even Abram Bergson's meticulous efforts to eliminate the upward bias and construct a fair measure of Soviet GNP growth come up with very respectable rates for 1928-55 in the range of 4.4-6.3 percent per annum.[19]

Robert C. Tucker has provided an insightful analysis of the Stalin revolution. The term "revolution from above" is applicable to the second revolution as a whole, including the phase in the later 1930s when massive terror transformed the single-party state inherited from Lenin into an absolute autocracy. Tucker pointed out that:

The revolution from above was a state-initiated, state-directed, and state-enforced
process, which radically reconstituted the Soviet order as it had existed in the
1920s. State power was the driving force of economic, political, social, and
cultural change that was revolutionary in rapidity of accomplishment, forcible
methods, and transformative effect. The statist character of this revolution is not
obviated by the facts that not a few willingly assisted it, most acquiesced in it,
and many were, in a career sense, its beneficiaries.[20]

Lenin was a state builder in the role of chief organizer of the soviet party-
state. He advocated and practiced revolution from above in repressing real or
suspected enemies of the new state. But Lenin did not see socialism mainly as
a state-building process. It was Stalin who "came to link, if not to equate, the
construction of socialism with state-building in an historical Russian sense."[21]
Stalin clearly saw the state as the main tool for industrialization. The thought
of Russia's backwardness and isolation in a dangerous world underlay Stalin's
warning in 1925 that the Soviet state must build armed strength to make it ready
for anything, and do so in a hurry. Stalin re-emphasized the idea that a
backward country would be beaten by stronger and more developed countries.
In order to avoid the miserable fate of being beaten because of weakness and
backwardness, industrialization must be carried out with the greatest possible
speed. According to Tucker, Stalin's goal was to augment state power quickly
by using the revolutionary state machine as much as possible. State power is
needed as the lever of transformation.[22]
Most Soviet leaders agreed on the necessity to industrialize; the difficult
question was how to do it. Nicholas Bukharin argued for industrialization
through an intensified NEP and encouraged Russian farmers to enrich
themselves. Leon Trotsky, on the other hand, emphasized that only high-tempo
industrialization could produce the rapid economic growth Russia required.
Trotsky also claimed that the building of socialism in Russia depended on the
triumph of the world revolution abroad. Attacking Trotsky, Stalin proposed the
popular slogan of "socialism in one country." He also criticized Bukharin's
proposal as too slow and dangerous. As the general secretary of the Communist
party, Stalin effectively used his control of party machine to eliminate organized
opposition to his programs. In 1928, Stalin reversed the New Economic Policy
and started forced collectivization and mass industrialization. The First Five-
Year Plan went into operation in October 1928, although its formal adoption
did not take place until the spring of 1929.
For Stalin, Soviet proletarian dictatorship should be the most mighty and
powerful of all hitherto existing state regimes. The revolution from above led
to the explosive growth of the centralized state during the First Five-Year Plan.
Economic expansion by Stalinist industrialization spurred growth of the Soviet
leviathan. All the far-flung projects were additions to the fund of state-owned
property. Their employees were servants of the state. Most came under

administrative subordination to great bureaucratic conglomerates, the people's commissariats.[23]

The leviathan dominated and intruded into all key aspects of sociopolitical and economic life. The will of the party also permeated the machinery of the state, and the state controlled its subjects to an unprecedented degree. The party, through the state, took charge of all public affairs. The state was the only employer; all independent sources of income were wiped out. Even the peasants (except for their garden plots) were now subject to state supervision.[24]

As the state swelled, the mass of the people "grew lean." They did so in the sense of being hungry much of the time, being overworked, struggling for items of simple necessity, and enduring all manners of hardship. But not all the people grew lean. Stalin introduced a policy of stratification and privilege that enabled higher-level functionaries and their families to lead relatively comfortable lives during that time of bleak austerity.[25] In order to control the movement of Soviet citizens, the internal passport system was extended to citizens throughout the USSR in 1933. As for the peasant majority of the population, the denial of passports made their enserfment complete. Soviet citizens were obliged to compulsory service to an unprecedented degree.

Building industrial and military power was the central task of the Stalin regime. The Japanese rulers had similar goals but they tried to achieve their ends with different means. When facing the threat of depression in the late 1920s, the emerging Japanese parliamentary democracy was not able to stand the pressures from below and above. The ultra-nationalists and militarists became more and more aggressive. In the early 1930s, Japan underwent militarization of the polity and the economy. From 1932 to 1945, the Japanese military dominated national political and economic life; this dominance reached its height during World War II.

There are sharp contrasts between the Russian and Japanese military. In both nations the military consumed a large portion of the state budget--from 21 percent to 48 percent in both countries between 1860 and 1913--and vast quantities of local resources, particularly in Russia.[26] To utilize the potentials of modern technology, the armies and navies became patrons of science and industry, and in order to make soldiers of peasants, they of necessity also became major educational establishments. Formed by strong political leaders, the Russian armed services were firmly subordinated to state authority, a tradition that survived 1917 and was transferred to the new revolutionary regime. Only when the state itself was in chaos--as during the turmoil of 1905 and the time of General Kornilov's attempted coup in the summer of 1917--was this subordination weakened, and then only briefly.

The Japanese military enjoyed special constitutional privileges of direct access to the throne. Moreover, its officers formed a caste that was increasingly separated by training and outlook from other interest groups. Openly committed to a role of "above politics," they simultaneously denied the validity of political constraints on the military, and ended by militarizing many aspects of civilian life. During the 1930s, military officers were able finally to surface as the strongest interest group in the state. Militaristic activities went out of civilian control from the time of the Manchurian Incident (1931) to the end of World War II.[27]

After the outbreak of the Sino-Japanese war in 1937, the Japanese military-controlled government extensively intervened in the economy. The supply of raw materials and the purchase of manufactured goods were tightly controlled by the government. Particularly after the surprise attack on Pearl Harbor which drew the United States into the war, Japan got into a stage of total mobilization of human and material resources for the war. In a sense, the Japanese war economy was a highly militarized command economy. The failure in the war also discredited the command system in the Japanese economy.

The rise of the Japanese military had deep historical roots. For more than 200 years before the Meiji Restoration, samurai stood at the top of social hierarchy in Japan. Militaristic thinking originating in the ancient past became very strong with the emergence of the samurai as the ruling class. The ethnocentrism of an island nation was transformed into a powerful force of nationalism in the nineteenth century as Japan encountered the West and felt compelled to transform its institutions and way of life in order to survive in the international arena of power politics. As Mikiso Hane put it: "The driving force behind the Meiji leaders was nationalism, and they never lost sight of their ultimate objectives in spite of the turbulence that buffeted them from all sides."[28] During the Meiji reform, many reform leaders came from the rank of samurai.

In addition to these factors, there were seeds for militarism in the Meiji system. According to Bradley M. Richardson and Scott C. Flanagan, there were at least three fatal flaws in the Meiji Constitution that posed major and perhaps insurmountable obstacles for the development of a parliamentary democracy which could deal with militarism effectively.

These were (1) the location of sovereignty in the person of the emperor rather than the people; (2) the failure of the Meiji political structure to subordinate clearly the military to the civilian authorities; and (3) the failure of the prewar constitution to integrate the political structure and decision-making processes or establish clear lines of authority and responsibility.[29]

The ambiguities in the Meiji political structure permitted the dramatic relocation of decision-making authority from the oligarchy to the parties and then to the military without any constitutional amendments or major structural reforms. As a result of the military prerogative of direct access to the throne, the military exercised virtually complete autonomy within its own sphere--military planning, administration, and combat operations. Moreover, the military could intervene in civilian and political affairs by withdrawing the army and/or navy ministers from the cabinet and refusing to supply a replacement unless its demands were met.[30] Army and navy ministers were only selected from the two highest ranks of officers on the active list. This practice guaranteed the military a significant influence in the cabinet. The military derived its very special position from the fact that the emperor was designated as commander-in-chief, in direct command of the armed forces. On the basis of this "imperial prerogative of supreme command," the military claimed independence from any civilian authority.

By the support of a strategy of nationalistic propaganda campaigns, by the intimidation and assassination of leading opponents, and by the use of foreign expansion programs, the Japanese military was able to displace the political parties and seize the dominant position in the governing coalition during the years 1936-45. Gordon Berger raised doubt on the stereotypes about military dominance of Japanese politics during that period.[31] However, substantial evidence indicates the decline of party power after 1932 and the final collapse of the party system in 1940. When there was direct confrontation between the military and political parties, the general tendency was that the military prevailed between 1932 and 1940.

The flames of nationalism, militarism, and imperialism were stoked by the economic and social frustrations felt by the masses as the depression brought them to the very brink of starvation. Hane pointed out the nature of Japanese militarism and ultranationalism:

> The ultranationalists generally favored expansion into the Asian continent, development of a powerful military force, and the creation of a totalitarian state that inclined toward national socialism. Consequently, they opposed liberal, individualistic values as well as the democratic, parliamentary concepts that had entered the country in the mid-nineteenth century. In concert with these attitudes, they rejected the basically Western, urban culture in favor of the traditional, agrarian way of life and values.[32]

While some Japanese militarists worshiped the traditional and rural life, Stalinists admired modern industrialization and urbanization. But they all rejected the mainstream Western political and philosophical ideas and democratic institutions. They both emphasized military over economic power.

When Japan first occupied Manchuria and established a puppet regime there in the early 1930s, the Japanese military authorities tried to establish a military-industrial basis without the participation of the *zaibatsu*, i.e., powerful family-controlled commercial and financial combines. Soon the military found out that they could not do well without financial and technical assistance from the *zaibatsu*. The established *zaibatsu*, such as Mitsui, Mitsubishi, Sumitomo, and Yasuda, closely cooperated with the military in the building of defense industries as the military gained ascendancy and arms expenditures began to increase. In contrast to the gains made by the *zaibatsu*, the small and middle-sized enterprises suffered a decline, particularly those engaged in the production of nonessential goods. This strengthened the monopolistic tendency of the Japanese economy in favor of authoritarian rule rather than pluralistic democracy.

The Stalinist revolution and the rise of militarism in Japan were two sharply contrasting phenomena. From the perspective of state-market relations, however, these two movements showed similar trends. For instance, one common feature of Stalin's USSR and militaristic Japan was the dramatic increase in the power of the state and the decline of the role of the market. In fact, the centralization of power was a typical practice not only in totalitarian and militaristic states but also in representative democracies during serious crises such as the Second World War. What made the cases of Stalin's USSR and militaristic Japan different was not only the degree, but also the nature, of the centralized control, i.e., party monopoly in the USSR and military domination in Japan.

State control of the economy in the USSR and Japan during the 1930s and 1940s was much more strict and comprehensive than that in any representative democracies. Furthermore, the Soviet party-state control of the economy was not just an emergency measure during a crisis situation but was a way of life. The end of the war did not bring fundamental change to the Stalinist system. Japan was defeated in the war and its highly militaristic centralized economy was reformed during the American occupation. Without the defeat and occupation, it would have been extremely difficult, if not impossible, to have reformed the Japanese economic system which was so deeply influenced by militarism. Thus, the postwar pattern of Japanese state-market relations was not a result of natural domestic evolution but a consequence of American occupation reform and Japanese adaptation to the fundamentally transformed world situation.

Science and Technology in Modernizing
Japan and Russia/USSR

Science and technology are central to modernization in general and industrialization in particular. Most Russian and Japanese reformers realized that it was absolutely critical for their nations to catch up with advanced Western states. The opportunity to learn from the advanced nations was a strategic advantage for the latecomers. However, the questions of what to learn and how to learn were not simple and could not be resolved automatically. State policies can heavily influence the innovation and/or transfer of science and technology. This section analyzes the role of the state in science and technology and the contribution of science and technology to the modernization of Japan and Russia.

The Meiji leaders clearly recognized the need for new skills and knowledge. In the "Five Articles Oath" they had stated: "Knowledge shall be sought throughout the world." As John Fairbank and Edwin Reischauer demonstrated, "The new leaders clearly saw that an organized system of education was a fundamental aspect of a modernized society and as early as 1871 created a ministry of education to develop such a system."[33] The government played an active role in developing a thoroughly modernized system of education. Insofar as borrowings from the West could contribute to strengthening the autocracy and increasing state power, they were accepted with alacrity.

In the early stage of modernization, what the Japanese feared and admired the most was Western military power. The Japanese reformers soon realized that such power was based upon modern science and technology. Thus, the survival of the Japanese nation largely depended on its ability to learn from the West in science and technology and the relating institutions. The Japanese reformers realized that any program of modernization would depend heavily upon the adoption of Western science, technology, and industrialization.

The borrowing of advanced technology from the industrialized nations of the West was crucial to the modernization of Japan and Russia. In Japan the importation and diffusion of Western technology received marked attention from the beginning of the Meiji reforms. Training programs were set up, technicians were brought in from abroad, and Japanese were sent to study in foreign countries. Modern machinery, embodying advanced technology, was imported in the process of building new industries. The Japanese became more and more proficient at adapting and even improving Western techniques for their own purposes. Improvement engineering has been a fine art in Japan.

Like Japan, Russia was confronted with the problem of modernizing on the basis of technology, ideas and institutions borrowed from the very Western states with which it was competing. The position as a latecomer permitted Russia to import techniques and institutions which had been developed elsewhere as a result of many years of experimentation and at great expense. With the aid of massive infusions of state support, Russia was able to make rapid progress and in isolated fields of endeavor surpassed its tutors.

Russian industrialization, especially in the late nineteenth century and early twentieth century, relied more on foreign entrepreneurs and foreign investment. As a result of the protective tariff of 1891, foreigners who wished to do business in Russia had to do it through direct foreign investment. The backwardness of the Russian economy and the tremendous opportunities for profit had a great appeal for the foreign investor. In the 1890s, foreign capital accounted for almost one-half of all new capital invested in Russian industry. In 1900 foreigners owned more than seventy percent of the capital in mining, metallurgy, and engineering.[34] This foreign investment greatly expanded the capital stock of Russia. Foreign technology was brought into Russia in the advanced capital equipment itself--and in the form of human capital: the foreign technicians and experienced businessmen and managers who came to Russia. As Gerschenkron argued, "Far from being irrational in conditions of a backward country, it was the modern Western technology which enabled the Russian entrepreneurs to overcome the disability of an inadequate labor supply and very frequently also the inferior quality of that labor."[35]

Under the impetus of the Five-Year Plans and the industrialization drive of the 1930s, the Soviet Union undertook a massive program of importing foreign technology. In addition to advanced technology, the USSR imported skilled workers, technicians, and engineering consultants. Almost 7,000 foreign specialists were reported to be at work in Soviet industry in 1932.[36] The Russians went on to combine borrowing with heavy investment in their own science and technology research and training programs. They tried hard to create an indigenous basis of research and development.

As in so many other areas, the state in Japan and Russia/USSR assumed principal responsibility in all phases for importing science and technology. In neither Japan nor Russia/USSR did such attention to advancement of the higher levels of knowledge lead to a neglect of the training of the middle levels of technical experts necessary to man an industrializing state. Within the system of formal education the two countries devoted close attention to a network of technical and vocational schools. In Japan, this program was consummated in the last decade of the century, whereas in Russia certain advances in the creation of these schools under the empire were greatly expanded by the heavily utilitarian educational policies of the Soviet regime.[37]

Lenin recognized that Russia was culturally a very backward country in comparison with Western Europe and North America. No less than a cultural revolution was required to transform Russia into a leading nation. According to Frederic J. Fleron, technological and industrial learning from the West was a key element of the broad "cultural revolution" for the Bolsheviks.

> In the Soviet case, industrialization and machine technology were not sufficiently present prior to 1917 to have "conquered nature" and broken down traditional society. For Lenin and the Bolsheviks, then, a central part of the thorough-going cultural revolution was full-scale industrialization and expansion of production capacity, which was accomplished with the importation of foreign technology and systems of factory organization to increase worker productivity.[38]

Were the Soviets able to build a new sociopolitical system by establishing its economic foundation with Western capitalist technology? Furthermore, how could the Russian technical intelligentsia, trained in the old system, serve the needs of the new "socialist" economy? According to Kendall E. Bailes, the Russian technical intelligentsia, in its origins, was a creation of the Russian state, one of the oldest groups being the Corps of Mining Engineers established by Catherine the Great in 1773 to manage state mines and metallurgical plants.[39] The Soviet Union continued the prerevolutionary practice of borrowing technology from the West. On the other hand, Bailes argued that the Soviet social relations connected with the use of such technology were in key respects quite different from those in the West. A major implication of this is that similarities in technology adopted by industrial societies do not necessarily determine the kind of social relations that may emerge.[40]

Bailes attempted to argue that what the Soviet Union did to industrialize demonstrated that it was possible to use Western capitalist technology in a socialist society without copying Western capitalist social and economic structures. But this argument was not supported with enough evidence. Bailes acknowledged that Soviet technology was essentially Western in nature. More importantly, the main attributes of "capitalist technical rationality" also had a deep impact on the Soviet Union.[41] It seems that it is impossible to copy Western technology without being influenced by Western institutions and ideas. Fleron has pointed out the inherent connections between modern technology and capitalism.

> As a product of its particular historical circumstances, the technology that developed under capitalism is a reification and concrete material manifestation of the dominant capitalist idea of maximizing control over labor in order to maximize profits. This control function is reflected not only in the machine itself, but also in the accompanying forms of technical rationality and technical infrastructure.[42]

In technological and industrial development, Soviet leaders stressed quantitative rather than qualitative growth. For instance, the automotive industry tended to grow primarily by expanding old enterprises. This practice "brought about growth without modernization. The expanded plants tended to produce at the same level of technology as the parent plants."[43]

The historical advantages of industrialization in conditions of backwardness also contained risks of over-reaction to certain aspects of modernization. As Gerschenkron pointed out, the tendency to exaggerate and overdo was everpresent in Russian industrialization. For example, the Soviet state planners relentlessly favored huge size in new plants. In many cases, smaller plant size would have been more rational. In addition, the very breadth and uneven development of industrialization kept creating bottlenecks; and the excessive bureaucratization of the economy absorbed an undue share of available manpower.[44]

The relatively fast per capita rate of growth achieved by Japan and Russia between the 1860s and the 1940s--surpassed before 1914 among major countries only by that of the United States, Sweden, and Germany; and unsurpassed in the 1930s--was achieved by converting existing institutions and by borrowing from the more developed countries.[45] In the realm of technology and specialized institutions, Japan and Russia relied extensively on the more modern West.

The efforts at creating a distinctive "Soviet science" and Soviet technology resulted in failure. According to Soviet Marxist theory, scholarship and learning were a part of the ideological superstructure of society deriving its characteristics from the economic base. As part of their cultural revolution, some ideological Soviet leaders tried to create a school of science fundamentally different from what was developed in the West. The historical development turned out to be the contrary; they did not create a "Soviet science." As Loren Graham has argued, "Science proved to be an element of continuity between Soviet and non-Soviet intellectual life. It reduced the exceptionalism of the Soviet Union and brought its intellectuals closer to the rest of the world and the rest of history."[46]

Science and technology are essential parts of modern civilization. In learning from the West in science and technology, Japan and Russia had to make necessary adjustments in their political and economic systems. In the Soviet era, the actual operation of the system was heavily shaped and influenced by imported Western technology and science. Science and technology cannot be separated from the large political and economic environment in which they were developed.[47] The state in Japan and Russia/USSR made enormous efforts in importing and utilizing Western science and technology. On the one hand, science and technology policies were heavily shaped by the state. On the other hand, imported science and technology had a deep impact on political and economic development in Russia and Japan.

Lessons from the Modernization of
Japan and Russia/USSR

When Japan and Russia began the modernization processes in the mid-nineteenth century, they were under serious military and economic challenge from more powerful Western states. Thus, defensive modernization was a common characteristic for both countries. Many scholars believe this notion of defensive modernization to be particularly relevant to Russia. As Gerschenkron said of the developmental process, "There is very little doubt that, as often before, Russian industrialization in the Soviet period was a function of the country's foreign and military policies."[48]

To what extent did Russia rely on the role of the market to accelerate economic development? To what extent did Japan use the market mechanisms to speed up its economic modernization? To what extent did the Russian government consciously limit and regulate the role of the free market? It is difficult to answer these questions precisely. From what we have learned from the above analysis, it seems that both the Meiji regime and the pre-revolutionary Russian government perceived a legitimate place for the market. However, both governments stressed the role of the state versus the "invisible hand." In retrospective perspective, it is natural for government leaders to emphasize the role of the state because that meant the increase of their power and authority over the economy and society.

Focusing on the role of the state, we can summarize major similarities between the state-building processes of Japan and Russia/USSR. In initiating modernization, the serfs were liberated in Russia and the class line between samurai and commoners was eliminated in Japan. These moves laid a keystone of the modern state, i.e., citizenship. Without legally equal citizens, it is impossible to establish a modern state. The removal of rigid class barriers not only facilitated social mobility but also provided free laborers for the growth of capitalist industry and commerce.

State power was used to establish the nationwide market in both Russia and Japan. Railway building was a prime example. State-led construction of railways not only encouraged industrialization but also greatly facilitated commercialization of the national economies of Russia and Japan. The two governments also removed domestic tariff barriers and promoted commerce.

Both Russia and Japan reformed the bureaucracy based on modern efficiency principles. The two countries had long traditions of gigantic bureaucracy and bureaucratism. However, there are fundamental differences between a feudal bureaucracy and a modern capitalist bureaucracy. Modernizers in the two countries transformed their bureaucracies based on modern rational efficiency norms. When the Bolsheviks seized state power, they quickly destroyed the tsarist bureaucracy and created a even bigger communist bureaucracy. Though communist bureaucracy was supposed to follow new ideological guidelines, it was not able to escape many key features of modern bureaucracy. In a sense, the communist bureaucracy was the combination of Russian tradition and an imported ideology.[49] The prewar Japanese bureaucracy was highly sophisticated and merit-oriented. The American occupation of Japan was an indirect occupation since most occupation reforms were carried out through the Japanese bureaucracy. Due to the nature of indirect rule, the American occupation did not fundamentally change the Japanese bureaucratic system. Nevertheless, the principle of popular sovereignty guaranteed by the new constitution made the bureaucracy to a large degree accountable to the elected national Diet.

Building a strong military and a powerful defense industry was a top priority for both Russia and Japan during their transition. As backward countries in comparison with the West, Russian and Japanese leaders shared a sense of urgency in upgrading their military technology. Defensive modernization had an inherent tendency of over-stressing military power. Thus, the success of defensive modernization by the latecomers might lead those countries to move on to the dangerous road of foreign expansion.

During their modernizing drive, Russia and Japan undertook foreign expansion. Russia aggressively expanded and tried to consolidate its huge empire. Stalin expanded the influence of the Soviet empire into Eastern Europe after World War II. Japan invaded Korea, China, and finally attacked Pearl Harbor in order to pursue its dream of East Asian-South Pacific domination. The rationale or excuse for foreign expansion was national security.

Direct involvement of the government in the early stages of industrialization was a key similarity of state capitalism of prerevolutionary Russia and Meiji Japan. But this similarity was short-lived because the two countries took sharply divergent paths of state involvement in the economy after World War I.

Contrasts between Russia/USSR and Japan were also very serious. It was much easier for the Japanese than the Soviets to achieve a strong sense of nationalism because of the cultural and racial homogeneity in Japan. The Russian empire was called a prison of nations in which ethnic conflict had been a constant theme in spite of and/or because of brutal repression of the regime. The Communist regime claimed that it achieved national unity. However, the "unity" formed by iron fists was not natural and was breeding seeds of deeper national and ethnic conflicts which would explode whenever state control over the society was significantly weakened.

It was relatively easier for Japan to defend itself because of its geographical locality. Japan had not been occupied by any foreign power before the American occupation from 1945 to 1951. Russia, in contrast, was often invaded by its more powerful neighbors. Russian rulers often felt threatened. In the old power games, one nation's security tended to be another nation's insecurity. Russia's relentless expansion and pursuit of its own security also constituted a serious threat to its many smaller neighbors.

While the Japanese government was able to keep peace and stability inside the nation, the Russian regime could not stop the growth of political and economic crises in the vast country. Russia went through violent revolutions and civil wars which destroyed the emerging market systems and gave birth to a totalitarian leviathan. The Japanese regime was able to attract the loyalty of a large portion of the population for most of the period of transition. Although changes brought about by the Meiji reforms were revolutionary, the Meiji Restoration was basically a peaceful movement. Even the militarization of Japan did not involve large-scale domestic bloodshed as took place in the Soviet Union.

The amount of violence involved in the state-building process in Russia/USSR was much greater than that in Japan. Coercion and violence were widely used in prerevolutionary Russia and especially in the Stalin era. In Gerschenkron's words, "Economic backwardness, rapid industrialization, ruthless exercise of dictatorial power, and the danger of war have become inextricably intertwined in Soviet Russia."[50] Starting from the forced agricultural collectivization and especially the "great purge," organized mass terror was systematically used by Stalin to control the party and the population at large. The use of state violence was relatively restrained in Japan, except for the suppression of the Communists and other left radicals. Nevertheless, the Japanese extensively used mass terror against people in their colonies.

There also were sharp contrasts in the decision-making styles of the two countries. The Russian tsar was an autocrat who ruled directly; the Japanese emperor did not rule but reigned. An oligarchy ruled Japan by consensus building among its members. In Russia, individual leaders played much more important roles. Democratic centralism was the operational principle of the Soviet Communist party. The essence of the principle was the centralization of power rather than the practice of democracy. The limited democratic element claimed by the principle was often violated by individual leaders. At the height of his power, Stalin often disregarded other leaders' opinions. On the contrary, consensus building was the norm of Japanese decision making. Even during the period of militarism, there was no single predominant leader in Japan as Stalin was in the USSR.

The Russians and the Japanese had different attitudes toward power and authority. Under normal circumstances, both Japanese and the Russians tend to defer to power and authority. But among Russians there also was an inherent latent tendency of rebellion and revolution.[51] This point was demonstrated by the repeated occurrence of revolt and revolution in Russia. The last Tsar Nicholas II was murdered by revolutionaries in 1918. From the Meiji Restoration to the end of World War II, the mythical belief in the sovereignty of the emperor was so deeply rooted in Japanese society that there was no serious threat to the imperial power at all. The effective use of traditional authority, particularly the imperial institution, greatly facilitated the peaceful transformation of agrarian Japan into an industrial power. Even the extreme militarists did not directly challenge the authority of the emperor. Different political forces struggled with each other in competition for the loyalty to the emperor. In Japan, the continuity of the state-building process after the Meiji Restoration was an outstanding case. In Russia, the 1905 and particularly the 1917 revolutions dramatically changed the pattern of development.

In economic activities, the Russians and the Japanese demonstrated that they had quite different degrees of entrepreneurship. Most scholars studying Japan found a strong work ethic and a tradition of entrepreneurship.[52] In contrast, some Russians show a love for literature but a low interest in entrepreneurship. A leading scholar of Russian studies observed:

> It could be argued that the existence of widespread social attitudes in Russia which were so patently unfavorable to entrepreneurship greatly reduced the number of potential entrepreneurs and thereby reduced the rate of economic development in the country. There is little doubt that there is some plausibility to such an argument. Even in the twentieth century, Russian university students showed a good deal of contempt for work associated with practical pursuits and particularly with business activity.[53]

Another persistent difference between Japan and Russia was their contrasting pattern in the use of resources, namely in Japan's "intensive" utilization of resources as opposed to Russia's "extensive" use.[54] This contrast was valid not just for the transitional period but also for postwar development. Sources of this difference were partly natural and partly human and ideological. Japan is a small and resource-poor nation, while Russia is a huge country with abundant resources. Development strategies of the two countries were based not only on the amount of resources available but also on ideological and cultural considerations.

The two patterns of modernization both were successful to a certain degree in terms of industrialization and modernization of the economy and society. But modernization created intense internal tensions. The interplay of such domestic tensions and international conflicts led to revolution in Russia and militarism in Japan.

Some tentative conclusions can be drawn by comparative studies of the historical development of Japan and Russia. First, there are different roads to modernization. With different cultural, social, economic and political backgrounds, Japan and Russia took different development strategies and different patterns of change. Nevertheless, both of them achieved impressive economic growth and substantial social change over a long period of time. Both Japan and Russia have gone through the process by which agrarian societies are transformed into industrial societies.

Second, the role of the state was very important in modernization. The Japanese government initiated modernization by reforming the economic and political systems, and by direct entrepreneurship at the beginning of industrialization. In the close interaction between government and business, the government has been very supportive to Japan's business, particularly to the big corporations. In Russia, the tsarist regime started the transformation to modern society by the liberation of the serfs in the early 1860s. After the 1917 Bolshevik revolution, especially since Stalin's revolution from above in the late 1920s, the Soviet state obtained absolute control over economic and social development. The centrally planned economy achieved high growth rates for several decades and transformed Russia into an industrial society, albeit one with an uneven pattern of development. In the advanced level of development, the command economy and authoritarian political system no longer work in any positive sense.

Third, high rates of long-term material growth necessitate high rates of short-term material sacrifice. In the Soviet case, this sacrifice resulted from a unilateral decision on the part of the state to transfer resources into the accumulation process as rapidly as possible in the first instance. This was engineered by taxation and a radical restructuring of the country's economic base. In the Japanese case, however, the government's role was less overtly coercive because the prevailing economic structure and conditions appear to have made the savings option attractive from both the firm's and the consumer's point of view.[55] In other words, the Soviet state managed the economy by predominantly administrative means, whereas the Japanese state tried to solve economic problems through the interaction of the state and the private sectors.

Fourth, borrowed technology could not be effective without making necessary adjustments in sociopolitical institutions. It is easier to borrow technology than to transfer political systems. Therefore, it is of strategic significance that the latecomers to modernization should reform their indigenous institutions in order to make them compatible with modern science and technology. The conversion of premodern institutions, particularly in the critical realm of politics, played a very significant role in Russian and Japanese modernization.

Fifth, state-building is critical to modernization. A country cannot achieve modernization without political development in general and political institutionalization in particular. This statement may appear to be an overgeneralization. Nevertheless, it is sufficiently demonstrated by the historical experiences of both Japan and Russia/USSR. A key for successful modernization in the two countries was the critical role played by their states. However, this comparative analysis of Russia/USSR and Japan also revealed the danger of over-emphasizing the role of the state. The state-builders, like the Stalinists and Japanese militarists, demonstrated a strong orientation to totalitarianism and authoritarianism. Thus, it is of vital importance for developing countries to build institutional mechanisms that can effectively deal with the stresses and crises of modernization. Only when these systems are properly institutionalized, can the danger for emergence of totalitarianism be avoided.

Sixth, the Soviet and Japanese experiences demonstrate that the suppression of the market forces by the state would necessarily lead to the growth of bureaucratic machines. During the transitional stages, the state increasingly dominated the market and resulted in the Stalinist command economy in USSR, and a highly militarized economy in Japan. When market forces were dominated by the party-state or the military, there would be no viable counterforces to check the abuse of power by the leviathan. A dynamic market economy is a reliable guarantor for the existence of pluralist interests in the society and a strong safeguard against the rise of totalitarianism in the state. But it is difficult to say that a market system will always be dynamic and well-functioning. Just as there are conflicts within the state, there are conflicts and potential crises within the market system. A stable and effective political system must be able to regularly release the inherent tensions between the state and the market. The dual task is to prevent the rise of a totalitarian state on the one hand and to avoid market failures on the other hand.

Japan and Russia/USSR were able not only to learn modern science and technology from the West but also to make substantial changes in their state-market relations. At the same time, each country kept strong traditional and national characteristics. By the end of World War II, there were two distinctive patterns of state-market relations in the USSR and Japan. Following the American occupation, Japan demonstrated a greater capacity for adapting to the technology-intensive methods of modernization. Soviet administrative methods proved to be more rigid. The highly centralized approach of the earlier period was slow to change and finally led to a deep crisis in the 1980s. The next chapter will examine the evolution of diverging patterns of state-market relations in the two countries from the end of World War II to the 1980s.

Notes

1. Cyril E. Black, et al., *The Modernization of Japan and Russia: A Comparative Study* (New York: Free Press, 1975), p. 7.

2. Cyril E. Black (ed.), *The Transformation of Russian Society: Aspects of Social Change Since 1861* (Cambridge: Harvard University Press, 1960); William Blackwell, *The Industrialization of Russia: An Historical Perspective* (New York, 1970); W.G. Beasley, *The Meiji Restoration* (Stanford: Stanford University Press, 1972); and Edwin O. Reischauer and Albert M. Craig, *Japan: Tradition and Transformation* (Boston: Houghton Mifflin, 1978).

3. Alexander Gerschenkron, *Economic Backwardness in Historical Perspective: A Book of Essays* (Cambridge: Harvard University Press, 1962); and Henry Rosovsky (ed.), *Industrialization in Two Systems: Essays in Honor of Alexander Gerschenkron* (New York: Wiley, 1966).

4. See Cyril E. Black, *The Dynamics of Modernization: A Study in Comparative History* (New York: Harper & Row, 1966); David A. Apter, *The Politics of Modernization* (Chicago: University of Chicago Press, 1965); Claude E. Welch, Jr., ed. *Political Modernization: A Reader in Comparative Political Change* (Belmont: Wedsworth, 1971).

5. Black, et al., *The Modernization of Japan and Russia*, p. 117.

6. *Ibid.*, p. 143.

7. *Ibid.*, p. 144.

8. *Ibid.*, pp. 171-172.

9. John K. Fairbank, Edwin O. Reischauer and Albert M. Craig, *East Asia: Tradition and Transformation* (Boston: Houghton Mifflin, 1973), pp. 514-517.

10. *Ibid.*, p. 518.

11. Barbara Molony, *Technology and Investment: The Prewar Japanese Chemical Industry* (Cambridge: Harvard University Press, 1990), p. 315.

12. Fairbank, Reischauer, and Craig, *East Asia*, p. 552.

13. Theodore H. Von Laue, *Sergei Witte and the Industrialization of Russia* (New York: Columbia University Press, 1963).

14. Merle Fainsod, "Summary and Review," in Black, *The Transformation of Russian Society*, p. 226.

15. Cyril E. Black, "The Modernization of Russian Society," in Black, *The Transformation of Russian Society*, p. 670.

16. *Ibid.*, p.678.

17. Gerschenkron, *Economic Backwardness in Historical Perspective*, p. 29.

18. Karl W. Deutsch, "Social Mobilization and Political Development," *American Political Science Review*, Vol. 55, No. 3 (1961), pp. 493-502; and Samuel P. Huntington, *Political Order in Changing Societies* (New Haven: Yale University Press, 1968).

19. Abram Bergson, *The Real National Income of Soviet Russia Since 1928* (Cambridge: Harvard University Press, 1962), p. 261.

20. Robert C. Tucker, *Stalin in Power: The Revolution from Above 1928-1941* (New York: W.W. Norton, 1990), p. xiv.

21. Tucker, *Stalin in Power*, p. 65.

22. Tucker specified the fundamental differences between Stalin and other Bolsheviks. The distinctiveness of Stalin's thinking entailed three further premises that together constituted the core of his approach. First, the engine of change could and should be the revolutionary use of state power. Second, the prime purpose of this revolutionary use of state power was the augmentation of state power. Third, because it was necessary to prepare quickly for a coming war, it was imperative to accomplish all these transformations at a maximally swift tempo. See Tucker, *Stalin in Power*, pp. 44-45.

23. *Ibid.*, pp. 104-106.

24. Theodore H. Von Laue, *Why Lenin? Why Stalin? A Reappraisal of the Russian Revolution, 1900-1930* (Philadelphia: Lippincott, 1964), pp. 215, 216.

25. Tucker, *Stalin in Power*, pp. 110-111.

26. Black, et al., *The Modernization of Japan and Russia*, p. 13.

27. See *Ibid.*, pp. 153-155.

28. Mikiso Hane, *Modern Japan: A Historical Survey* (Boulder: Westview Press, 1986).

29. Bradley M. Richardson and Scott C. Flanagan, *Politics in Japan* (Boston: Little Brown, 1984), p. 6.

30. *Ibid.*, p. 10.

31. See Gordon Mark Berger, *Parties Out of Power in Japan: 1931-1941* (Princeton: Princeton University Press, 1977).

32. Hane, *Modern Japan*, p. 249.

33. Fairbank, Reischauer and Craig, *East Asia*, p. 531.

34. Black, et al., *The Modernization of Japan and Russia*, p. 183; and John P. McKay, *Pioneers for Profits: Foreign Entrepreneurship and Russian Industrialization, 1885-1913* (Chicago: University of Chicago Press, 1970).

35. Gerschenkron, *Economic Backwardness in Historical Perspective*, p. 127.

36. Black, et al., *The Modernization of Japan and Russia*, pp.183-184. See Kendall E. Bailes, *Technology and Society under Lenin and Stalin: Origins of the Soviet Technical Intelligentsia*, 1917-1941 (Princeton: Princeton University Press, 1978); Bruce Parrott, *Politics and Technology in the Soviet Union* (Cambridge: MIT Press, 1983); and Antony C. Sutton, *Western Technology and Soviet Economic Development, 1917 to 1930* (Stanford: Hoover Institution,

1968), and *Western Technology and Soviet Economic Development*, 1930-1945 (Stanford: Hoover Institution, 1971).

37. Black, et al., *The Modernization of Japan and Russia*, p. 225.

38. Frederic J. Fleron, Jr. (ed.), *Technology and Communist Culture: The Socio-Cultural Impact of Technology under Socialism* (New York: Praeger, 1977), p. 5.

39. Bailes, *Technology and Society under Lenin and Stalin*, p. 25.

40. *Ibid.*, p. 408.

41. For an analysis of the particular attributes of capitalist technical rationality, see Fleron's introduction and conclusion to Fleron, *Technology and Communist Culture*, esp. pp. 3-4.

42. *Ibid.*, p. 408.

43. John P. Hardt and George D. Holliday, "Technology Transfer and Change in the Soviet Economic System," in Fleron, *Technology and Communist Culture*, p. 201.

44. Gerschenkron, *Economic Backwardness in Historical Perspective*, p. 149.

45. Black, et al., *The Modernization of Japan and Russia*, p. 236.

46. Graham, *Science and Social Order in the Soviet Union*, p. 2.

47. See Fleron, *Technology and Communist Culture*, esp. the introduction and conclusion.

48. Alexander Gerschenkron, "Problems and Patterns of Russian Economic Development," in Michael Cherniavsky (ed.), *The Structure of Russian History* (New York: Random House, 1970), p. 303.

49. Frederic J. Fleron, Jr. and Lou Jean Fleron, "Administration Theory as Repressive Political Theory: The Communist Experience," *Telos*, No. 12 (1972), pp. 63-92.

50. Gerschenkron, *Economic Backwardness in Historical Perspective*, p. 29.

51. Lucian W. Pye and Sidney Verba (eds.), *Political Culture and Political Development* (Princeton: Princeton University Press, 1965), esp. the chapter on Japan by Robert E. Ward and the chapter on the Soviet Russia by Frederick C. Barghoorn. See also Theda Skocpol, *States and Social Revolutions: A Comparative Analysis of France, Russia, and China* (Cambridge: Cambridge University Press, 1979).

52. See Ezra Vogel, *Japan as Number One: Lessons for America* (Cambridge: Harvard University Press, 1979); and James Billington, *The Icon and Axe: An Interpretive History of Russian Culture* (New York: Knopf, 1966).

53. Gerschenkron, *Economic Backwardness* in Historical Perspective, pp. 61-62.

54. For a discussion of the distinction between intensive and extensive patterns of economic development, see Egon Neuberger and William J. Duffy, *Comparative Economic Systems: A Decision-Making Approach* (Boston: Allyn and Bacon, 1976), p. 170.

55. David K. Whynes, *Comparative Economic Development* (London and Boston: Butterworths, 1983), p. 236.

3

Postwar Patterns of State-Market Relations

The Second World War had a profound impact on many aspects of world history. The Soviet Union suffered huge human sacrifices and enormous material losses but emerged as a giant military and political power second only to the United States in the postwar world. Japan initially expanded its empire but finally was defeated by the Allied forces and occupied by the United States. To a large degree, the results of the war significantly changed the domestic and international situation for both Japan and the USSR, and opened a new chapter in state-market relations within the two countries.

The Trading State Versus the
Military-Territorial State

Postwar Japanese sociopolitical and economic development is dramatically different from that of the prewar case. In order to reveal major sources of this revolutionary change, we must examine the important transitional period: 1945-1952. During the seven years, under the Supreme Commander for the Allied Powers (SCAP), Japan was transformed from a defeated fascist power into a democratic society. Japan was totally defeated at the end of the Second World War. Unlike in Europe, the Soviet Union did not have substantial influence in Japan. History offered the U.S. an extraordinary opportunity to reform Japan. The power of the SCAP was subject to remarkably few restraints. Robert A. Scalapino stated the aims of American occupation: "Japan was to be recreated as a democratic, parliamentary state, with the widest range of political protections for its citizenry and the fullest competition which a market economy would allow."[1]

A major goal of the occupation reforms was demilitarization of Japan. The toll of war casualties and the shame of defeat had already made deep impacts. The trials and purges of war criminals further reduced the power of the Japanese military. The Occupation authorities also removed many old conservative politicians from political participation and opened the way for a new generation of leaders. Although many of the new leaders had been involved in prewar politics, they were people with political orientations different from that of the war-time Japanese rulers. Article 9 of the new constitution declared that "the Japanese people forever renounce war as a sovereign right of the nation" and that "land, sea and air forces, as well as other war potential, will never be maintained."[2] This article was later interpreted as prohibiting Japan to build an armed force exceeding the basic need for self-defense. As a result, the deeply rooted Japanese military tradition was greatly weakened.

The cornerstone for the democratization of Japan was the new constitution of 1947. Drafted by General Douglas MacArthur's staff, this constitution reflected America's tradition, experience, and political and social values. It is truly remarkable that this constitution has worked fairly well in practice and has survived intact so far as formal amendments are concerned. Theoretically, it is always difficult to transplant any political system from one country to another. The adaptation of U.S. ideas to Japan is worth careful examination.

The prewar Japanese political system was by the standards of the time predominantly authoritarian. The postwar Japanese institutions and behaviors compare favorably with those of other contemporary democracies. In this sense, there is no doubt that fundamental changes took place in Japan. The new constitution stripped the imperial institution (emperor) of all its divine rights and sovereign attributes. Electoral rights were extended to women and youth; before the reform only one-quarter of the population could vote, after the reform about half of the population had the right to vote. Analyzing the significance of the new constitution for democratizing Japan, Robert E. Ward argued:

> In addition to substituting popular for imperial sovereignty, the new constitution also conferred all legislative authority on an elective bicameral Diet, provided extensive and detailed protection for civil and human rights, minimized, if not eliminated, the role of the military, created a powerful cabinet chosen by and responsible to the Diet, gave constitutional sanction to local autonomy, and endowed the judiciary with more extensive authority. These new institutions in turn brought about pronounced changes of a democratic sort in the performance characteristics of the Japanese government.[3]

Besides all the basic changes, there also are continuities between prewar and postwar Japan. In a certain sense, the Allied occupation was an "indirect occupation" in which the Japanese government survived defeat and continued to administer all domestic affairs of state, though subject to the authority of the SCAP. The occupation did not seriously try to change the prewar role and functions of the Japanese bureaucracy. The general orientation of the bureaucracy was conservative. It was a conservative force and an important part of continuity in postwar Japan.

The restructuring of the Japanese economy encompassed the following elements:

1. Land reform: According to a plan put through in 1948, absentee landlords were required to sell all their land to the government, and even cultivating landlords in most parts of Japan had to sell any land above ten acres. Once the state acquired the land, it was resold cheaply to the tenant farmers.

2. Labor reform: When Japan surrendered, the SCAP believed that a strong and independent union movement was essential to democratization. Trade unions were formed and were given the rights of collective bargaining and strike.

3. Business reform: The prewar Japanese economy was dominated by big-business combines (the *zaibatsu*). The SCAP tried to end excessive concentration of economic power through the reform of the *zaibatsu*. However, the business reform met strong resistance from Japanese business and government. The American Occupation authorities stopped the business reform when "recovery" replaced "reform" as the chief U.S. goal for Japan as a result of the growing tension between the United States and the Soviet Union.[4]

Japanese economic recovery was slow through 1948, with real GNP not even back to its 1931 level. By 1951, the United States had pumped more than $2 billion into the Japanese economy. The Korean War (1950-1953) brought Japan an opportunity for economic growth. Orders poured in, production expanded, and even foreign exchange grew plentiful as U.S. special procurement in Japan added its impact to that of U.S. aid. By the mid-1950s the United States had spent about $4 billion in Japan for the special procurement. The United States and Japan signed the peace treaty in 1951 and the Occupation ended in 1952. The two sides also signed a security pact which provided for the protection of Japan.

In the early 1950s, the Japanese government decided to establish industries in Japan which required intensive employment of capital and technology, industries that in consideration of comparative cost of production should have been inappropriate for Japan at that time. A MITI (Ministry of International Trade and Industry) official recalled in 1972:

From a short-run, static viewpoint, encouragement of such industries would seem to conflict with economic rationalism. But, from a long-range point of view, these are precisely the industries where income elasticity of demand is high, technological progress is rapid, and labor productivity rises fast.[5]

This long-term strategy began to receive its payoff in the late 1960s. For instance, Japan's motor vehicle production grew from 2 percent to 17 percent of world total from 1950 to 1970; Japan's steel production rose from 2 percent to 16 percent of the world total in the same period of time.[6]

In sharp contrast to the rise of the trading state in Japan, there was the further strengthening of military territorial orientation in the Soviet Union. The victory over Hitler and the establishment of the pro-Soviet regimes in Eastern Europe greatly boosted Soviet leaders' confidence in their military machine and the centrally planned economy. According to their logic, if the centrally planned economy could support the enormous war efforts against the once powerful fascist enemy, the same system would enable them to compete with Western nations in the postwar era. Therefore, there was no need for fundamental reform in the economic system following the partial demobilization of the gigantic Soviet Red Army.

In Japan, the postwar national consensus was economic catching-up with the West. For the Soviet regime, the top priority was to achieve military and strategic parity with the United States. The single-minded pursuit of nuclear strategic parity with the U.S. was achieved by the Brezhnev regime in the 1970s. However, the Soviet nuclear build-up was accomplished by sacrificing the civilian industries and consumer interests. No wonder there was such a joke in Moscow: it took less time for a Soviet leader to make a trip to outer space than for an ordinary Soviet citizen to make a daily trip to the stores.

Many pre-Gorbachev Soviet leaders perceived military forces, especially their strategic nuclear arsenal, as the chief indicator of national power. Following the tradition established by Stalin, they tended to favor military over civilian sectors, heavy over light industries, and state over consumer preferences. As a result, the USSR remained a minor player in the world market when it entered the 1980s as a military superpower competing with the United States. In both the volume and content of foreign trade, the Soviet Union behaved more like a Third World country rather than an industrial power. Military and political expansion of the Soviet Union in Eastern Europe did not benefit the USSR economically. In fact, the Soviet Union often provided raw materials and energy at prices lower than the world market prices to its partners in the former Council of Mutual Economic Assistance. What made matters worse was the extensive Soviet military and economic support of radical regimes around the world in its global competition with the West.

Such support was extremely costly. For instance, the Soviet Union provided Cuba annual military and economic aid of around $3 billion in the 1980s. The Soviet invasion of Afghanistan cost not only billions of rubles but also thousands of Soviet lives. The war resulted in enormous human and material sacrifices for the Afghans.

The over-extension of military, economic, and political power had led to the fall of one empire after another. Japan over-extended its power in a desperate attempt of building the so-called "Great East Asian Co-prosperity Sphere." Japan invaded China in 1937 and then directly challenged the United States at Pearl Harbor and in the Pacific war. The Japanese military adventure ended in a total failure in 1945. At the end of World War II, the USSR was a victorious military and political power. It swiftly and forcefully extended its influence into Eastern Europe. Soviet leaders also fought hard to achieve strategic parity with the United States. However, the over-extension of Soviet power in the world arena put enormous burdens on the Soviet economy. Foreign policy strains greatly intensified conflicts of state-market relations. It is ironic (or dialectic) that forty years after the end of World War II, the former defeated Japan emerged as a leading economic power with the most advanced technology. Although retaining or even strengthening its military forces, the Soviet Union was still economically under developed and entering a deep crisis.

The Endogenous and Exogenous Variables

Every economic system is influenced by endogenous and exogenous factors. The degree of a regime's ability to control is the main difference between endogenous and exogenous factors. While the regime can modify endogenous factors, it has little or no control over the exogenous factors. Even the exogenous factors that can be influenced are slow to change. For instance, existing workforce skills are endogenous; they can be transformed in the long run. Institutional and organizational variables are endogenous. The regime can reform them in the short run. Technical infrastructure is an objective and endogenous variable. It is changeable in the long term. In contrast, the existing international system is an exogenous factor. The Soviet regime did not have much control over the international system. Ed A. Hewett stated it clearly:

> Exogenous factors are either unchangeable or take a long time to be changed. Exogenous factors such as the weather, raw material and energy reserves, and accumulated capital stock (both human and physical) also influence the performance of the system, whatever its configuration. Variations in Soviet climatic conditions, which can be large, not only cause agricultural output to fluctuate, but also create disruptions in transport, which in turn add to bottlenecks in the economy.[7]

While the USSR was a cross-continental empire, Japan is an island nation. The Soviet Union's size was sixty times that of Japan. On the one hand, the enormous Soviet mass land created difficult problems for both administrative work and market exchange. The problems were especially serious in communication and transportation. Japan as an island nation has an excellent domestic transportation system symbolized by the high-speed railways connecting major cities and seaports. With a highly developed ocean-going industry, Japan has had few problems in sending manufactured goods abroad and importing raw materials. On the other hand, the USSR was blessed with rich natural resources. This seemingly great asset encouraged the Russian and Soviet tendency of extensive use of raw materials. Japan is a resource-poor country which is heavily dependent on foreign supply of raw materials. However, this apparent liability has created a national sensitivity to utilizing resources intensively and efficiently.

The Soviet Union was a multinational empire including more than one hundred nationalities; Japan is a highly homogeneous society. With only one-sixtieth the size of the USSR, Japan has a population more than 40 percent of the Soviet population. The Soviet political system was "federal in form and socialist in content" (Stalin); Japan has a unitary system. While the Soviet Union was the leader of the former Eastern bloc, Japan has been a minor player in strategic terms under the protection of the United States.

An economic system can be analyzed in the framework of the formal versus the de facto or informal systems. The Soviet economic system consisted of a formal system and a de facto system: "the system described in laws and decrees, which represents the way that Soviet leaders would have the economic system operate (the formal system), and the system as it actually operates, sometimes at complete variance with the existing laws and decrees (the de facto system)."[8]

The guiding principle behind the design of the Soviet economic system was that the Communist party should have institutionalized control of all major aspects of economic activity in the USSR. This goal clearly dominated other possible considerations, most notably economic efficiency. The CPSU controlled the economy through several mechanisms. For instance, the party appointed important personnel in economic administrative organizations and enterprises. Party organizations at different levels had their own *nomenklatura* lists.[9] Administrators and managers understood this and worked in favor of the party leaders' preference. The CPSU also controlled the agenda and set priorities for the national economy. Strategic goals of the economy and the most important policies of national development were decided by the Politburo. Furthermore, party organizations and party members within ministries and enterprises were responsible for monitoring the implementation of party policy. Ministries and local party organizations were held responsible to see that the plans were fulfilled in "their" enterprises.

A core feature of the Soviet formal system was its emphasis on centralized planning. The planning process was central to the Soviet economic system, performing many of the functions that markets perform in Western economies. It passed information on production possibilities and consumer preferences among the various actors.[10]

However, the Soviet economic system actually worked in a way quite different from this design. For instance, although the formal system excluded party organizations at all levels from involvement in the operational side of the economy, the CPSU in fact played a vital role. Such involvement took place at both the central and local levels. Another problem was the uncertainty of raw material supply. In order to avoid the unknowns, each enterprise and each ministry tended to develop autarky and vertical integration. When the formal system was not able to function satisfactorily, there emerged the so-called informal adjustment mechanisms. These were economic practices outside the formal system, such as the shadow economy, the second economy, and *blat*.[11] The informal adjustment mechanisms have developed to such a degree that they became an indispensable part of the de facto system and corollary of the formal system. The command economy could not operate without the assistance of the informal adjustment mechanisms.

The Japanese economic system differs from that of the Soviet Union in many aspects. First, there is a strong tendency in favor of consumer preference as reflected in the widely used phrase "the consumer is the king." Second, the state does not own and run the bulk of the economy. Third, the Liberal Democratic Party does not directly intervene in economic life as the Soviet Communist Party did. Fourth, the market plays a substantial role in resource allocations in Japan. Finally, the Japanese economic system encourages and strengthens a strong work ethic within the work force.

In the Japanese system, the lines between the formal and the informal system are not clear-cut. The formal system is legal-rational, while the informal system is highly personalistic. Daniel I. Okimoto has defined the Japanese state as a "network state," i.e., one able to exercise power only in terms of its network of ties with the private sector.

> The existence of various organizational structures in the Japanese economy gives MITI numerous levers, or points of access, by means of which to intervene in the marketplace. In the same vein, bureaucratic power is also relational in the sense that it emerges from the structure of LDP-bureaucracy-interest group alignments and the political exchanges that take place among them. The secret to the power of the Japanese state is thus embedded in the structure of its relationship to the rest of society. In this sense, Japan is a societal state.[12]

In the early 1960s, the Japanese government developed a National Income Doubling Plan and initiated an industrial restructuring. Unlike the Soviet case, the Japanese state did not purely rely on administrative commands to carry out its plans. However, the Japanese government did make loans available. In short, we should neither overstate the extent of the pure market mechanism nor underestimate the political side.

The Ministry of International Trade and Industry (MITI) plays a central role in Japanese economic development. MITI has the power to sanction the import of goods as well as the import of foreign technologies. It decides what industry the government will help to build. Furthermore, MITI also has a strong influence on Japan's banks. That is, the banks look to MITI for leads on what investments to make, knowing that the suggested investments would enjoy state protection and support. Besides MITI, another agency with a role in economic growth is the Economic Planning Agency (EPA), which was set up in 1946 at the SCAP's request. The EPA makes long-term socioeconomic development plans. "What might be called the dynamic part of Japan's planning is based on a very careful analysis of production trends abroad. The object is to see what are the production patterns in countries richer than Japan."[13] Although being an agency responsible for formulating economic development strategies, the EPA is much less powerful than the Soviet Gosplan. In fact, the EPA is often subjected to the influence of MITI and the Ministry of Finance.

Key factors in the postwar Japanese economic growth were the quality and quantity of the skilled workers, engineers, managers, and civil servants produced by the educational system. The educational level in prewar Japan was already comparable or even higher than that of many Western countries.[14] However, prewar education was heavily influenced by imperialist and militarist indoctrination. Fundamental reforms in education were carried out during the Allied occupation. Quality education has always been a national priority of the Japanese government.

Cultural heritage also contributed to Japan's economic growth. Max Weber's proposition of the Protestant ethic should be modified to reflect the Japanese case. The tradition of working hard and saving more helped Japanese businesses to invest and grow. Many Japanese workers have a deep sense of loyalty and belonging to their factories. Such sense is further strengthened by the lifetime employment system existing in some large enterprises. Workers often go to work early and stay overtime without receiving extra pay. In some cases, Japanese managers regularly seek advice from technicians and workers. The close interaction among managers, engineers, and workers has facilitated the growth of productivity. One might argue that Japanese cultural heritage contains elements that are functionally equivalent to the Protestant ethic analyzed by Weber.

In addition to systemic and cultural differences, there are differences between the patterns of technological development in Japan and the USSR. Types of machine technology are different in Japan and the Soviet Union in the postwar era. Japan did not rebuild its industry on the technical basis of the 1930s; the Soviet Union did. That type of industrial technology developed in the 1920s and 1930s reached its pinnacle during the Second World War. But the Soviet Union rebuilt its postwar industry on the basis of prewar technology. The Soviet increases in industrial output were chiefly due to vast infusions of labor and capital. Hence, the USSR lagged behind when Japan and other advanced industrial democracies were entering a new technological revolution.

Dramatic shifts in the international system have had contrasting impacts on both Japan and the USSR. In the early postwar era, Japan had little choice as a defeated power. Japan quickly became a highly successful "trading state" because its leaders and people made a conscious decision to enrich the country through domestic production and foreign trade. Strong U.S. support facilitated Japanese entry into the Bretton Woods system. On the contrary, the Soviet Union was excluded from the world trading system dominated by the United States and other Western powers.

The Japanese government did have control over some endogenous factors. For instance, the U.S. had not told Japan what kind of industry to build. The economic transformation of Japan after 1945 offered the most spectacular example of sustained modernization in several decades, outclassing almost all of the existing "advanced" countries as a commercial and technological competitor. One major reason for the Japanese miracle was its strong commitment in achieving the highest levels of quality control, and borrowing (and improving upon) sophisticated management techniques and production methods in the West.

The devastation of World War II left Japan's per capita income in 1950 at less than three-fourths its prewar level. With rapid economic growth, per capita income attained the prewar level in the mid-1950s and doubled this level by 1963. Between 1963 and 1973 its gross domestic product grew at the fantastic average of 10.1 percent a year, far in excess of that of any other industrialized nation. Even the oil crisis in 1973-1974, with its profound blow to the world economy, did not prevent Japan from achieving impressive annual growth of 4.1 percent between 1973 and 1985.[15] Steadily, relentlessly, its trade surpluses increased; its share of world production and market expanded. When the Allied Occupation ended in 1952, Japan's "gross national product was little more than one-third that of France or the United Kingdom. By the late 1970s the Japanese GNP was as large as the United Kingdom's and France's combined and more than half the size of America's."[16] Only the USSR in its most dynamic years had achieved anything like that degree of growth, but Japan had done it far less painfully and in a much more impressive, broader-based way.

The Soviet Union evolved along a very different route from the 1950s to the 1980s. In this period of dramatic economic growth for Japan, the Soviet Union not only maintained a strong army, but also achieved nuclear-strategic parity with the United States, developed an ocean-going navy, and extended its influence in various parts of the world. Yet this persistent drive to achieve strategic military equality with the Americans on the global scene created enormous socioeconomic strains in the economy and society. As a result the USSR suffered from increasing economic difficulties after the 1970s.[17]

In contrast to the gigantic Soviet military spending which consumed up to 20-25 percent of Soviet GNP, Japan has spent only around one percent of its GNP in national defense. After the disaster of World War II, Japan adopted an American-drafted Constitution that renounces war and narrowly circumscribes the role of the military in Japanese society. Given the circumscribed role of the military, Japan has been forced to rely heavily on the United States for both nuclear and conventional protection and for the defense of its vital strategic interests abroad. Under the 1960 Treaty of Mutual Cooperation and Security, the U.S. promised to defend Japan in case of attack. As Paul Kennedy pointed out, being able "to redirect its national energies from militaristic expansion and its resources from high defense spending, Japan has devoted itself to the pursuit of sustained economic growth, especially in export markets."[18]

Japan's concern for economic security is certainly understandable, given the country's almost total lack of raw materials, its geographic isolation, and the trauma of its prewar experiences. Closely related to economic security--indeed, an integral aspect of it--is Japan's growing integration in the international system and the Japanese perception of vulnerability. Japan largely depends on not only the continuous supply of raw materials from abroad but also the stability of the world trading system for its survival and development.

Kennedy, Joseph Nye, Richard Rosecrance, and other scholars have debated on the changing nature of world power.[19] In the long term, many people believe, economic power and technological innovation count more than military power. In the age of rapid technological change, the Soviet Union was losing its national power when it continued to lag behind the West in key technological sectors. National security was always a top concern for the Soviet leadership. New political thinking rejected nuclear deterrence as the key guarantee for world peace. As Gorbachev stated clearly in 1987, the "fundamental principle of the new political outlook is very simple: nuclear war cannot be a means of achieving political, economic, ideological or any other goals."[20] The new Soviet thinking emphasized political rather than purely military methods of achieving national security. It also put much more emphasis on developing the national economy as a whole rather than expanding the military-industrial complex.

The "Developmental State" and the "Authoritarian Welfare State"

Although it is always difficult to generalize the nature of a particular state in a simple phrase, many analysts have attempted to do so. An appropriate catch-word helps to highlight the essential features of a particular system. The risk of oversimplification in using such catch-words or phrases could be reduced by adding qualifying conditions to the terms. By focusing on state-market relations, we shall argue that the postwar Japanese state has been mainly "developmental." The Soviet state evolved from Stalinist totalitarianism to Brezhnevian "welfare-state authoritarianism."

Some analysts attribute Japan's economic success to its unique pattern of government-business interaction. The essential characteristic of the Japanese government-business relationship is that the business community and the various government departments have been in close communication with each other from the days of the Meiji Restoration. The result is a style of industrial development which has allowed Japanese business considerable initiative and independence even when subject to administrative guidance facilitated by a variety of government aids and incentives.[21] Thus, Japan's planning and development model sharply differs from that of the Soviet Union which was characterized by the bureaucratic domination with little room for market forces to work.

Chalmers Johnson argues that the Japanese state is a developmental state which differs from both the Western pluralistic state and the Soviet-type centralized state.

> As a particular pattern of late development, the Japanese case differs from the Western market economies, the communist dictatorships of development, or the new states of the postwar world. The most significant difference is that in Japan the state's role in the economy is shared with the private sector, and both the public and private sectors have perfected means to make the market work for developmental goals. This pattern has proved to be the most successful strategy of intentional development among the historical cases.[22]

Building on the theoretical constructions of Max Weber ["market economy" (*Verkehrwirtschaft*) versus "planned economy" (*Planwirtschaft*)] and Ralf Dahrendorf ["market rationality" versus "plan rationality"], Johnson focused our attention on the differences between what he termed "plan rational" and "plan ideological" economies.

> Economies of the Soviet type are not plan rational but plan ideological. In the Soviet Union and its dependencies and emulators, state ownership of the means of production, state planning, and bureaucratic goal-setting are not rational means to a developmental goals (even if they may once have been); they are fundamental values in themselves, not to be challenged by evidence of either inefficiency or ineffectiveness.[23]

From Johnson's perspective, Japan is plan rational, and the Soviet Union was not. The Japanese government gives greatest precedence to a concern with the structure of domestic industry and with promoting the nation's international competitiveness. The existence of an industrial policy implies a strategic, or goal-oriented, approach to the economy. Following the Meiji Restoration of 1868, Japan emerged as a developmental, plan-rational state whose economic orientation was keyed to industrial policy.

Industrial policy, according to Robert Ozaki, refers to a complex of "policies concerning protection of domestic industries, development of strategic industries, and adjustment of the economic structure in response to or in anticipation of internal and external changes."[24] Those policies are formulated and pursued by the Japanese government in the cause of the national interest, as the term "national interest" is understood by government officials. Viewed in comparative perspective, Okimoto argues,

MITI's industrial policy has emerged from a distinctive set of regime characteristics. Of these, perhaps the most unusual are the long period of Liberal Democratic Party (LDP) domination, the weakness of labor-based political parties, and the lightness of Japan's defense burden. In few other large industrial states can one find any one of these characteristics--not to mention the combination of all three.[25]

The LDP was in power between 1955 and July 1993. Contrary to its name, the Liberal Democratic Party is neither liberal nor democratic. It is a very conservative party in which a few factional leaders decide major policy for the party. The president of LDP has been elected through negotiation within a very small group of factional leaders. When the president was chosen, he would be elected prime minister by LDP Diet members who were under the constraint of strong party discipline. These Diet members usually depend upon their factional leaders for political and financial support. On the one hand, the LDP domination of Japanese politics in since 1955 has provided a high degree of continuity of the pro-business and pro-export policy. On the other hand, strong internal competition among four or five big factions within the party has allowed the existence of limited pluralism and a possibility for alternative policy to emerge. Furthermore, the LDP must take the influence of opposition parties into account.[26] Therefore, LDP domination of Japanese politics is not comparable to the CPSU's monopoly of power before the Gorbachev era.

The comparative weakness of organized labor has had a profound effect on the postwar development of the Japanese economy. Japan pursued "the fastest pro-producer route to economic growth. Only after doubling output every seven or eight years did the LDP government turn belatedly to the task of upgrading the country's welfare programs."[27] Without militant demands from organized labor, Japan also has managed to escape the trap of protecting industries no longer capable of competing against low-cost producers in latecomer countries.

Japanese government officials are skeptical of the complete free market principles. "Although the market imparts substantial impetus to long-term economic efficiency, it offers no guarantee that broader social, political, or economic security interests will be served." Thus, to "derive optimal outcomes, the visible hand of the state must work in conjunction with the invisible hand of the market."[28] The state is to Japanese society the source of collective identity, guarantor of continuity, guardian of common interests, and main vehicle for reaching collective goals.[29]

In contrast, the Russian/Soviet state has evolved from a developmental state via totalitarianism to an authoritarian welfare state. Welfare-state authoritarianism is a concept developed by George Breslauer to characterize the Soviet regime under Brezhnev. In Breslauer's view, that regime was authoritarian rather than totalitarian for a number of reasons. First, it had moved far in the direction of a form of "corporate pluralism" within the political elite. Second, it had expanded and regularized opportunities for specialist input into decision-making processes on social and economic issues. Third, it had abandoned the use of mass terror as an instrument of policy, had de-politicized many realms of social life, and allowed a considerable measure of physical security and privacy for the politically conformist. Thus, whereas the regime had retained its mobilizational character, it no longer engaged in totalitarian forms of mass mobilization.[30] According to Breslauer, the welfare-state policy includes:

> ...a basic commitment to minimal and rising levels of material and social security, public health, and education. Equally important, its commitment to welfare includes an egalitarian commitment to job security and subsidized prices for basic commodities--even at the cost of considerable economic inefficiency and failure to develop entrepreneurial initiative.[31]

The Soviet authoritarian welfare state made people dependent upon the state for job security and for political promotion and economic improvement. The level of material welfare, or the quality of public health, was not in accord with many Western definitions of a welfare state, but the term "welfare state" was useful in differentiating the social policies of the Brezhnev era from Stalinism.

A related conceptualization of the Soviet system was Kenneth Jowitt's "neotraditionalism." Jowitt's focus "is the Soviet party's loss of organizational integrity; i.e., regime corruption." Thus, a phenomenon like the "second economy" will be "understood as a central component in the neotraditionalization of a novel form of charismatic organization and rule--the Leninist party-regime, in this case the Soviet regime."[32] Jowitt disagreed with Reinhard Bendix's suggestion that "Communist dictatorships" are "clearly outside Weber's tripartite division" of traditional, charismatic, and legal-rational authorities. Jowitt intended to demonstrate that Weber's "tripartite division" when appropriately reformulated was, in fact, the most useful basis for understanding the nature of Leninist regimes. According to Jowitt, the Soviet regime could best be seen as "an institutionally novel form of charismatic political, social, and economic organization undergoing routinization in a neotraditional direction, one quite consistent with its political organization and ideological self-conception."[33]

In the neotraditional society, party and state bureaucrats believed that political power could give the right to everything. The phrase "money is rubbish" spoken by a Communist commissar reflected the contemptuous attitude to the market and to money making typical of party men who saw their power as opposed by the power of the market.[34] As a result, there was a strong anti- market sentiment among Soviet officials. Jowitt pointed out:

> Communist cadres opposed the ethos as well as the power of the market *system* as a source of contamination, as a mode of existence that is undignified, demeaning, and inappropriate. In short, ideal as well as material interests supported the party's charismatic orientation to economic action.[35]

Building on Jowitt's theoretical construction of communist neo-traditionalism, Andrew G. Walder has developed a detailed case study of work and authority in Chinese industry. Walder also provided some insightful comparative analyses of the Soviet and Chinese cases. For instance, he stressed the significance of "a system of clientelism," "particularism," and the "network of instrumental-personal ties" in the two countries.[36]

The prevalence of *blat* in social interactions is another expression of the charismatic-traditional quality of the Soviet polity and economy. *Blat* typically refers to ties of reciprocity, not to impersonal, strictly accountable exchanges of standardized value. *Blat* relationships and exchanges are status-type substitutes for the impersonal predictability and standardization of a market economy and electoral polity. Both the tsarist and Soviet leadership work with a traditional, and concrete, fixed amount in priority areas (e.g., court expense for Catherine, missiles or heavy trucks for Brezhnev), and the "rest" is practically if not ideally "left over" for those who are cunning or "economical."[37] In economic relationships, many Soviet managers prefer face-to-face deals over impersonal contracts.

In the Soviet system, success and failure of enterprises, as well as individuals, were socialized. This was reflected in the widely heard joke "They pretend to pay us, we pretend to work." The authoritarian welfare-state limited people's opportunity for political participation and entrepreneurial activities, but it also provided a safety net of minimal economic security. The Soviet state under Brezhnev lost its initial "developmental" nature; what it emphasized was "trust in cadres" and stability. Brezhnev's policy led to the stagnation of political and economic life.

In the era of stagnation, however, the struggle between the modernizers and the conservatives was intensified in the USSR. In the postwar period, those Soviet leaders who advocated greater stress on consumer goods (butter over guns) lost to those who advocated a strong military orientation. For instance, Malenkov lost to Khrushchev; Kosygin lost to Brezhnev. This pattern did not change until Gorbachev came to power in 1985.

The Contrasting Cultural Traditions

Without examining cultural variables, we cannot fully understand either the Russian/Soviet authoritarian tradition and the emphasis on a safety net against socioeconomic uncertainties, or the Japanese emphasis on national economic security and development. Therefore, we shall study the interaction between cultural traditions and state-market relations in spite of the unusual complexity often involved in cultural analysis. Lucian Pye and Sidney Verba suggest that the concept of political culture provides a useful basis for examining the links between social and economic factors and political performance. Samuel

Huntington points out that political culture can be an important independent variable in explaining political change.[38] Understanding political culture also is important for explaining changes in state-market relations.

What is political culture? According to Archie Brown, a political culture "consists of the subjective perception of history and politics, the fundamental beliefs and values, the foci of identification and loyalty, and the political knowledge and expectations which are the product of the specific historical experience of the nations and groups."[39]

Robert C. Tucker defined political culture more comprehensively: "a culture is a society's customary way of life, comprising both accepted modes of thought and belief and accepted patterns of conduct. Political culture is everything in a culture that pertains to government and politics."[40] In studying political culture in Cuba, Richard Fagen viewed political culture as embracing "patterned ways of life and action as well as the states of mind that sustain and condition these patterns."[41] In other words, political culture contains both beliefs and behavior.

In essence, political culture "consists of the system of empirical beliefs, expressive symbols, and values which defines the situation in which political action takes place."[42] According to Pye and Verba's often quoted definition, the concept of political culture suggests that:

> the traditions of a society, the spirit of its public institutions, the passions and the collective reasoning of its citizenry, and the style and operating codes of its leaders are not just random products of historical experience but fit together as a part of a meaningful whole and constitute an intelligible web of relations. For the individual the political culture provides controlling guidelines for effective political behavior, and for the collectivity it gives a systematic structure of values and rational considerations.[43]

Cultural explanations are essentially explanations of differences. On the one hand, different patterns of political change can be explained to a certain extent by cultural difference. On the other hand, different patterns of political change also bring changes into political culture. One of the controversies within the discipline of comparative politics concerns the appropriateness of explaining political behavior in terms of culture as opposed to more "structural" considerations. The separation of cultural and institutional factors may be justified for analytical purposes. If political institution is the structural aspect of political system, political culture is the psychological aspect of the same system. In real life, it is always difficult to separate the two aspects of the political system.

One of the most salient characteristics of pre-democratic Japanese political culture was the extent to which ordinary citizens felt themselves "subjects" of political life, rather than active participants in it. No longer is this the case among large segments of the public. The affluence and mass educational attainments of the postwar era have given the individual Japanese the resources associated with a greater tendency to participate in public life. Consciousness of one's ability to take advantage of those opportunities and resources has proceeded apace: protest, both within and outside the law, has been a frequent occurrence in postwar politics.[44]

Although many continuities can be observed between prewar and postwar political culture in Japan, it is important to appreciate the degree of change in political life and socialization patterns in these two periods. The overall prewar tendencies were toward authoritarian or "subject" attitudes about the relationship of the ordinary citizen to political life. It is quite clear that the early postwar period witnessed a sharp break with known political tradition. The sum effect of the American Occupation reforms, and the growing and self-conscious concern for "democratic behavior," was to at least disseminate the norms of popular government throughout Japanese society.[45]

In contrast, there was no such fundamental cultural transformation in the USSR in the early postwar period. De-Stalinization under Khrushchev was only a limited liberalization. Brezhnev re-strengthened many "patriotic," "heroic" prewar or war traditions. A real cultural revolution in the Soviet Union did not begin until the *glasnost* of the late 1980s.

Nevertheless, ideology as part of the political culture did experience some changes. Although there were changes in "petty ideology," in David Joravsky's terminology, Soviet "grand ideology" remained intact before Gorbachev's reform.[46] Under Khrushchev, the view took shape that the "dictatorship of the proletariat" had given way to a "state of the whole people." During the Brezhnev era, the notion of "developed socialism" degenerated into an apologia for the status quo. The open-minded Andropov emphasized that the USSR was only at "the beginning" stage of "developed socialism." Gorbachev finally abandoned "developed socialism" as a central concept.

Brown contended that the Soviet Union did not have a unified political culture, but it did have a dominant one.[47] In other words, there were certain values, fundamental political beliefs, and perceptions of history shared by a majority of the population. Because political culture is historically conditioned, the long-term authoritarian character of the Russian and Soviet state constitutes a serious impediment to political change of a genuinely democratic nature. Gorbachev made increasing use of the term "political culture." He identified as a major defect of existing Soviet political culture the lack of tolerance and respect for contrary opinions. "We are now going through the school of democracy afresh. We are learning. Our political culture is still inadequate. Our culture in debate is insufficient, and also inadequate is our respect for the point of view even of our friend and comrade. We are emotional people."[48]

To a certain degree, political culture is independent of the political system. Thus, while a political system may be destroyed, the culture underlying that system may continue to exist. For instance, after the breakdown of the tsarist state, elements of the Russian political culture did not perish completely.[49] On the other hand, political culture sometimes can go ahead of the political system because of the relative independence of the former from the latter. Therefore, civic culture began to emerge in Soviet and post-Soviet Russia before the establishment of a civic political system, i.e., a pluralist state.[50] It is increasingly clear that the emerging civic culture plays a positive role in the political reform.[51]

It seems that differences in political culture do matter in deciding the pattern of political change, and state-market relations. Japan's political change since the Meiji Restoration can be seen as a process of integrating the traditional Japanese culture into the mainstream of the world civilization and vice versa. The Japanese have been successful in modernizing their socioeconomic and political systems while keeping distinctive national characteristics. In Russia, modernizers and Slavophiles have been struggling with each other regarding how to deal with Western values. When Lenin came to power, he tried to separate "culture the ideology" (which should be rejected) from "culture the civilization" and "culture the knowledge" (which may be absorbed).[52] Lenin's attempt at creating a new Soviet culture was frustrating. Stalin forcefully engaged in building socialism within one country. He combined some elements of Russian tradition, particularly the compulsory state service, with the Bolshevik elitist spirit and highly centralized party system to create the state-centered system. The phrase "We are all servants of the state" reflected Stalin's mentality.

In Russian tradition, there was a strong emphasis on the tsar or tsarina as a powerful leader, e.g., Peter the Great or Catherine the Great. Stalin developed the cult of personality around Lenin and later replaced it with the cult of Stalin himself. Khrushchev attacked the cult of personality and started de-Stalinization. However, Khrushchev also attempted to build a cult of personality for himself. The shadow influence of this traditional emphasis on a strong leader could be seen even during the failed coup in August 1991. Many demonstrators against the coup shouted "Yeltsin! Yeltsin!" instead of "Democracy and Freedom!"

There was no comparable cult of personality for Japanese political leaders except the emperor. The Japanese emperor was used as a symbol of national unity. But for the most part during its history, the emperor did not engage in political decision making. In other words, the emperor reigned over rather than ruled the country. The majority of Japanese leaders, including the Meiji reform leaders, kept a low profile and respected consensus building. The Japanese emphasis on consensus building and collective leadership is in sharp contrast to the Russian/Soviet tradition of emphasizing powerful individual leaders.

Both Japan and Russia/USSR states had a tradition of putting state interests above individual interests or civil liberty. Russia/USSR in particular had a tradition of building the "compulsory service state." Peter the Great in the early eighteenth century started the process of building Russian industry and expanding its military. In the state-building process, the regime initiated the binding of all classes in compulsory state service. The emancipation of serfs in 1861 was an effort at unbinding social classes to the state. As Tucker has pointed out:

Although it witnessed a considerable liberalization of Russian life, the autocratic, authoritarian, centralized, bureaucratic state structure that evolved in the state-building process was too well entrenched, its repressive powers too formidable, and history-bred submissiveness of the people too enduring, for the processes of change to work their way to fruition peacefully.[53]

The February 1917 revolution ended the tsarist regime but was unable to produce an enduring democratic state. The provisional government was soon overthrown by the Bolsheviks. "Soviet Communism had been designed by its principal founder as in essence a new culture containing within itself a system of party-state power."[54] By reversing the New Economic Policy, Stalin opened a new state-building process centering on forced-draft industrialization with emphasis upon heavy industry and military-industry power. The authoritarian welfare state was similar to the tsarist state in binding all social classes in serving the state. The unbinding of social classes in compulsory state service did not begin until the mid-1980s.

Stephen Burant analyzed the influence of Russian tradition on the political style of the Soviet elite.

Upon assuming power in 1917, the Bolsheviks sought to effect a cultural revolution in Russia. However, traditional Russian culture exercised a significant impact on the demeanor, outlook, and style of the Soviet leadership. In their behavior, Soviet rulers betray a conservatism, a disdain for ingenuity, and even a crudity that bears similarity to the work ethic of the Russian peasantry, and that conflicts with the conscious, resolute, ideologically driven personality of the new socialist man first described by Lenin.[55]

In Russian and Soviet culture, there were elements of risk aversion. Risk aversion extended into economic development as well, as entrepreneurs were few and far between. Russia's leaders felt the continual need to obtain revenues and strengthen their political control. The Soviet state offered "guaranteed social order and womblike economic security. It not only provides housing and utilities at very low cost, it furnishes this basic material security no matter how unproductive Soviet citizens may be."[56] The risk aversion attitudes were reflected in the widespread fear of the uncertainties of the market and the lack of exchange culture. The Bolsheviks inherited and developed this deep rooted tradition. "Although Lenin presented socialism as a successor to Western European capitalism, his program rally implied a different path of development--a path emphasizing old communal values and an absence of the insecurity of the market." As a result, Jerry Hough continued to argue, "the protection of frightened people from unsettling market forces meant the creation of monopolistic ministries that totally protected the country's industrialists from foreign competition."[57] Under welfare-state authoritarianism, the state was supposed to protect people from the unpredictability of market cycles. Instead of bringing the USSR to a position of world leadership, autarky and protectionism meant that the country began to fall further and further behind.

In Japan, the Meiji reformers overcame the fear of market insecurity by initiating state capitalism first and then selling state enterprises to private entrepreneurs. Of course, there was state capitalism under the last two tsars, but the Bolsheviks destroyed it. In the late 1920s, the world economic crisis created enormous strains and tensions in Japanese society and the economy. Xenophobia and nationalist military officers and bureaucrats designed a program of "political totalitarianism at home and territorial aggression abroad."[58] Japan's attempt at establishing economic autarky and military territorial expansion ended in a complete failure in World War II. After the war, the U.S. Occupation treated Japan leniently. Within a few years of Japan's surrender, the United States was embroiled in the Cold War. The U.S. provided Japan with loans, technology transfers and access to the vast American market to speed economic recovery and growth. Thus, it is no exaggeration to claim that the Allied Occupation substantially transformed not only the Japanese political and economic systems but also brought new elements of culture into Japan. Postwar Japan regained and further developed its exchange culture and trading strategies. In the 1980s, Japan attained a level of industrial development second only to the United States, even surpassing it in some areas.

Most traditional cultures are undergoing changes in the age of the communication revolution. The development of communication and transportation technology has greatly enhanced the scope and speed of cultural exchange. The ease of communication helps the spread of global political culture. A trend of "internationalization" is becoming more influential in Japan, while nationalist sentiment is also growing in some sections of the society.[59] If the former trend continues to gain support over the latter, Japan will become a country that is easy for other countries to live with. In Russia, the struggle between modernizer and anti-Westernizer has been intensified in the recent years. Common human values, part of the global culture, are gaining ground in Russia and other post-Soviet republics. With more independent tendencies developed in various republics, the rise of pluralist culture is more promising. However, dangerous Slavophilistic sentiment represented by the "Pamyat" should not be ignored.[60] If the reformers cannot overcome or at least neutralize the extremely nationalistic and anti-Western sentiments among the Slavophiles, then a return to dark days of the past is one possible scenario.

Learning from the Past and *Perestroika*

Reforming the Soviet economy was a central task of *perestroika* (restructuring). Since the mid 1950s, there have been several serious efforts at reforming the centrally planned economic system. However, all the past efforts, including the 1957 *sovnarkhoz* reforms under Khrushchev and the 1965 Kosygin reforms, resulted in failure. Gorbachev initiated a new cycle of reform. One of his advantages was the lessons that could be learned from the past. Gorbachev gave voice to the importance of this learning when he stated: "In carrying out a radical economic reform, it was important to preclude the repetition of the past mistakes which in the 1950s, 1960s, and 1970s doomed to failure out attempts to change the system of economic management."[61] In order to better understand *perestroika*, we shall analyze some key lessons from the past.

The 1957 Khrushchev reform was the first effort to change the Stalinist command economy. The major approach was replacing the ministerial system with *sovnarkhozy* (regional economic councils). It was designed to eliminate the "departmentalism" of the ministerial system, replacing it with a rational division of labor within and between regions. "In fact localism soon began to assert itself as *sovnarkhozy* quite predictably favored their own enterprises over others, the result being a potentially disastrous move toward a fractionated, regionally based, autarky divided among 100 or so 'economies'."[62] Khrushchev heavily relied on administrative method to reform the administrative organizations. In particular, he saw the party organization as a tool of reform; he did not realize that the bureaucratized party organization itself was an obstacle for reform. In Breslauer's words, what Khrushchev engaged in was only "deconcentration," not genuine "decentralization."[63]

The 1965 reform was the only effort at a comprehensive reform in the USSR before Gorbachev. This reform was better prepared than the Khrushchev reform. In 1962 there was a debate led by Evsei Liberman. Liberman advocated the elimination of unwarranted central interference in enterprise activities and the use of material incentives in promoting productivity. The basic measures of 1965 reforms were an administrative reform reinstituting the ministerial system and an overhaul of the enterprise incentive system. The Kosygin reform reduced the number of obligatory targets reaching enterprises from around forty to eight and replaced gross output with sales as the leading success indicator. Unfortunately, the reform was dead by the early 1970s. Brezhnev's concern with industrial reorganization in 1973 and the 1979 reform decrees did not produce positive results.

The reasons for failures of the past reforms are complicated, but new reformers can learn from the following key factors:

1. The Soviet economic system was a complex one with many interrelated parts. In order to achieve success, a reform should not touch just part of the system; it must be comprehensive. In other words, a successful restructuring of the Soviet economic system must be an overhaul rather than a partial reform. Ideally, it would be desirable to carry out a comprehensive reform at once. In reality, a successful reform often can only be implemented step by step. To implement a comprehensive

reform program, reformers must keep a strategic perspective while adapting to specific conditions.

2. Administrative reorganization alone cannot solve the real problems. Neither the elimination of the ministerial system in 1957 nor the re-establishment of it in 1965 helped to solve the problems of departmentalism or localism. The administrative reform must be accompanied by a cultural and political reform. The real problem is the source of power. A true decentralization of power should start with building democracy at the enterprise level by giving workers the right to elect managers and to participate in major decision making. Decentralization of power cannot succeed without a corresponding reduction of responsibility. In the early reforms including the 1973 and 1979 economic reforms, no effort was made to reduce the responsibilities of the administrative organs even when their power was deconcentrated. As a result, the administrative organs always found ways to regain control of "their" enterprises.

3. Former reformers did not fully appreciate the importance of market mechanisms. Their emphasis was on improving or "perfecting" the central planning system (administrative methods) rather than replacing it with market mechanisms (economic methods). Thus, no serious price reform was carried out.

4. "Revolution from above" alone does not work. Revolution from above is a historical tradition in Russian society. However, the failures of the 1957 and 1965 reforms demonstrated that this traditional strategy did not work under the contemporary situation. A key reason for the failures of the two reforms was the lack of popular support from below.

5. It is necessary for the reform leaders to have independent power bases. Khrushchev's failure partly resulted from losing support in the Politburo and finally his deposition from the party leadership in 1964. Kosygin, chairman of the Council of Ministers, never gained strong support from General Secretary Brezhnev. In fact, it was Brezhnev who applied the braking mechanism to the Kosygin reforms. Thus, it is of vital importance for today's reformers to create their own independent power bases.

6. It is necessary to re-negotiate the social contract. The social contract in the authoritarian Soviet welfare-state system provided economic security and required relatively equal distribution of incomes. Economic security, which was reflected in the absence of involuntary unemployment, and egalitarianism have become major sources of disincentive for productivity. Without renegotiating the social contract, the past reformers were not able to find enough individual initiative and incentive for technological innovation and economic development.

The failure of the past reforms led to a period of stagnation in the Soviet Union. Stagnation was reflected in many aspects including Brezhnev's policy of trust in cadres and his theory of the "developed socialism" which meant only fine-tuning the system. The result was the intensification of conflict between the formal economy of the state and the markets of the de facto economic system that resulted in deepening of the contradictions in the Soviet system. Gorbachev pointed out the consequence of this situation when he observed in 1987 that "the gap in the efficiency of production, quality of products, scientific and technological development, the production of advanced technology and the use of advanced techniques began to widen, and not to our advantage."[64]

After the death of Brezhnev in 1982, Andropov started a serious debate on the economic system. His successor Chernenko acted as only a caretaker. When Gorbachev was elected general secretary of the CPSU in March 1985, he opened a new chapter of Soviet politics. Our next chapter will analyze *perestroika* with an emphasis on marketization and democratization.

Notes

1. Robert Scalapino, "The American Occupation of Japan--Perspectives after Three Decades," *Annals of American Academy of Political and Sciences*, Vol. 428 (1976), p. 105.

2. "The Constitution of Japan," in Kyoko Inoue, *MacArthur's Japanese Constitution: A Linguistic and Cultural Study of Its Making* (Chicago: University of Chicago Press, 1991), p. 275.

3. Robert E. Ward, "Conclusion," in Ward and Sakamoto Yoshikazu (eds.), *Democratizing Japan: The Allied Occupation* (Honolulu: University of Hawaii Press, 1987), p. 430.

4. Bruce R. Scott, John W. Rosenblum, and Audrey T. Sproat, *Case Studies in Political Economy: Japan 1854-1977* (Harvard Business School, 1980), pp. 125-126.

5. Quoted in *Ibid.*, p. 138.

6. *Ibid.*

7. Ed A. Hewett, *Reforming the Soviet Economy: Equality versus Efficiency* (Washington: Brookings Institution, 1988), pp. 94-95.

8. *Ibid.*, p. 99.

9. The *nomenklatura* system was established in the 1920s and existed until the deepening of *perestroika* in the late 1980s. Jerry Hough described the system: "Each party committee had its list of posts, called *nomenklatura* in Russian, and personnel could not be appointed or elected to these posts or removed from them without the agreement of the specified party committee." Jerry Hough, Russia and the West: Gorbachev and the Politics of Reform (New York: Simon and Schuster, 1988), p.160.

10. Hewett, *Reforming the Soviet Economy*, p. 15.

11. *Ibid.*, especially chapter 4. For a discussion of different market mechanisms existing in the USSR, see Aron Katsenelinboigen, "Coloured Markets in the Soviet Union," Soviet Studies, Vol. 29 (1977), pp. 62-85. For an analysis of the significance of informal adjustment mechanisms in the Soviet economy, see Jerry Hough, *The Soviet Prefect: The Local Party Organs in Industrial Decision-making* (Cambridge: Harvard University Press, 1969).

12. Daniel I. Okimoto, *Between MITI and the Market: Japanese Industrial Policy for High Technology* (Stanford: Stanford University Press, 1989), p. 226.

13. Scott, Rosenblum and Sproat, *Case Studies in Political Economy*, p. 137.

14. See Ronald Dore, *Education in Tokugawa Japan* (Berkeley: University of California Press, 1965); and Marius B. Jansen and Lawrence Stone, "Education and Modernization in Japan and England," *Comparative Studies in Society and History* Vol. 9 (1967), pp. 208-232.

15. Bela Balassa and Marcus Noland, *Japan in the World Economy* (Washington: Institute for International Economics, 1988), pp. 3-6.

16. Ezra Vogel, *Japan as Number One: Lessons for America* (Cambridge: Harvard University Press, 1979), pp. 9-10.

17. Paul Kennedy, *The Rise and Fall of the Great Powers: Economic and Military Conflict from 1500 to 2000* (New York: Vintage Books, 1987), pp.385-391, 429.

18. *Ibid*, p. 459.

19. For two conflicting views on the nature of world power, see Kennedy, *The Rise and Fall of the Great Powers*; and Joseph S. Nye, "The Changing Nature of World Power," *Political Science Quarterly*, Vol. 105, No. 2 (1990), pp. 177-192.

20. Mikhail Gorbachev, *Perestroika: New Thinking for Our Country and the World* (New York: Harper and Row, 1988), updated edition, p. 126.

21. Scott, Rosenblum, and Sproat, *Case Studies in Political Economy*, p. 134.

22. Chalmers Johnson, *MITI and the Japanese Miracle: The Growth of Industrial Policy, 1925-1975* (Stanford: Stanford University Press, 1982), p. viii.

23. *Ibid.*, p. 18.

24. Robert S. Ozaki, "Japanese Views on Industrial Organization," *Asian Survey*, Vol. X, No. 10 (1970), p. 879.

25. Okimoto, *Between MITI and the Market*, p. 232.

26. Gerald L. Curtis, *The Japanese Way of Politics* (New York: Columbia University Press, 1988).

27. Okimoto, *Between MITI and the Market*, p. 233.

28. *Ibid.*, p. 12

29. *Ibid*, p. 226.

30. George W. Breslauer, "On the Adaptability of Soviet Welfare-State Authoritarianism," in Erik P. Hoffmann and Robbin F. Laird (eds.), *The Soviet Polity in the Modern Era* (New York: Aldine de Gruyter, 1984), pp. 219-245.

31. *Ibid.*, p. 220.

32. Kenneth Jowitt, "Soviet Neotraditionalism: The Political Corruption of a Leninist Regime," *Soviet Studies*, Vol. XXXV, No. 3 (1983), pp. 275-297.

33. *Ibid.*, p. 278.

34. Alec Nove, "Is There a Ruling Class in the USSR?", *Soviet Studies*, Vol. XXVII, No. 4 (1975), p. 625.

35. Jowitt, "Soviet Neotraditionalism: The Political Corruption of a Leninist Regime," p. 279.

36. Andrew G. Walder, *Communist Neo-traditionalism: Work and Authority in Chinese Industry* (Berkeley: University of California Press, 1986), pp. 162-165.

37. Jowitt, "Soviet Neotraditionalism: The Political Corruption of a Leninist Regime," pp. 279, 280.

38. Lucian W. Pye and Sidney Verba (eds.), *Political Culture and Political Development* (Princeton: Princeton University Press, 1965). Samuel P. Huntington, "The Goals of Development," in Myron Weiner and Samuel P. Huntington (eds.), *Understanding Political Development* (Boston: Little Brown, 1987), pp. 3-32.

39. Archie Brown, "Introduction," in Archie Brown and Jack Gray (eds.), *Political Culture and Political Change in Communist States* (New York: Holmes & Meier, 1977), p.1.

40. Robert C. Tucker, *Political Culture and Leadership in Soviet Russia: From Lenin to Gorbachev* (New York: W. W. Norton, 1987), p. vii.

41. Richard R. Fagen, *The Transformation of Political Culture in Cuba* (Stanford: Stanford University Press, 1969), pp. 5-6.

42. Pye and Verba, *Political Culture and Political Development*, p. 7.

43. *Ibid.*

44. Takeshi Ishida and Ellis S. Krauss (eds.), *Democracy in Japan* (Pittsburgh: University of Pittsburgh Press, 1989), p. 329.

45. Bradley M. Richardson, *Political Culture of Japan* (Berkeley: University of California Press, 1974), pp. 13-14.

46. For a discussion of Joravsky's distinction of grand ideology and petty ideology, see "Introduction" to part 3 of Erik P. Hoffmann and Frederic J. Fleron, Jr. (eds.), *The Conduct of Soviet Foreign Policy* (Hawthorne: Aldine, 1980), p. 94.

47. Archie Brown, "Ideology and Political Culture," in Seweryn Bialer (ed.), *Politics, Society, and Nationality Inside Gorbachev's Russia* (Boulder: Westview Press, 1989), p. 17.

48. *Pravda*, July 15, 1987, p. 1.

49. Edward L. Keenan, "Muscovite Political Folkways," *The Russian Review*, Vol. 45 (1986), pp. 115-181; and Stephen R. Burant, "The Influence of Russian Tradition on the Political Style of the Soviet Elite," *Political Science Quarterly*, Vol. 102, No. 2 (1987), pp. 273-293.

50. For an analysis of cultural development in the Soviet Union, see Alec Nove, *Glasnost In Action: Cultural Renaissance in Russia* (Boston: Unwin Hyman, 1989). For a discussion of the emerging pluralism in the Soviet Union, see Stephen F. Cohen and Katrina Vanden Heuvel, *Voices of Glasnost: Interviews with Gorbachev's Reformers* (New York: W. W. Norton, 1989), pp. 107, 195.

51. S. Frederick Starr, "Soviet Union: A Civil Society," Foreign Policy, No. 70 (1988), pp. 26-41; and Gail W. Lapidus, "State and Society: Toward the Emergence of Civil Society in the Soviet Union," in Bialer, *Politics, Society, and Nationality Inside Gorbachev's Russia*, pp. 121-147.

52. See Carman Claudin-Urondo, *Lenin and the Cultural Revolution* (Atlantic Highlands: Humanities Press, 1977).

53. Tucker, *Political Culture and Leadership in Soviet Russia*, p. 111.

54. *Ibid.*, p. 48.

55. Burant, "The Influence of Russian Tradition on Political Style of Soviet Elite," p. 288.

56. John M. Joyce, "The Old Russian Legacy," *Foreign Policy*, No. 55 (1984), p. 140.

57. Hough, *Russia and the West*, pp. 9, 10.

58. Michael A. Barnhart, *Japan Prepares for Total War: The Search for Economic Security, 1919-1941* (Ithaca: Cornell University Press, 1987), p. 20.

59. Edwin O. Reischauer, *The Japanese Today: Change and Continuity* (Cambridge: Harvard University Press, 1988), pp. 395-412.

60. The Pamyat [Memory] Society advocates very aggressive Russian nationalism and anti-Semitism. For a discussion of the nature and influence of Pamyat, see Cohen and Heuvel, *Voices of Glasnost*, pp. 65-66.

61. Gorbachev, *Perestroika*, p. 70.

62. Hewett, *Reforming the Soviet Economy*, pp. 225-226.

63. George W. Breslauer has made a distinction between "deconcentration" and "decentralization."

The post-Stalin effort to deburden higher levels of administration of excessively detailed planning is not decentralization, but deconcentration. Decentralization, or "marketization," would require the extension to local executives of genuine autonomy from party or ministerial intervention, and the establishment of markets as coordinating devices. Neither Khrushchev nor Brezhnev stood for this.

See Breslauer, *Khrushchev and Brezhnev as Leaders: Building Authority in Soviet Politics* (Boston: George Allen & Unwin, 1982), p. 4, note 5.

64. Gorbachev, *Perestroika*, p. 70.

4

Perestroika and the
Push Toward Marketization

Perestroika (restructuring) was an ambitious program of systemic transformation. The term *perestroika* is subjected to various interpretations. Its meaning changed along dramatic evolvement of domestic and international contexts. In the broadest sense, *perestroika* referred to the combination of a revolution from above and a revolution from below. The dynamic interactions between the two revolutions profoundly transformed the nature of the Soviet system and eventually led to the total collapse of the USSR. While destroying the old regime, *perestroika* did not succeed in creating a viable new system. The deepening of socioeconomic crisis resulted in rejection of the administrative command system and the push toward marketization. Russia today is facing a dual challenge, i.e., resolving the vital question of who controls the supreme power of the state on the one hand, and making painful but necessary transition to the market on the other hand.

Most pre-Gorbachev leaders believed that the Soviet economic system could be workable with some modification. When he came into power as the general secretary of the CPSU in March 1985, Gorbachev grossly underestimated the profound conflicts between the state and market in the Soviet Union. Without knowing what kind of change was required, he started with moderate reform but was forced into more and more radical positions by the rise of popular pressure and the deepening of the economic crisis. The growing tension within the authoritarian welfare-state system dragged Soviet society into a profound crisis. Sources of the crisis include the conflict between equality and efficiency, as well as contradictions between the formal and the informal systems.

In the early stage of *perestroika*, the main focus was on how to make the existing system work, rather than on how to create a totally new type of state-market relationship. In fact, the very idea of market was quite alien and remote to the Soviet leadership, which had been used to the administrative command system. Some reform-minded intellectuals started the market debate in 1987. As the Soviet economy continued to deteriorate, reformers were forced to search for viable alternatives to the command economy.

By the end of 1990, most Soviet reformers realized that marketization was the only viable alternative for the Stalinist system. According to the famous Shatalin 500-day plan, the right to property is to be realized through denationalization and privatization, giving over state property to citizens.[1] The plan stated that a market-oriented society was dictated by the "universal nature of laws of economic and social development. The attempt to impose a different scenario, a unique path for one country, goes counter to the logic of history, is doomed from the outset."[2] This reflected a full dropping of the claim that Marx had discovered a universal law of human development.

Many serious problems must be resolved during the transition to the market. According to the Shatalin plan, the transition to the market should combine institutional reforms, the beginning of privatization and decentralization, with the first steps of stabilization. Then prices will be liberalized step by step. "Destatization" is a key to a successful market transition because the new market relations simply cannot develop without lifting the command structure imposed by the authoritarian state. The "demonopolization" of the large state enterprises is going on simultaneously. The convertibility of the ruble must be completed. A foreign exchange market is to be created. Finally, the market economy is developed on the basis of private ownership of the means of production.[3]

The democratization of the Soviet state and the growth of a pluralist political culture were necessary steps for creating and improving the new pattern of state-market relations in the USSR. Each of the tasks listed in the transition plan is very difficult to accomplish. The transition to the market needs many years of hard work rather than a short period of time. In addition to the enormous amount of work involved in the structural and institutional reforms, the deeply rooted patterns of people's thinking and behavior also must be transformed in order for Russia to enter the mainstream world civilization.

Gorbachev first embraced and then rejected the 500-day plan. The political risks of marketization were big problems for the Soviet leaders. It seemed that Gorbachev was facing a no-win situation. Were he to give up control over the economy, he might lose political power. If the economy collapsed, his rule would be ended too. The economic system is interconnected with political and belief systems; it is difficult to reform only one system without changing the others. The fact of the matter is that without reforms in other fields, purely economic reforms cannot create a viable economic system.

The market economy has its own logic. The market needs its supporting systems, particularly the legal constitutional framework which provides legal protection and predictability for market activities. On the contrary, the highly rigid and non-independent legal system supporting the centrally planned economy is incompatible with the market economy. The creation of the legal foundation for the market economy takes time.

Stalin destroyed the New Economic Policy along with its already limited market mechanisms and established the centrally planned economy by commands and coercion. As a result of *perestroika* and especially the dramatic changes in 1991, the administrative command system has been dismantled mainly by political means. Having lived under socialism for almost three-quarters of a century, do older Russians still remember the old way of doing business? Even if they do remember the past, pre-revolutionary Russians did not have a dynamic market system from which the post-communist generations could learn. Can the younger generations learn how to do business in ways alien to the environment in which they grew up? Will they be able to make the necessary adjustments to market mechanisms? Answers to these questions should be both political and economic in nature. The establishment of a new market economy cannot be accomplished by political means alone. Economic means, particularly the growth of entrepreneurship of hundreds and thousands of individuals, are absolutely essential for building a market-oriented system.

Nationalism was an explosive factor influencing the changing nature of the Soviet state. The centralized Soviet state was partly designed to control the multinational empire. When Gorbachev started *perestroika*, he did not fully take the nationality factor into account. Thus, when the demand for independence grew among the Baltic and other republics, the threat of national disintegration became a big challenge for further political and economic reforms. When the Soviet Union finally collapsed after the failed coup in August 1991, one challenge is how to deal with the relationships between political disunion and economic integration or disintegration.

Dramatic developments during and after the August coup in 1991 sufficiently demonstrated that *perestroika* and *glasnost* have changed the nature of the Soviet state. Radical reforms have undermined traditional authority and the legitimacy of the pillars of the Soviet party state: the Party, the army, the KGB, and the central bureaucracy. The centralized political and economic institutions have lost power and authority. But democratic values and systems have not been firmly established in Russia and other post-Soviet states. Institutionalization of the democratic processes is still an urgent task facing the Russian reformers. The most challenging task is to establish a constitutional government in a society with a weak tradition of the rule of law. At the same time, feelings of ethnic exclusiveness have revived. This does not mean each post-Soviet republic is democratic, however. Ethnic conflicts, if not contained, may lead to social crisis even civil wars. If the reformers cannot successfully deal with the economic crisis, economic and social problems may constitute obstacles for further democratic changes. This chapter examines the dynamics of *perestroika* and the debate on marketization.

The "Pre-crisis Situation"
and the Sources of Reforms

In the Brezhnev era of stagnation, intensification of conflicts between the state and the market led to the decline of economic growth rates, further bureaucratization of the party state, and widespread passivity of the populace. In the last two decades, the Soviet economy compared unfavorably not only with Western countries and Japan, but also with the newly industrialized areas like South Korea and Taiwan. An alienated generation of Soviet citizens turned away from the formal system and resorted to the informal system to satisfy their needs and solve problems. The drastic growth of illegal and extra-legal economic activities deepened the crisis of the economic system.

The Novosibirsk Report, written by Tat'yana I. Zaslavskaya in 1983, revealed many serious contradictions in the Soviet system. According to the report, the basic features of the Soviet economic management system were formed in the 1930s. The characteristics of the system included: a high level of centralization in economic decisions, the weak development of market relations, the centralized regulation of all forms of material incentives for labor, and most importantly, the public ownership of means of production. "All these features reflect the predominance of administrative over economic methods, of centralization over decentralization."[4] However, the state of the productive forces in the 1980s was different from the 1930s not only quantitatively, but also qualitatively. Therefore the system of productive relations was becoming more and more of a brake on the progressive advancement of the productive forces which were characterized by intensive rather than extensive growth. This contradiction was obviously reflected in a tendency toward a noticeable decline in the rate of growth of national income.

Conflicts between the state and the market are major sources of Gorbachev's economic reforms. The conflicts are reflected in the following aspects. One basic problem was the decline of economic growth rates. Soviet economist Abel Aganbegyan stated that there was no growth from 1980 to 1985.[5] If Soviet military expenditure in real terms grew in the early 1980s as is widely accepted (by three percent a year according to the CIA), and there was no economic growth, the military share of the GNP would have been increasing, which would have implied a much greater Soviet internal conflict over allocation of resources than has been perceived in the West.[6] The major disappointment with the administrative command system was that it did not produce the level of economic growth and efficiency anticipated of it. This was a key factor responsible for the economic crisis and for the search for alternatives. During his rule, Brezhnev conducted a policy in favor of the military program but at the expense of economic growth. That policy had a very negative effect on the civilian and consumer sectors of the Soviet economy.

The Soviet central planners relied heavily on political considerations and government indicators rather than economic rationale and market signals to make crucial decisions of resource allocations. Largely because of the lack of accurate information about supply and demand, the Soviet government tended to make plans from the "achieved level." Such practice led to tension and even antagonism between planners and managers. Difficulty in information problems increased rather than decreased with the growth of economic scale and intensity. The existence of such problems partly explained why the seemingly strong Soviet state was actually weaker than the Japanese state in economic affairs. Both information overload (inability to process and use a large amount of information) and the lack of information (due to a strong tradition of high secrecy regarding socio-economic data, some of the most basic statistics are lacking for Soviet scholars and decision-makers) created big troubles for the Soviet central planners.

A related but more far-reaching issue was the widening technological gap between the Soviet Union and advanced Western countries. There were structural disincentives in the Soviet system. The administrative methods of management ignored the demands of economic laws and stifled innovation. The Scientific and Technological Revolution (STR) was a big slogan for the Soviets even during the 1970s.[7] But this once hopeful trend did not turn in favor of the Soviet Union. Western countries made much more progress in science and technology.[8] Systemic obstacles in the Soviet Union created great difficulties for the progress of science and technology. Problems were particularly serious in food production and distribution, which dramatically affected consumers.

While the Soviet economy was not able to satisfy people's demand, the popular expectation for higher living standards was increasing with the spread of urbanization and the growth of mass education. The emergence of civil society in the Soviet Union after the 1960s weakened the Soviet state. It seems that the centrally planned economy can only work in a strong state and a weak civil society. A growing civil society and relatively weak state favor the development of the market economy. On the other hand, a dynamic market will significantly contribute to the growth of pluralist groups and interests which form the economic foundation of a civil society and democratization.

The growing popular demands for change gradually reached the leadership. Leadership succession offered an opportunity for policy change in contests of authority building. In a classic analysis of authority-building strategies of Khrushchev and Brezhnev, George Breslauer discovered that policy innovations often come out of the power struggles during leadership succession.[9] Competing leaders often provide alternative policies on key political and economic problems. For Gorbachev, a leader with different training and outlook than his predecessors, *perestroika* was seen as the most effective strategy for authority building. Contrary to Gorbachev's anticipation, *perestroika* undermined the legitimacy and authority of the communist party state. It was ironic that

Gorbachev lost power because of both his successes and failures in reforming the old system.

In conjunction with domestic forces for change, foreign policy strains and new thinking provided a catalyst for dramatic transformation. The failure of the Soviet adventure in Afghanistan and the costly strategic competition with the United States dramatically increased the military burdens on the Soviet economy and society. In addition to all the important endogenous variables, the new political thinking and changes in the international system have contributed significantly to *perestroika*.

What is new political thinking? The roots of new political thinking lay in Soviet domestic and international developments. "The Soviet Union's relative decline on the international scene, combined with its domestic crisis, created a situation that required an urgent reassessment of the strategic direction of Soviet security and foreign policies."[10] The intellectual and theoretical origins of new thinking could be found in the academic and theoretical debates that had been going on for decades in the Soviet Union. Allen Lynch documented the de-utopianization of Soviet thinking about international relations.[11] It was significant that these debates became public in the age of *glasnost* and new thinking directly influenced Soviet foreign and domestic policy.

Gorbachev's report to the 27th Party Congress in February 1986 contained a concise statement about new thinking. The basic themes have been repeated and developed by Gorbachev and his associates since then. New political thinking includes the following innovative statements regarding several vital issues:

1. A recognition of the existence of global problems that can only be resolved by cooperation on a global scale. "Global problems that affect all mankind cannot be solved through the efforts of a single state or group of states."[12]

2. The interdependence of states. "Despite the profoundly contradictory nature of the world today and the fundamental differences among the states making it up, it is interconnected and interdependent and constitutes a definite integral whole."[13]

3. The rejection of nuclear deterrence as a durable guarantor of peace. If the nuclear arms race continues, even parity will cease to be a restraint on conflict.

4. The nature of current weaponry makes defense by military-technical means alone impossible. "Ensuring security is becoming more and more a political task, and it can be accomplished only by political means."[14] In the context of U.S.-Soviet relations, security can be maintained only if it is mutual. No nation's security can be achieved at the expense of another country.

A philosophic reason underlying new political thinking is the claim that universal human values are higher than narrow class values. At the United Nations in December 1988, Gorbachev stressed the importance of human values and argued that differences in ideology should not be allowed to affect relations between states.

Alexander Dallin was among the first to provide a framework for analyzing the linkage between Soviet foreign policy and domestic politics. He pointed out:

> The most explicit linkage of the new foreign policy orientation with domestic priorities is Gorbachev's own assertion, in various formulations, that at a time of essential, stressful, and far-reaching domestic reforms the Soviet Union needs an international environment that is unthreatening and predictable, permitting Moscow to avoid both potentially dangerous crisis and additional demands on scarce resources.[15]

What did Gorbachev mean by arguing that *perestroika* drives Soviet foreign policy? The essence of the argument could be summarized as the following: there was an increasing gap between the level of productive relations and the level of productive forces. The superstructure had become an obstacle for further development of productivity. The Soviet economy was going down compared with most market economies; the rate of growth was declining compared with its own past performance. Consequently, the Soviet Union was losing its superpower status. The trend could not be stopped without a resurgence of the Soviet economy following fundamental reforms. In fact, Gorbachev said that the Soviet Union was a superpower which did not act like one. In order to conduct domestic reforms, it was necessary to make basic adjustments in Soviet foreign policy.

Reforms in Eastern Europe and in China provided some stimuli for Soviet reforms. The Chinese have successfully introduced the market prices system for agricultural goods and many daily consumer goods. The dynamics of market forces have been pushing the Chinese economy forward in the last decade. Gorbachev initially did not pay much attention to the Chinese reforms. He overemphasized the differences between the USSR and China. In retrospective, if the Soviet reformers started with an agricultural reform. Increased agricultural output and more consumer goods might satisfy people's needs and create a strong popular basis for further economic reforms. Poland and Hungary have gone a long way in marketization and privatization.

The success of economic reforms in the long term depends on building a well-functioning market economy. The integration of the former command economy into the world economy is very significant because autarky can no longer work in the contemporary world. The only way to succeed is to build an innovative and competitive economy that can survive and excel in the world market.

From Acceleration to *Perestroika*: Stages of Reform

Compared with his predecessors, Gorbachev was an innovator and a reformer. Even before he became the general secretary, Gorbachev proposed economic reform as the basis of social reform at the December 1984 Plenum of the Central Committee of the CPSU. The key word was *uskorenie* (acceleration), the opposite of Brezhnev's stagnation. *Uskorenie* was pointing to the speed rather than the nature of change. If the fundamental system was wrong, accelerating changes would not solve the problems but expose the weaknesses of the system. Gorbachev was elected as the general secretary in March 1985. From the April 1985 Plenum on, socioeconomic reform gradually shifted to sociopolitical reform. "*Glasnost*" became the key phrase. At the 27th Party Congress of February 1986, Gorbachev proposed *perestroika* as the major policy, which represented a radicalization of socioeconomic reform. After the January Plenum in 1987, *perestroika* was linked to deepening of democracy.

In June 1987, two central reform documents were adopted, the "Law on State Enterprises" and the "Basic Provisions for the Fundamental Restructuring of Economic Management," and a large number of subordinate decrees ensued. By this time, Gorbachev came to understand that unless the big state enterprises acted more independently, there could be no successful economic reform. Under the new law, the role of the ministers in Moscow was to be curbed and the role of the plant managers out in the field to be expanded. Managers were promised that each year they could set aside a larger and larger share of production, which they could sell on their own at whatever price they could negotiate in the market. The share of output retained by the state in the form of state orders was to shrink to seventy percent. However, in absence of market mechanisms, the managers had much difficulty in finding customers or obtaining necessary supplies. Thus, most managers strongly asked for the continued protection of the central ministries rather than moving to the market by themselves. Most enterprise managers were delighted therefore when their ministries continued to insist on control of not 70 percent, but often 90 percent or even 100 percent of the factory's output. The failure of the Law on State Enterprises intensified the economic crisis in the USSR.[16]

The 19th Party Conference in June 1988 was a significant move in the direction of implementation of radical political reform. Elections for the Congress of People's Deputies and the president were held in 1989. The introduction of democratic competitive election was very significant in breaking the communist monopoly of power in the Soviet Union. With removal of constitutional guarantee of the "leading and guiding role" of the CPSU, there emerged a real opportunity for the rise of meaningful oppositions. The rise of legal opposition leaders and organizations is a critical condition for democratic development.

The work on a more radical reform started in earnest in the summer of 1989, and the USSR Supreme Soviet adopted the Basic Guidelines for Economic Stabilization and Transition to a Market Economy in October 1990. Therefore, the years 1988-90 form a natural period of deepening economic crisis and preparations for a more radical reform. The year of 1990 witnessed hot debates on the marketization and privatization of the Soviet economy. After a few months of setback, new programs of dramatic transformation of the Soviet centrally planned economy into a market-oriented economy were once again under serious consideration. However, large-scale marketization and privatization did not begin until the final collapse of the Soviet Union.[17]

Economic reform was at the heart of *perestroika*. Without significant success in the economic field, no comprehensive reform could succeed and last. Pressures were building on the Soviet leaders to satisfy Soviet citizens' basic needs and improve people's living standards in order to maintain popular support for reforms. Poor socioeconomic infrastructure was a serious problem. By some estimates, 50 percent of the food produced in the agricultural sector never make it to the marketplace due to transportation bottlenecks.

The reformers demanded enterprises to compete in the international market, but many enterprise managers were not willing to do so. Or, if they were, the Soviet infrastructure could not support them. Conflict of interests and the struggle for power were interconnected during the reform process. Power struggles often created deadlock obstructing meaningful reforms. Precious time and human energy were wasted while popular discontent was spreading.

Market mechanisms cannot exist in a vacuum. A market-oriented economic culture is necessary for the establishment and development of a well-functioning market. In this sense, market reforms also involve cultural change. Among the major tasks of cultural change, two stand out as top priorities: replacing the command culture with exchange culture, and replacing a passive, non-participatory mentality with the principle of popular sovereignty. Political reforms should transform the traditional dependency of the Russian/Soviet people on the state. The traditional Soviet state was powerful but not effective. To regulate a market economy, the state needs qualitatively different skills than what the Soviet state bureaucrats had.

The destruction of the old Soviet state is a necessary step for building a new state compatible with the market economy. The most fundamental principles for the old system were the *nomenklatura* system and democratic centralism. When these principles were eliminated, the power base of the party state was undermined.

Perestroika as a comprehensive reform program includes both a revolution from above and a revolution from below. The transformation of state-market relations has been reflected more in changes in the state structure than in the economy. Major progress in *glasnost* and democratization has profoundly transformed the Soviet party state. The introduction of democratic election and the emergence of the Congress of People's Deputies undermined party sovereignty and started building popular sovereignty. Furthermore, the establishment of the new presidency provided an independent power basis for the state leader versus the party chief. Not incidentally, Gorbachev was able to resign as general secretary of the CPSU but remain as president of the USSR after the coup in August 1991 for a few more months.

During the years of *perestroika*, though with many twists and turns, the political and economic reforms as a whole were becoming more and more radical. However, the reformers did not prevent the eroding of the "precrisis situation" into a deep economic crisis. By 1990, the living standard of the Soviet people was lower even than that of 1985. The gap of technological development between the Soviet Union and the advanced market economies was not narrowed but enlarged. A huge government budget deficit developed. The consumer market was in a total disarray which resulted in widespread shortages of consumer goods. Popular discontent was growing every day. *Perestroika* stood at a crossroad. The Soviet leaders were facing risks in marching toward the market, while there seemed no way to turn back to the Stalinist centralized planning system. The failure of the coup and the collapse of the conservative wing in the central leadership provided an opportunity for radical reformers to push forward marketization.

Why Did *Perestroika* Fail?

By 1991, it was obvious that Gorbachev's reforms resulted in a big failure. The traditional centrally planned system had been weakened, but many central and local bureaucrats were still struggling to preserve their power and privileges. On the one hand, the central plans ceased to play critical roles as they used to do in the economy. On the other hand, a market system was still lacking and there was little chance that a well-functioning market could be established in the near future. Soviet economic performance between 1985 and 1990 was the worst in the postwar period in terms of growth rates. No progress was made toward the goal of reducing the economic and technological gaps with the West; rather, those gaps widened. Soviet manufactures were no more salable in Western markets in 1990 than they were in 1984. The long-suffering populace became more miserable, and far more vocal. Major strikes and episodes of ethnic violence erupted, further damaging the economy.[18]

During his years in power, Gorbachev made many serious policy mistakes. Economic conditions began to deteriorate at an accelerating pace, particularly after 1988. If the Brezhnev era was officially referred to as a period of stagnation, then Gorbachev brought the Soviet economy to a total collapse. By 1991, the USSR found itself with a depression. The drop in Soviet GNP exceeded 10 percent. The collapse of the economy hastened what eventually became a process of political disintegration.

What are the major reasons for the failure of Gorbachev's economic reforms? There is no simple answer to this question. The following factors are responsible for the deepening of the economic crisis.

Inconsistent policies and indecision at critical points led to the breakdown of the old system and the lack of a well-functioning new system. The chaos created by the reforms has taken a heavy toll. The Soviet economy had been a command economy for more than half a century. When it was finally broken up, the economy totally lost its direction. Planners are no longer in control. Producers have little information about supply and demand. Even when they had sufficient information about market trends, entrepreneurs would still encounter a lot of difficulties in searching for raw material suppliers and finding buyers. The distorted price system constituted a big obstacle for shifting toward the market. Market mechanisms have not developed yet, while the centrally planned system is no longer in place. Chaos and crisis occurred.

There were ideological, strategic, and tactical differences among the reformers. Generally speaking, there were fewer true reformers than conservatives. This was true at least at the initial stage of the reform. What makes things more complicated is that reformers themselves are divided. Timothy Colton identified three reform orientations: minimum reform, moderate reform, and radical reform.[19] The actual divisions in the reform camps were much more diverse than the clear-cut pattern described by Colton. Thus, the reformers often could not unite to fight against the conservative forces. On the contrary, when the interests of the conservatives were threatened by the reforms, the conservatives were able to join forces to fight against the reformers. The aborted coup of August 1991 changed the balance between the conservatives and reformers.

One critical problem was the lack of laws that underlie a competitive and pluralistic economic and political system. Although many reformers have realized the significance of the legal framework and have been working hard to establish one, it is extremely difficult to build a legal system in a society without a tradition of the rule of law. A deep-rooted Russian tradition is the tendency of loyalty to a person rather than to political, and particularly legal, institutions. This has created a serious obstacle for building a law-based society and establishing legal-rational norms.

For a long time, pricing formed the central battleground for Soviet reformers and conservatives. Some reformers rightly saw a reform of the price system as a condition for the success of economic reform, and they were confident their views were correct both in theory and practice.[20] The conservatives, on the other hand, felt confident in their struggle over pricing, because of support from ideology, the bureaucracy, and the population at large. As a result of this intense struggle, it was harder to compromise on pricing than on many other issues. As long as the price system was not fundamentally improved, rational criteria for the efficiency of an investment could hardly be found.

One serious weakness in the welfare-state authoritarianism was that there was no clear-cut lines for winners and losers. Gorbachev realized this problem and tried to correct it. But he did not succeed in establishing universalistic rules for winners and losers. A closely related issue is that there are no clear-cut lines between power and responsibility.

The reformers encountered enormous difficulty in making organic links with the world economy. On the one hand, Soviet products were generally of low quality and could not be sold on the world market. On the other hand, the Soviet Union was not a member of key international economic organizations like the International Monetary Fund and the General Agreement on Tariffs and Trade. The Soviet Union did not enjoy most favored nation status with the United States. The West did not totally lift many trading barriers created during the cold war. As a result, the Soviet Union had a lot of obstacles to overcome before entering the world market as a "normal" trading partner.

The existence of cultural and ideological barriers also retarded the transition to the market. For instance, the conservatives consciously stimulated popular fear of the market. This is part of the Russian/Soviet political culture. The defining characteristics of Soviet political culture include fear of disorder or chaos, and the resulting emphasis placed upon order.[21] In short, traditional Russian/Soviet cultural values have strong elements against the establishment of a market system.

According to Breslauer, political ideology contributes to explaining the persistently *partial* nature of reform, for it allows opponents to legitimize opposition to the social, political, and institutional costs of marketization. The Soviet official ideology was antithetical to allowing markets to perform primary coordinating functions for the economy or the polity. It condemned private ownership of the means of production as the defining characteristic of an exploitative, capitalist social system. It extolled instead the virtues of central planning and the "leading role of the Party." What's more, protection of the working people against market insecurities resonated powerfully in a Leninist political order. Thus, the social, political, and institutional consequences of marketization have repeatedly been invoked to argue for alternatives to radical reform as the appropriate response to economic crisis. A central thesis of the conservatives is the protection of working people against market insecurities or injustice (inflation, insecurity of employment, inequality).[22] These have become deeply ingrained in Soviet thinking outside the major Westernized cities.

The Gorbachev regime made perilous mistakes such as the emphasis on the "human factor", the use of traditional methods, and the campaign against drinking. At the initial stage, Gorbachev believed in reform within the system rather than reform of the system. Hence, *uskorenie* (acceleration) became a key theme which emphasized the speed rather than the nature of change. When the

Soviet economy and society were moving in the wrong direction, acceleration could only make matters worse. It turned out that the "enormous reserves" were not easily activated within the old system, whose combination of bottlenecks, rigidity and vested interests prevented most attempts at improvement. The jacking up of the growth targets in the five-year plan for 1986-90 was unrealistic. The campaign against alcohol appeared to have had several positive effects in the short term, but it was difficult to sustain it and market imbalances were exacerbated. The failure and ineffectiveness of the many traditional measures were spectacular. Most means had been tried before, though not so energetically for the last two decades. The view that the administrative command system was good, but poorly managed, received a serious blow.[23]

In its ambitious search for improvements, the regime neglected one of its most fundamental tasks: to maintain some balance between supply and demand. The widespread shortages of basic consumer goods gravely undermined popular support for further experiments in economic reform.[24] In the long run, today's difficulties may provide rationale for fundamental reforms. At present, the loss of balance between supply and demand is no doubt a major economic failure. The widespread shortages of goods and the lack of market mechanisms resulted in the prevalence of the seller's market and consequent severe inflation.

At a deeper level, there were additional obstacles for radical reforms. When economic reform touches the public ownership (state ownership) of the means of production, the resistance to reform increased dramatically. When political reform started to remove the Communist party's monopoly of power, the resistance to reform from the conservative side became stronger. It took huge amounts of work to overcome these obstacles. These two issues were not adequately dealt with until late 1991. The party and the central government apparatus were the beneficiary of the centrally planned economy. The reforms were threatening the privileges and power of many bureaucrats. Thus, reforms had to be defended against intimidating branch ministries. Most party-state bureaucrats, especially the central planners, have lost their privileged jobs as the reforms went forward. The training and skills of most Soviet cadres are incompatible with what are needed in a market economy.

The reformers seized the initiative, but they were not alone on the stage. The central authorities could accept limited experiments, but as the reform movement advanced, institutional resistance was mobilized. As Anders Aslund pointed out, almost all central economic bodies were exposed as fundamentally conservative.[25] The whole infrastructure for trade and marketization was missing.

A painful reality involved the lack of independent enterprises and individual initiatives. For a long time, the reformers only demanded "a considerable increase in the economic independence" of enterprises, and nonsensically advocated "an optimal relationship between the central management and the operative independence" of enterprises. In order to ensure enterprises their independence, massive cuts in the intrusive state bureaucracy were needed. In

1986, public administration involved 17.7 million people, of whom 2.4 million worked in managerial positions above enterprises. The basic reformist aim should have been to guarantee the operative independence of enterprises from interference by superior state bodies and the Party.[26] Even when administrative interference is reduced or removed, the growth of free enterprise in Russia and other former Soviet republics will take a long time because entrepreneurial spirit is very weak.

The lack of vision and theoretical guidance in the leadership further compounded inconsistency of reform policies. The constantly changing political and legislative processes allowed little precision or coordination. The reform was not consistent in theory, because of a lack of theoretical conceptualization and impotence in general. On the one hand, Gorbachev claimed that he would support private and family farming. On the other hand, he strongly opposed any form of privatization of the land. Although encouraging the use of market mechanisms, there were all kinds of restraints on what could be sold and who could sell it. In spite of frequently making demands of fundamental economic reforms in public speeches, Gorbachev often gave only halfhearted support of radical reform policies.

The depths of the Soviet economic crisis, and the inability to avert it despite the moderate reforms of the past, became necessary preconditions for the Soviet commitment to marketization. But they were not sufficient conditions. Due to the highly centralized nature of the Soviet political and economic system, major policy changes were closely related with political competition among key political leaders and their collective learning process. There has been no consensus regarding the speed and scope of marketization and privatization. The debate on marketization has been further complicated by a power struggle between reformers and conservatives.

The Debate over Marketization

The initial period of *perestroika* gave the Soviet people great hope. But unfulfilled promises and broken dreams created a deep sense of frustration among the population. Reformers began to question the basic principles of the centrally planned system. Nikolai Shmelev's breathtaking attack on the Soviet economic system in June 1987 broke most taboos on planning, calling its foundations "economic romanticism": "Today we have a shortage [economy], unbalanced on virtually all accounts and in many ways unmanageable, and to be completely honest, an economy which almost does not yield to planning, and which in any case does not accept scientific-technical progress."[27]

The eternal alternative to central planning is the market. A substantial number of Soviet economists were convinced market economists, but they were reticent about expressing this view until 1988. In a forceful advocacy of the market, Aleksander Yakovlev noted that "money-commodity relations" could not exist without a market. Yakovlev criticized "scholastic" disputes for having missed that the "market has historically been formed as an objective and social reality" and went on to call the market a "natural, self-regulating mechanism."[28] This was an obvious reply to Yegor Ligachev, who had just argued that the market brought about chronic unemployment and social stratification. When fewer academic economists supported central planning in the press, Gosplan officials themselves had to defend the vested interests of their organization.

Most radical reformers realized that it was necessary to replace the administrative command system with market mechanisms. "To shift to the market" was the catch-phase of the 500-day plan and the government program of the fall of 1990. Such a shift was also declared at the outset of the watered-down but officially approved final Gorbachev document: "There is no alternative to switching to a market."[29] All these programs also included at least an eventual liberalization of price formation, and the opening of the Soviet economy to free international exchange.

A comparative analysis of the Shatalin plan and other transition plans is required to understand the nature of the debate on marketization. In summer 1990, Russian President Yeltsin promised to bring order from chaos by installing a market economy in 500 days, and at the same time to give substance to the hitherto empty concept of a "union of sovereign republics." Gorbachev moved in late July to cut a deal with Yeltsin. On August 2, he announced the formation of a working group of 13 members, including both his and Yeltsin's top advisers. The leader of the group was academician Stanislav S. Shatalin. Thus the draft produced by the working group in late August was called the Shatalin plan.

The Shatalin plan began by reconstituting the Soviet Union as a confederation, which would then grant power to the center. It called for a rapid dismantling of the administrative command system and "destatization" of public assets. Yeltsin strongly supported the plan and presented it to the Supreme Soviet of the Russian Republic, which then proceeded to adopt it. Gorbachev first supported the Shatalin plan but soon backed away from his commitment to it. He considered the plan too radical and too risky. To follow the plan would effectively destroy the economic control of the central government. By denying the center its authority to tax, for instance, power would shift to the republics at the expense of the union.[30]

In comparison with the Shatalin plan, an earlier reform proposal developed by Leonid Abalkin (the director of the Institute of Economics of the Academy of Sciences) and revised by Prime Minister Nikolai Ryzhkov in late 1989 was much more cautious. For example, Shatalin's plan had a fixed 500-day timetable. The Ryzhkov-Abalkin plan would require about five years. Moreover, the Ryzhkov-Abalkin plan would retain control of the center along with most of the existing ministry bureaucracies. The Shatalin plan would give the republics much more power and authority, particularly the power to tax and the authority to own their own natural resources within their boundaries.[31] In short, the Ryzhkov-Abalkin plan was much more conservative than the Shatalin plan in both the scope and speed of marketization.

In September, Gorbachev asked his economic adviser Abel Aganbegyan to integrate the Shatalin plan with the Ryzhkov-Abalkin plan. On October 16, Gorbachev came back to the Soviet parliament with a "Presidential Plan," which he fully supported. Although retaining the four stages of the original Shatalin Plan, the Gorbachev plan prepared by Aganbegyan drops any mention of 500 days. It is therefore not so much a plan as it is a statement of intent so general as to be unobjectionable to the various factions in the debate. On October 19, 1990, the Supreme Soviet of the USSR passed the Gorbachev plan as guidelines for economic stabilization and transition to the market.

It is significant to examine the key points of the Shatalin plan because it is controversial and influential. According to the plan, reform efforts should be concentrated on the following tasks:

1. Demonopolization of the state economy, and the privatization and development of entrepreneurship. Demonopolization implies that the state shall no longer engage in direct control over economic units.
2. Development of market and market infrastructure, introduction of new mechanisms for establishing economic ties, and promotion of entrepreneurship.
3. Demonopolization of the economy and abolition of the institutional framework that had been formed under the command system and today stands in the way of the market development.
4. The removal of the state control over prices and transition to free price setting on the basis of supply and demand patterns.[32]

The Shatalin plan has a time table of 500 days in a four-stage development. In stage one, the first 100 days of the 500-Day Plan, the Soviet Union would be reconstituted as a voluntary economic union. Along most of the lines of economic reform the republics should act on their own without any interference from the Center. The plan calls for demonopolization of the state economy by selling off state assets, and reorganization of the large state enterprise into joint stock companies. It also calls for the privatization of small shops and consumer services. The budget of the military and the KGB should be reduced by 10 to 20 percent.

During stage two (100th-250th day) the pace of destatization and privatization would accelerate, tight monetary and fiscal policies would continue, and the first moves toward price liberalization would be taken. The main aim of the second stage is to "remove state control over the majority of equipment, consumer goods and services, and to keep inflation under control using the financial and credit policy."[33] The liberalization of price controls would be one of the key components of this stage. Decentralization and privatization would be concerned particularly with trade, food supply and services.

For the third stage (250th-400th day), the principal task "is to reach market stabilization for consumer goods and the means of production. Likewise, we should widen market relations and arrange a new system of economic relations."[34] The plan foresees serious socioeconomic problems during the transition process. The emerging market will bring into being many problems of a different nature than the problems that existed in the Soviet command system. For instance, inflation, price instability and unemployment will deepen the economic crisis if they are not dealt with adequately. Ruble convertibility also is a challenging issue in the transition.

In stage four (the last 100 days), the key task is "to consolidate the stabilization of the economy and of finances to prompt the creation of a self-regulating competitive market."[35] By day 500, if all goes as planned, 70 percent of Soviet industry would be operating generally without subsidies, in a competitive environment, managed by bodies independent of any direct state supervision, or directly by private individuals. Eighty to ninety percent of construction, auto transport, trade, food and other services would be in mostly private hands. Most prices for goods and services would by decided by supply and demand. In short, the Soviet Union would have a rudimentary market economy. Most important, basic institutions would be in place to allow the further development over the following years of a truly complex and rich set of market institutions.[36]

Marie Lavigne points out that the Shatalin program has some very serious drawbacks. The first is price reform. The second is the future of the public sector. What about the part that will not be dismantled or closed down? How will it be managed? Is shareholding an adequate answer? Will the enterprises owned by holding companies or other state enterprises be automatically more efficient? The combination of public ownership and private management methods that is a distinctive feature of the French industrial system is still unknown in the USSR, even as a concept. Though the program insists on its social component, the treatment of the "non-market" sector is remarkably vague. What is supposed to be privatized and what is to remain public in the fields of health care, education, culture, and environmental protection? How is this sector to be financed?[37]

The Gorbachev Plan approved by the Supreme Soviet on October 19 was a result of compromise between the Shatalin plan and the Ryzhkov-Abalkin plan. The Gorbachev plan declared that the "choice of switching to the market has been made--a choice of historic importance to the fate of the country. The whole question is how to move toward the market, how to choose the most reliable and correct paths."[38] In fact, however, the Gorbachev plan backed off from more radical reforms and took a more cautious stand. For example, it completely dropped the timetable as defined by the Shatalin plan. At the time when the plan was passed, Abalkin expressed the view that the main concern was to create prerequisites for the transition to a market. "But creating an effective economy will take no less than a decade and perhaps the life of a whole generation."[39] Gorbachev also retreated on price reform and the decision to allow enterprises to operate without government subsidies. Republic rights would be curbed and their powers defined by an "interregional economic committee." In the end, Gorbachev decided to increase his authority as president of the USSR rather than to decentralize power as suggested by the Shatalin plan. The central and republics leadership became more divided. Although being passed in the Supreme Soviet, the Gorbachev plan did not gain support from more and more independent republican leaders like Yeltsin. As a result, Gorbachev was not able to implement the plan. The Soviet Union was heading to deeper political and socioeconomic crisis as the conflicts between the center and republics intensified and the economy continued to deteriorate.

The August 1991 coup was a desperate attempt by the anti-*perestroika* forces to reverse the disintegration of the Soviet Union. Opposite to the coup organizers' intention, the dramatic events led to the total collapse of the Soviet Union and provided new ground for even more radical reforms. After the failed coup, there was a sense of euphoria among radical reformers. Yeltsin and other nationalistic leaders seized the opportunity and quickly and decisively dismantled the centralized Soviet party-state.

Obstacles to Overcome

When the old system has ceased to function and the new system has not yet been established, the pain and trauma of transition are strong and often appear to be unbearable. In the transitional stage, the Russian people are facing many serious challenges. Whether or not these obstacles can be overcome will determine future state-market relations in Russia and other post-Soviet republics.

First, destatization and state-building. On the one hand, *perestroika* is a process of dismantling the highly centralized Stalinist state. On the other hand, there is a great need for a democratic state which is effective in terms of providing the legal and constitutional framework for the market. Without legality, without constitutional guarantee, there can be no long-term stability and predictability in the economy. Therefore, the establishment of such a legal constitutional state system is a prerequisite for the market. It is an extremely challenging task to establish a legal foundation for the market economy in a society lacking the tradition of the rule of law.

Obviously, it is easy to talk about the need for a regulatory state that facilitates the operation of the market. It is extraordinarily difficult to build such a state on the infrastructure left behind by more than half a century of command administrative domination. The problem of uncertainty concerning state authority is not simply a problem of uncertain political relationships. The traditional Soviet legal theory envisioned a unified state power--organic in nature and indivisible--and the structures of Soviet state authority formed according to this theory were indeed very integrated and overlapping. As a study by leading Western experts in 1990 pointed out:

> The effective functioning of a market-based system is dependent upon the existence of clearly defined and reasonably broad property rights, the ability of market participants to freely exchange property rights through a system of legally enforceable agreements, and the existence of a system which provides reasonably secure and predictable enforcement of such agreements.[40]

Second, political disunion and economic integration. Nationalist emotions were rising and the demands for independence were growing in the later stage of *perestroika*. Political disunion became a reality when all the fifteen former Soviet republics claimed independence by the end of 1991. When the newly independent states are defending their sovereignty, they need to have a certain degree of economic integration with other republics, however. One legacy of the centrally planned economy is the unbalanced interdependence of the republic economies. For instance, Kazakhstan is a major supplier of agricultural goods, while Russia provides most heavy industrial equipment. The pattern of unequal distribution of raw materials and natural resources also facilitates exchange among different republics. Under the centrally planned economy, most resource allocations were achieved by administrative mechanisms controlled by the centralized bureaucracy in Moscow. When the republics consolidate their independence, the rules of the game must be fundamentally changed. How to achieve an appropriate degree of economic integration without compromising political independence of the sovereign republics is a truly challenging task.

Third, the lack of policy mechanisms and inadequate understanding of the market principles. A major difficulty in establishing competitive market mechanisms in the Soviet Union was the resistance on the part of the administrative apparatus to relinquish power. There is a lack of fiscal, monetary, and professional infrastructures for the transition. There are also educational and even mental barriers in understanding and internalizing the mechanics and essence of the "invisible hand" behind the market as a regulating tool rather than an anarchical one. These and others factors contributed to the economic crisis that has been building for a long time and has dramatically intensified since 1989, which makes further advance much more difficult. The prospects of solving such problems in the near future are not bright.

Fourth, practical and ideological difficulties in changing the ownership of the means of production. Another major economic change that has been initiated is in the structure of ownership and property rights, mostly of productive assets. In addition to the practical difficulties involved, any significant change in ownership or the structure of property rights must overcome the major ideological barrier of the sanctity of public ownership of the means of production, and of the closely related dogma against "exploitation." Although losing their credibility now, these ideas have been obstacles for market-oriented reforms for a long time. Ownership of the means of production in the USSR was formally vested in the people as a whole. In the name of the people, the state, through its various agencies and ministries at different governmental levels, exercised the basic rights of enterprise ownership, making production and pricing decisions and determining how the capital stock would be used, maintained, and augmented. Nevertheless, fundamental aspects of ownership were missing for those who have exercised these rights: especially, the ability to buy and sell enterprise assets and a related personal stake in the long-term value of those assets. Soviet planners placed the principal emphasis on maximizing immediate physical production, with little concern for the waste of capital and other inputs this might entail.[41]

Fifth, overcoming political risks of marketization. Transition to the market involving the removal of the "safety net" has met strong resistance from unskilled workers. The party and state bureaucrats who do not possess adequate management or technical skills that are valuable in a market economy are also frightened by the transition policies. Political risks for the transition to the market represented a serious concern for Gorbachev. In responding to a claim that unfettered marketization would set the Soviet economy right in a month, Gorbachev shot back sarcastically that "such a market will bring all people out into the street within two weeks and they will sweep away any government, no matter how much it professes loyalty to the people."[42] A thorough market reform would benefit immediately only a "highly skilled enterprising vanguard" of Soviet society that amounts at most to one-third of the labor force. A prudent reform government cannot afford to abandon the remaining majority of the population, and run the risk of it becoming the chief constituencies of an opposition challenge from the left or right.[43]

Sixth, encouraging competition, getting rid of protectionism, and entering the world market. Soviet industry used to be one of the most protected in the world. If the transition to a market economy is to succeed, these barriers to competition must be dismantled, and the Russian government must act vigorously to encourage trade rather than to thwart it. How to build links with the world economy is a key task for the Russian reformers. Key problems include quality, access to markets, technological know-how, and desirable products. Leaders of the newly independent states should act quickly to introduce an effective framework of antimonopoly laws and regulations along with the institutions to enforce them. The establishment of a well-functioning market economy will lead to the opening up of the republics to international trade and investment and their integration into the world trading system.[44]

Seventh, demilitarization and transfer of resources from the military to civilian sectors. The Soviet economy was highly militarized for more than half a century. The military-industrial complex in the USSR used to enjoy governmental supplies of the best human and material resources available in the country. After the collapse of the centralized Soviet state, a serious challenge to Russia and other former Soviet republics is how to convert the military and heavy industry into a civilian consumer industry. It will take a long period of time for the new republics to develop competitive consumer industries that can produce quality goods and provide efficient service to their consumers.

The centrally planned economy was established to deal with a particular set of problems. Now there are new situations, new institutions, and new problems. The successes and failures of the Soviet system in solving past problems created new problems.[45] The accumulation of such problems and the loss of political dynamism and creativity resulted in systemic crises which led to the disintegration of the USSR.

Most pre-Gorbachev reformers believed that the Soviet economic system could be workable with some modification or moderated reform. Gorbachev and Yeltsin realized that the Leninist-Stalinist system could no longer work without a fundamental and comprehensive reform. The appropriate word to describe this phenomenon is revolution. It took a revolution from above led by Stalin to build the centralized economic system. The dismantling of the system and the transition to the market is also revolutionary. Of course, the two revolutions have a fundamentally different nature and direction.

A new wave of discussion about marketization came after the failed hard-liner coup in August 1991. In an era of drastic shifts on the political scene and economic policy, it is important to analyze possible state-market relations in the post-Soviet states. Due to historical, geographic, and political reasons, it is most promising for the Baltic republics to make the transition to a market economy rapidly. In the long run, the most significant events should be observed in Russia. The current struggle between the reformers and the conservatives might produce different scenarios. We shall make some cautious observations.

The basis of the centrally planned economy has been removed. The party state and its economic planning organs have collapsed. Thus, the command economy has lost its organizational mechanisms. At the same time, the political and legal bases for the market economic are only at the initial stage of the building process. Enormous difficulties stand in the way of a well-functioning market economy.

There are conflicts between those who want to dismantle the state economy and build a free market and those who want to combine large parts of the state sector with a market economy. Market socialism also had a certain degree of appeal to some Russian citizens. They want the benefits of a dynamic market economy. At the same time, other citizens are demanding the protection of the state against economic insecurity coming with market forces.

Democratization is a decisive factor in determining future state-market relations in Russia. The very question of marketization is both a political and an economic issue. The success or failure of the transition plan largely depends upon whether or not the reform leaders can obtain and maintain significant popular support for their reform programs, and whether or not they can persuade the majority of citizens to endure the sacrifices and pain during the transition. Ideally, real democratization must move toward political decentralization and representative government. If the newly independent states cannot solve basic socioeconomic problems, however, it will be very difficult for democracy to grow against the strong Russian/Soviet authoritarian tradition. Thus, democratization can be successful only if it goes hand in hand with economic development and not as its substitute.

In addition to the political and legal foundation for marketization, economic skills and technical competence are gaining vital significance for moving toward the market economy. This implies that post-Soviet societies need a new generation of leaders with high skills and new perspectives. It is true that the younger generations in these societies are better educated and more open minded than their predecessors. However, re-education is an urgent task even for the young people because their educational backgrounds, acquired under the Stalinist system, are often incompatible with a pluralist state and the market economy.

Russian President Yeltsin decreed a shift to market prices for goods and services starting January 1992. The Russian government adopted a program of privatization. It stated that by the end of 1992, up to 70 percent of all enterprises in the sphere of services, trade and public catering are to become nonstate enterprises. But very soon the initial sense of euphoria was gone. Most reformers realized that democratization and marketization were far more complicated and difficult than what they anticipated. There emerged a growing sense of frustration and pessimism.

In the first half of 1992, Yeltsin gambled that Egor Gaidar's economic shock therapy, liberalization and stabilization would break the power of the ministries and the industrial lobby by forcing bankruptcies and looser control from the center. When the Gaidar plan met increasing resistance, Yeltsin had to sacrifice Gaidar in favor of more moderate reformers.

By the end of 1992, privatization had made some progress in services, housing and agriculture, but had hardly touched medium- and large-scale industry. In October, only 4 percent of all industrial enterprises and 5 percent of trade and service enterprises were in private hands. About 10 percent of Moscow's housing had been privatized. There were over 170,000 private farms cultivating about 3 percent of the arable land. There has been no consensus regarding the speed and scope of privatization. A widespread phenomenon is so-called *nomenklatura* privatization. For instance, a state research institute spun off a private company, installed the secretary of its former Communist Party as president and then sold the firm more than 100 IBM-clone computers at ridiculously low, state-subsidized prices. The company then began selling off the computers at market prices, up to 100 times the purchase prices. Such *nomenklatura* privatization could be described as the grabbing and looting of state-owned property of, for and by the old communist elite.

The European Bank for Reconstruction and Development (EBRD) estimates that real gross domestic product in Russia declined by about twenty percent in 1992, while inflation averaged 1,450 percent. During 1992 industrial production fell by 24 percent. Money had become almost useless; the ruble, which was rated at 162 to the dollar in August 1992, had fallen to 649 to the dollar by March 1993, and further fallen to about 1000 to the dollar by June 1993.

In the meantime, the power struggle between Yeltsin and the Russian parliamentary Chairman Ruslan I. Khasbulatov intensified. Russia faced a profound, but historically familiar crisis of authority. The political revolution that swept Russia after the failed August 1991 coup expelled the Communist Party from power and left the Soviet Union in ruins. But the revolution did not settle the most fundamental issue of political power--in whom and in what institution does legitimacy rest? For a period of time, both the president and the Soviets had a claim to authority. It was similar to the dual power period between the February and October of 1917. During that nine-month interregnum, power rested simultaneously in the liberal Provisional Government and the Socialist-led Soviets. Without resolving the present constitutional crisis, it is difficult to make significant progress in either democratization or marketization. In September 1993, Yeltsin dissolved the Congress of People's Deputies and called for the election of a new parliament in December 1993. The Congress rejected Yeltsin's demand and attempted to establish a competing center of executive power. In early October, Yeltsin used military force to defeat his opponents. It appears that Yeltsin has won the power struggle. However, it is still too early to see clearly what impact Yeltsin's use of force will have on state-market relations.

A key test of the Russian leadership is whether or not they can overcome the widespread sense of pessimism and political apathy among groups of people. Many Russians are afraid of imminent outbreaks of public disorder, followed by a dictatorship. Many sense the possibility of an imminent crisis--economic collapse, mass hunger, another coup, the rise of a nationalist dictatorship.[46] The future of democratization and marketization depends heavily on the skills and visions of the Russian leadership as well as economic recovery and growth. According to Samuel Huntington, the two most decisive factors affecting the future consolidation and expansion of democracy will be economic development and political leadership. "Economic development makes democracy possible; political leadership makes it real."[47]

The shift from the command economy to market mechanisms and the gradual integration of the Russian economy into the world economy will strengthen economic interdependence between the East and the West. In the long run, a Russian economy fully integrated into the world economy will be more competitive than it is today. But for the West, a strong economic competitor is less dangerous than an economically poor and militarily powerful adversary. Japan is an economic superpower. But most Western countries do not feel threatened by Japan in a military or political sense despite the fact that they are conscious of the economic challenge from the Japanese.

Notes

1. The Shatalin Working Group formed by a joint decision of Mikhail S. Gorbachev and Boris N. Yeltsin, *Transition to the Market: Part I (The Concept and Program)* (Moscow: Cultural Initiative Foundation, 1990), p. 6.

2. *Ibid.*

3. *Ibid.*

4. "The Novosibirsk Report," *Survey*, Vol. 28, No. 1 (1984), p. 89.

5. Abel Aganbegyan, *The Challenge: Economics of Perestroika* (London: Hutchinson, 1988), p. 2.

6. Anders Aslund, *Gorbachev's Struggle for Economic Reform* (Ithaca: Cornell University Press, 1991), p. 17.

7. See Julian M. Cooper, "The Scientific and Technical Revolution in Soviet Theory," in Frederic J. Fleron, Jr. (ed.), *Technology and Communist Culture: The Socio-Cultural Impact of Technology under Socialism* (New York: Praeger, 1977), pp. 146-179; and Erik P. Hoffmann and Robbin F. Laird, *Technocratic Socialism: The Soviet Union in the Advanced Industrial Era* (Durham: Duke University Press, 1985).

8. In most new technologies, there was a substantial Soviet lag behind U.S. performance. According to a 1986 analysis by the U.S. Department of Defense, in the twenty most important basic technology areas the U.S. was superior in fourteen, the Soviet Union was superior in none, and in six areas there was a rough equality. See Russell Bova, "The Soviet Military and Economic Reform," *Soviet Studies*, Vol. XL, No. 3 (1988), pp. 388-389.

9. George W. Breslauer, *Khrushchev and Brezhnev as Leaders: Building Authority in Soviet Politics* (Boston: George Allen & Unwin, 1982).

10. Seweryn Bialer, "The Domestic and International Sources of Gorbachev's Reforms," *Journal of International Affairs*, Vol. 42, No. 2 (1989), p. 290.

11. Allen Lynch, *The Soviet Study of International Relations* (Cambridge: Cambridge University Press, 1989).

12. *Soviet Foreign Policy Today: Reports from the Soviet Press* (Selections from the *Current Digest of Soviet Press*, third edition, 1989), p. 16.

13. *Ibid.*

14. *Ibid.*, p. 17.

15. Alexander Dallin, "Gorbachev's Foreign Policy and the 'New Political Thinking' in the Soviet Union," in Peter Juviler and Hiroshi Kimura (eds.), *Gorbachev's Reforms* (New York: A de Gruyter, 1988), pp. 100-101.

16. Marshall I. Goldman, *What Went Wrong with Perestroika* (New York: W.W. Norton, 1991), pp. 139-142.

17. For a chronology of *perestroika*, see "Chronology of Noteworthy Events, March 11, 1985-July 11, 1991," in Ed A. Hewett and Victor H. Winston (eds.), *Milestones in Glasnost and Perestroika: Politics and People* (Washington: Brookings Institution, 1991), pp. 499-536.

18. Gertrude E. Schroeder, "The Soviet Economy on a Treadmill of Perestroika: Gorbachev's First Five Years," in Harley D. Balzer (ed.), *Five Years That Shook the World: Gorbachev's Unfinished Revolution* (Boulder: Westview Press, 1991), p. 45.

19. Timothy J. Colton, *The Dilemma of Reform in the Soviet Union* (New York: Council on Foreign Relations, 1986).

20. See Nikolav P. Shmelev, "Rethinking Price Reform," in Ed A. Hewett and Victor H. Winston (eds.), *Milestones in Glasnost and Perestroika: The Economy*, (Washington: Brookings Institution, 1991), p. 153.

21. Archie Brown, "Ideology and Political Culture," in Seweryn Bialer (ed.), *Politics, Society, and Nationality Inside Gorbachev's Russia* (Boulder: Westview, 1989), pp. 1-40; Tucker, *Political Culture and Leadership in the Soviet Union*; and Stephen Burant, "The Influence of Russian Tradition on the Political Style of the Soviet Elite," *Political Science Quarterly*, Vol. 102, No. 2 (1987), pp. 273-293.

22. George W. Breslauer, "Soviet Economic Reform Since Stalin: Ideology, Politics, and Learning," *Soviet Economy*, Vol. 6, No. 3 (1990), pp. 254, 255, 258, 259.

23. Aslund, *Gorbachev's Struggle for Economic Reform* (Ithaca: Cornell University Press, 1991), p. 88.

24. Gertrude E. Schroeder, "'Crisis' in the Consumer Sector: A Comment," in Hewett and Winston, *Milestones in Glasnost and Perestroika: The Economy*, pp. 408-414.

25. Aslund, *Gorbachev's Struggle for Economic Reform*, p. 111.

26. *Ibid.*, p. 116.

27. Quoted in Aslund, *Gorbachev's Struggle for Economic Reform*," p. 124.

28. *Ibid.*, p. 125.

29. "Basic Guidelines for the Stabilization of the National Economy and the Transition to a Market Economy," *Pravda*, October 18, 1990, in Foreign Broadcast Information Service (FBIS), *Daily Report on the Soviet Union*, October 22, 1990, p.45.

30. Goldman, *What Went Wrong with Perestroika*, p. 221.

31. *Ibid.*, pp. 218-219.

32. The Shatalin Working Group, *Transition to the Market*, pp. 18-19.

33. *Ibid.*, p. 29.

34. *Ibid.*, pp. 31-32.

35. *Ibid.*, p. 35.

36. *Ibid.*, pp. 35-36.

37. Marie Lavigne, *Financing the Transition in the USSR: The Shatalin Plan and the Soviet Economy* (New York: Institute for East-West Security Studies, 1990).

38. "Basic Guideline for the Stabilization of the National Economy and the Transition to a Market Economy," p. 46.

39. *Izvestia* October 21, 1990, in *Current Digest of the Soviet Press* Vol. XLII, No. 42 (1990), p. 7.

40. International Monetary Fund, the World Bank, Organization for Economic Co-operation and Development, and European Bank for Reconstruction and Development, *A Study of the Soviet Economy* (Paris, IMF, 1991), Vol. 2, p. 295.

41. IMF et al., *A Study of the Soviet Economy*, Vol. 2, p. 19.

42. Quoted in Patrick Flaherty, "The State and the Dominant Class in the Soviet Perestroika," in Paul Zarembka (ed.), *Research in Political Economy*, Vol. 12 (Greenwich and London: JAI Press, 1990), p. 275.

43. Flaherty, "The State and the Dominant Class in the Soviet Perestroika," p. 275.

44. IMF et al., *A Study of the Soviet Economy*, Vol. 2, pp. 29, 41.

45. See Alfred G. Meyer, "The Soviet Political System," in Hoffmann and Laird, *The Soviet Polity in the Modern Era*, pp. 753-770.

46. Harley Balzer, "Russia: Not Apocalypse, but Purgatory," *Christian Science Monitor*, July 20, 1992.

47. Samuel P. Huntington, "Democracy's Third Wave," *Journal of Democracy*, Vol. 2, No. 2 (1991), p. 33.

5

The Japanese Model:
Limits and Lessons for Russia

The dramatic growth of the Japanese trading state in the postwar era has attracted increasing attention from the international community. In searching for lessons from Japan, some scholars have identified unique features of state-market relations imbedded in Japanese tradition and culture. If cultural and traditional variables account for the Japanese success, there are reasonable concerns over the applicability of the Japanese experience elsewhere.

Those doubts may be especially relevant to efforts to use Japan as a guide for Russia's struggle toward a market-oriented economy. The question of learning from Japan has been raised in Russian intellectual and policy circles.[1] Gorbachev talked about a "cardinal" change in the functions of the centralized Soviet economic bureaucracy. During his visit to Japan in April 1991, Gorbachev argued that the USSR could learn much from Japan, especially in the fields of technological innovation and economic competitiveness. Since the demise of the Soviet Union, Russian reformers have continued to look to Japan for economic lessons.

Are, in fact, such lessons from Japan applicable to Russia and other countries with a command economy? Or, on the other hand, do they not fit because of Japan's peculiar cultural and traditional characteristics? In particular, questions must be raised about the sources of the strength of the Japanese state and the vitality of the Japanese market; about the Japanese solutions to conflicts between market and state; and about the political mechanisms that the Japanese government uses to control, regulate and facilitate the market exchange.

The answers to those questions require a brief examination of the reasons the constitutional framework established during the Allied Occupation of Japan has remained stable for four decades. Nine main factors may be noted: (1) The transfer from imperial sovereignty to popular rule has taken root in the Japanese citizenry. (2) The high degree of modernization by 1937 provided a partial socioeconomic basis for postwar development. (3) Having suffered enormously during World War II, most Japanese people sincerely supported the peace constitution characterized by Article 9's restriction of investments to civilian, rather than military, development. (4) The alliance with the United States in the Cold War strengthened Japan's links with the West, not only in military and economic aspects, but also in the patterns of political thought and behavior. (5) The growth of the middle class and the emergence of civil society in Japan solidified popular support for the democratic constitution. (6) The existence of truly independent economic and political forces in Japanese society has obstructed the growth of political authoritarianism. (7) The conflict and compromise among the powerful LDP factions strengthened pluralist elements in the party. (8) The weakness of the radical opposition has contributed to the stability of the Japanese political system. (9) The country's marked social homogeneity averted any real crisis of integration.

Furthermore, the constitution developed on the basis of a solid, but not stagnant state. Its solidity ensured underlying administrative stability. The deeply-rooted tradition of excellence in the state bureaucracy arose from the long-standing ability of key government ministries to recruit the top graduates from elite universities.[2] Yet, stagnation was avoided, because the constitution provides for competitive elections, because the LDP political dominance before 1993 existed within a traditional emphasis on consensus decision-making that allows room for a viable opposition, and because the competition among LDP factions ensured some degree of choice.

Besides the Japanese state, Japanese society is an essential element in the context of economic development that must be considered in asking what the Russians can learn from the Japanese, and, especially, what the Russians probably cannot learn. In other words, there may be cultural, historical, and political limitations on the transferability of the Japanese experiences. For example, the homogeneity of Japanese society contrasts to Soviet multinationality. If social homogeneity favors the growth of a united market and political stability, Russia and other successor states should have a better chance for a successful transition to the market and democracy than did their antecedent. However, evidence supporting the correlation between homogeneity and democracy is insufficient. The case of the United States may suggest that ethnic diversity can enhance political democracy.

Another crucial consideration concerns the circumstances in which Japan became a highly successful trading state. They include a fundamental and far-reaching shift in the international system: Japan's defeat in World War II and subsequent alliance with the United States. Japanese policy makers were very flexible in adapting to the new situations. Japan's defeat forced Japanese leaders to abandon their traditional military territorial adventurism and adopt a trading strategy. In other words, they revised the Meiji slogan "enrich the country and strengthen the army" to a single-minded pursuit of economic development. National consensus has supported economic growth as the central task for Japan.

In contrast, the Soviet Union was a World War II ally and Cold War foe of the United States. Transformation to a "trading state" was not feasible in such conditions of international isolation. The Soviet Union could not follow Japan to build a trading state, not only because of different domestic factors, but also due to the sharply contrasting international contexts. Even if Soviet leaders had wanted to build a trading state, they would have had great difficulties because Soviet manufactured goods were not competitive in the international market.

The recent history of Russia somewhat parallels the earlier Japanese experience. Russia "lost" the Cold War and has formed a de facto entente with its former enemy. Russian President Boris Yeltsin and U.S. President Bill Clinton discussed building a "partnership" between the two countries at the July 1993 Tokyo economic summit. Russia's reduction of military emphasis and its promotion of trading elements are creating conditions fundamentally similar to Japan's situation after 1945, although Russia will likely remain a military and political power for the foreseeable future.

The differences between Japan and Russia are enormous. However, cultural and historical differences do not exclude the possibility of learning from others. Having a tradition fundamentally different from that of the West, Japan still succeeded in learning from the West and became a highly developed country politically and economically. This chapter argues that Russia can follow Japan's example and draw lessons from it as Japan learned from the West. In particular, it sees special opportunities in the following specific areas: indicative planning, industrial policy, private ownership, pragmatism, intensive growth, separation of state and party, and international competition.

Indicative Planning Versus
Administrative Command Planning

Indicative planning is a key link in Japanese state-market relations. Government plans identify the strategic targets, provide guidance for industrial policy, and bolster confidence of the investors and entrepreneurs. At the same time, the enterprises do not have to follow each step defined by the Economic Planning Agency because indicative planning is not compulsory. Thus, there is room for the growth of entrepreneurship.

Japanese planners seriously consider basic market principles. Plans are adjusted according to changes in basic trends of supply and demand. A main objective of the plans is to attain balanced growth. The Economic Planning Agency is responsible for the formulation of national economic development plans. The government plans provide information to private entrepreneurs and, combined with the keen competition for the market share among enterprises, have often led to rapid expansion of the economy. In some cases, government plans acted as a brake on over-competition rather than as a stimulant for growth. The plans also have opened up consideration of the economic implications of education and social security and have had an important influence upon policy-making in these fields. State-orientation of the plans are integrated with market-orientation, i.e., consumer orientation, in indicative planning.

According to Kazuo Sato, in carrying out indicative planning, the government has a number of policy instruments at its disposal. Key policy instruments include the following. (1) Expenditure policy is a very potent policy instrument at the disposal of the government. (2) Tax policy designed to promote savings is needed to finance capital formation. (3) The national government is engaged in extensive off-budget activity, based on funds collected by the Postal Savings System. (4) Subsidizing an industry is another way of favoring an industry that needs special protection. (5) Credit policy supports entrepreneurship. (6) Research and development policy strongly favors strategic technology innovation and application. (7) Agricultural policy protects Japanese farmers' interests and solidifies the conservative rural votes to LDP. (8) Trade policy effectively promotes Japanese exports worldwide.[3]

Another kind of policy instrument is administrative guidance. The Japanese government often intervenes in the private sector by issuing official notifications and instructions which instruct private agents on how to behave on certain subjects. Some of these notifications are based on laws and others are not. Even in the former case, Japanese laws tend to be so broadly stated that a wide scope of interpretation is possible. Hence, official notifications are vital in setting precedents. In certain instances, official interpretations have even proved to have been illegal or extra-legal. The often-cited cases can be found in MITI's industrial structure policy, which recommended the formation of cartels in violation of the Anti-Monopoly Law. Another instance of government intervention is MITI's regulation of large-scale retail stores, based on the Large-Scale Retail Store Law in force since 1974. In a broad sense, a unifying interpretation of Japan's structural economic policy is that it has been principally pro-producer. Producers' interests are put ahead of consumers' interests.[4]

Chalmers Johnson's distinction between plan-rationality and ideology-rationality is a useful research tool.[5] Generally speaking, Japanese planning is based upon economic rationality. Soviet planning, in contrast, was based upon political and ideological consideration. In the Soviet system, most important orders originated from the Politburo of the Communist party and the Council of Ministers, but additional directives to the enterprise could come from regional or local party and government bodies. All these orders from governmental or supervisory bodies were supposed to be in accord with the plan, which emanated from Gosplan or its subordinate agencies. The highly centralized direction that proved quite effective in mobilizing Soviet society during the early five-year plans became an obstacle to adaptation when a greater complexity of society called for more flexibility and technological innovation.

Without fundamental changes in its planning system, the Russian economy could not be transformed from a centrally planned economy to a market-oriented economy, or a "plan-oriented market economy." As the Russians are trying to make a shift from administrative command planning to indicative planning, strategic indicative planning was one field that they should learn from the Japanese.

Restructuring the planning system must involve changes in both the style and substance of planning. The style of planning refers to the methods and forms of planning. The substance of planning refers to its contents and scope. There are enormous differences between Japan and Russia in both aspects. Changing the substance of planning is more critical than transforming the style of planning. However, without changes in style, the new substance cannot express itself properly. There is an organic connection between style and substance. Therefore, the power, authority, responsibility, and accountability of planning organizations, and their relations with other state organizations and particularly the emerging independent economic actors, must be restructured.

Five-year plans were a hallmark of the Soviet administrative command economy between 1929 and 1991. When the Soviet planning system was undergoing restructuring, it was necessary to re-examine the strengths and especially the weaknesses of the Soviet planning system. It seemed that the Soviet planning system functioned relatively well during the period of extensive growth from the 1930s to 1950s while it met increasing troubles after the 1960s.[6]

Obviously, if the plans are to be workable, they must be close to real life, and must reflect the "objective demands" of the economy and society. At the stage of intensive economic growth, it is impossible for the central planning agency to collect all necessary information about supply and demand and then to make specific plans for allocations of human and material resources, and the production and distribution of all major products. There are simultaneously problems of information overload and information scarcity. A feasible way for the Russian planners to avoid the dilemma is to dramatically reduce the scope of state planning, to drastically change the bureaucratic style of planning. Changes in the planning system involve changes in the information system. Market prices, instead of plans, should be the core information. Market prices, reflecting supply and demand, are going to be the most significant indicator for planners, producers, traders, and consumers.

The Japanese case has demonstrated that indicative planning is more suitable and compatible with intensive economic growth than is command planning. Intensive growth needs more individual initiatives and creativity. The accelerated pace of the scientific-technological revolution demands greater flexibility on both planners and producers. Although the Russians cannot copy the Japanese planning system, they can learn key lessons about how to formulate and implement "indicative plans" by examining and imitating the Japanese planning processes.

As the world economy becomes increasingly interdependent, it is difficult for any central planners within a nation-state to predict, not to say control, the trend of the world economy. In this context, indicative planning with its flexibility can be adjusted to shifts in the global economy. On the other hand, the traditional administrative command planning is doomed to fail in the increasingly diversified and interdependent world economy.

Industrial Policy Versus
Administrative Control of Industry

Since the Meiji reforms, the Japanese government has played a quite active role in economic planning and development. Many scholars, like William Lockwood and Herman Kahn, assign a central role to government management in Japanese economic development.[7] Johnson emphasizes that a "state attempting to match the economic achievements of Japan must adopt the same priorities as Japan. It must first of all be a developmental state."[8] The Ministry of International Trade and Industry (MITI) quickly turned its attention to developing a dynamic, export-promoting and import-retarding industrialization strategy after World War II. It is therefore useful to inquire in greater detail into the mechanisms and levers employed for implementing the policies of Japan's economic bureaucracy.

Whereas the Japanese bureaucracy often takes its own initiative in formulating economic policy, it maintains very close relations with the business community. Economic bureaucrats from MITI and other state agencies regularly meet with representatives from the business community. The Japanese bureaucracy is deeply concerned with active industrial policy. The basic promise is that the private sector alone does not have sufficient vision, coordination, resources, and risk-bearing ability to conduct its affairs in an optimal manner. To alleviate bottlenecks, to avert over-production, to anticipate market shifts, and to develop new technology, the government is needed to assist in the sharing of information, pooling of resources, and the overall collaboration of efforts. As a result of the successful implementation of this approach, MITI has publicly introduced the concept of a plan-oriented market economy system.[9] In postwar Japan, the government tended to decide how many firms there should be in a given industry and then set about to arrange the desired number. Prioritized sectors have enjoyed benefits from special depreciation and favorable tax rates. Since the 1980s, the priorities of the economic bureaucracy have shifted to new technologies and broader social environmental concerns, but the preponderant state function of guiding and facilitating economic development is still visible.

According to Johnson, there are two kinds of industrial policy: functional and sectoral. Functional industrial policy means the role of government is in educating the labor force, building the roads and infrastructure on which industry depends, legislating incentives to reward savers and investors, developing an environmentally sound energy policy, and supporting research and development for the technologies of the future. Sectorial industrial policy aims at helping new industries to become competitive and assisting in the orderly retreat of those that can no longer compete. Industrial policy is not a plan to protect or enrich private industry; it is, rather, the recognition that the economy is too important to be left entirely to private interests.[10]

Industrial policy results from an intense and continuing interaction between business and the government bureaucratic apparatus. Each sector of the Japanese economy has a client relation to a ministry or agency of the government. The client relations in the USSR were similar in appearance but different in essence from that in Japan. The key was that Soviet economic actors were not independent players with their own ownership and autonomy.

To a certain degree, both Japanese and Soviet governments were pro-producer rather than pro-consumer. However, there are fundamental differences between the two. The Japanese state favors market/consumer-oriented producers. A key criterion for the Japanese government to judge a producer is its ability to compete in the world market. The Japanese government always takes market factors into consideration. While some producers may just focus upon short-term gains or losses on the market, the government formulates long-term strategic policies and provides administrative guidance to the producers. Industrial policy makes organic connections between state preferences and market preferences.

The Soviet state, in contrast, did not think much about consumer preferences or about international competitiveness and quality. State interests, as understood and interpreted by the party-state leaders, dominated Soviet decision making on economic planning and development. Most industries were directly owned and controlled by the party-state. The administrative control of the state economy led to a crisis situation. The Soviet Union did not have industrial policy as practiced by the Japanese.

During the transitional stage, the Russian government is rapidly giving up its control over the state enterprises. Most enterprises are confronting great difficulties in adapting to a post-command and primitive market environment. Under such circumstances, it is difficult but necessary to formulate an industrial policy that will help the emerging winning industries and reduce pains of the losing industries. The lack of industrial policy might prolong the chaotic situation and further intensify a transitional crisis. Thus, Russia needs an industrial policy that can promote productivity and efficiency of the consumer oriented sectors.

Private Ownership Versus State Ownership

In analyzing state-market relations, the most fundamental issues involve the relations between the patterns of ownership and the performance of the economy. A classic question in the study of political economy is the controversy of private ownership versus public ownership, and the related issue of efficiency versus equality. Is privatization a prerequisite for the transition toward a market economy? Or, can private ownership survive and thrive without a well functioning market? It seems that private ownership and the market are mutually supportive and interdependent.

The Japanese economy is predominately privately owned. At the initial stage of modernization (1860-1880), the Japanese government directly engaged in industrial undertakings. When the government-owned enterprises demonstrated inefficiency and a budget deficit developed, the Japanese government had to sell off most of the government enterprises to private business. In the contemporary world, most advanced market economies are predominantly based upon private ownership of the means of production. The Japanese case demonstrated well that the state can play a significant role in economic development of the market-oriented economy based upon private ownership. This fact is contrary to the Soviet official ideology which claimed that the contradictions between the socialized mass production and the private ownership of the means of production would necessarily lead to profound economic conflict and crisis.

The aim of the Communists was the abolition of private property. The state-owned economy in the USSR did not create greater wealth or a greater degree of equality than the capitalist Japanese economy. In comparison with the Russians, Japanese citizens have enjoyed better consumer goods, greater opportunity for education and training, more chances to travel abroad, and broader rights in electing their political leaders. Private property provides people with a sense of personal independence and an economic basis for political freedom and civil liberty. State ownership often leads to political control of the management, production, and distribution of goods, to the predominance of state preference over consumer preference in resources allocation, to corruption among officials in charge of state-owned property, and to a huge waste of human and material resources because of the lack of or low degree of personal care over public property. A cautionary note is due here. Private ownership itself does not guarantee a clean government. In fact, the Japanese government, especially the LDP politicians, are notorious for many scandals involving political corruptions.

"Self-interest" is a key for studying economics and politics. It seems that private ownership reflects more closely the self-interest of the people involved. For example, Sony Corporation's owners and stockholders have developed a sense that Sony is "their" company. All of them have a stake in enhancing the company's productivity and profits. In a Soviet factory, the party-picked and party-supervised managers cared less about the factory than about the "*blat*" or connections with their superiors. Many Soviet workers had little sense of being the "owners" of their factories.

Ownership of the means of production is closely related with the style and process of decision-making. Public-owned companies tend to be highly bureaucratized, over-staffed, and slow in decision-making. Private enterprises are often managed by professional rather than political officials. These professional managers usually can make timely decisions reflecting the needs of the market.

Gorbachev was slow to realize the links between privatization and marketization. He had a strong personal commitment to public ownership of land. Even after the failed coup of August 1991, Gorbachev still claimed that he had deep faith in basic socialist values. Yeltsin has openly declared marketization and privatization as policy goals of the Russian government. However, how to develop a market economy based mainly upon private ownership in Russia and other newly independent states is a challenging problem. The Soviet economy was dominated by public ownership, mainly state ownership, for more than seventy years. One of the most difficult questions in *perestroika* is how to change people's thinking and behavior, i.e., the culture regarding the ownership of the means of production. Just as there are different forms of private ownership in Western market economies, there can be different forms of ownership in Russian and other former Soviet republics. Looking at Japanese ownership will provide potential models for the reformers.

Pragmatism Versus Ideological Rigidity

Most Japanese leaders are very pragmatic and not bound by ideology.[11] Since the Meiji Restoration, the Japanese have been extraordinarily flexible and adaptive to new ideas and new situations. Consequently, they have excelled in learning from others while keeping their distinctive national characteristics. As Hugh Patrick and Henry Rosovsky have argued:

> Japan's historical experience and value system have resulted in a school of pragmatic thinking supportive of close and harmonious government-business relations. One thinks immediately of emphasis on the group rather than the individual, on cooperation and conciliation aimed at harmony, on national rather than personal welfare. The right of the government to lead, and to interfere where necessary, has substantial basis in ideology as well as in historical experience.[12]

Economic ideology can be a means of establishing norms of economic behavior and of legitimizing economic institutions and practices, yet the Japanese are careful not to attach too much importance to it. In Japan, the ideology is not well articulated and its role in directly shaping the economic system is not large;

it is pragmatically focused on what succeeds in achieving desired goals.[13] When a doctrine comes into conflict with the reality, the Japanese would not hesitate to discard it. They believe that theory is grey while life is ever dynamic.

In contrast, many Soviet leaders were highly ideological and were used to living by doctrines rather than learning from life. Many of them became prisoners of doctrines that exaggerated the potential danger and injustice of the market. One fundamental aim of the Soviet system as defined by official doctrine was to eliminate capitalism, including the private ownership of the means of production and the market as a central place of exchange. Soviet leaders, following Marxist and Leninist doctrine, tried to eliminate the market. Even though the efforts had proven a total failure, it took a long time for Soviet leaders to face the facts and revise their doctrine.

If the Russians want to survive and succeed in the world market, they must first build a competitive domestic market. In order to do so, they should learn from the Japanese pragmatism and get rid of their out-dated doctrines. De-ideologization is a key task for the Russians to catch up with the modernization processes in advanced market economies. Most Russian leaders and academics have become less ideological and more open-minded in recent years. Nevertheless, there is a gap between talking about and acting on pragmatism.

Recent trends in Russia suggest that an increasing number of people there are becoming more pragmatic. First, hard facts of life have taught many Russian citizens a good lesson about the devastating effects of rigid doctrines. The reformers want to get rid of the ideological burdens and liberate themselves. Second, pluralism has begun to take root in the emerging civil society. Many people have become more critical, analytical, and realistic than ever before.[14] *Glasnost* has contributed to the growth of free thinking and the decline of the official ideology. However, the emerging pluralism in Russia and other post-Soviet republics is strongly ethnic in nature and not necessarily conducive to political compromise and an effective legal framework.

Worldwide experiences have demonstrated the strengths of pragmatism. Japan is an outstanding case of the triumph of pragmatism. China's economic reforms, particularly the household responsibility system, have gained remarkable results. "Practice is the sole criterion of truth" has been a cardinal principle guiding the Chinese reforms. On the other hand, rigid ideology has obstructed the growth of productivity. This is especially true in the age of technological revolution. When the processes of technological innovation and productive application are being transformed so dramatically, how can a doctrine developed a hundred years ago remain effective and retain vitality without significant revision? With the collapse of the CPSU, its official ideology has lost its legitimacy and credibility. Many Russians are searching for new ideas; some are looking to the West, some are looking to Japan, and some are going back to the Russian legacy for inspiration. The battle of minds will have significant impact on future development.

Intensive Growth Versus Extensive Growth

The basic difference between Japanese and Russian resource utilization is the intensive versus extensive approach. Japan increased output by a greater input of skills as Russia sought to achieve the same results by a greater input of material resources and manpower. When it comes to advanced development based on high technology which requires individual initiative and technological innovation, the Stalinist system and the extensive strategy no longer work.

Since the 1970s, Soviet leaders had argued for intensive rather than extensive growth, but they failed to achieve intensive growth. What were the major obstacles for the Soviets to make the necessary transition? Related with problems discussed in the previous chapters, the following factors are significant.

The habit of thinking of Russia/USSR as a large country with almost unlimited natural resources has encouraged the practice of expanding outputs by increasing the amount of inputs. The centralized resources allocation and utilization system was political-oriented rather than economic-rational. Its major purpose was to concentrate, consolidate, and expand state power without careful calculation of the costs. For convenience of the central planners, gross output was the key indicator for economic performance for a long time. Thus the emphasis was on quantity rather than quality. The more materials a plant uses, the heavier and bigger a product was, the higher the achievement of the producer. Traditional overemphasis on the size of heavy and defense industry granted managers in those sectors easy access to human and material resources. Division "A" industry was supplied with good materials without much consideration of the cost-benefit calculation.

For more than half a century, Soviet industrial managers were well protected against foreign competition. Protectionism reduced the desire as well as the pressure for producing better goods with less resources. The long-term shortage of consumer goods and the existence of the sellers' market had allowed the continuous production of low quality goods because many poorly manufactured goods were still in demand. Bureaucratic conservatism was deeply rooted in the administrative command system. The *nomenklatura* system ensured the tendency for the bureaucrats to please their superiors, to keep order and stability rather than to encourage creative work of their employees, and to make innovative changes. Furthermore, the lack of real incentives for technological innovation enlarged the technological gap between the former USSR and advanced countries. In the USSR, there was a huge gap between research and production partly due to the bureaucratic separation of research institutions and factories.

As Russia shifts from extensive to intensive growth, it is imperative to examine the fundamental causes of intensive growth in Japan. The small size of the island nation (in comparison with Russia) and scarcity of natural resources have given the Japanese a deep sense of a crisis situation and a strong desire to survive and excel in the world. Japan is almost totally lacking in many important raw materials. The country imports over 90 percent of all of its energy, virtually all of its oil, iron ore, and a substantial portion of its foodstuffs. Even a hundred years ago, Japanese agricultural production was already quite intensive. Such historical emphasis on intensive growth of agriculture has been sustained in the contemporary industrial and post-industrial era.

The close links between the domestic market and the world economy, a result of the export-driven growth strategy, have compelled the Japanese to manufacture better and cheaper goods with fewer inputs. As discussed earlier, private ownership plus the strong identification of many employees with their companies have established deep concern for property and other resources. Thus, there is much less waste of materials in Japan than in Russia.

With strong support of the Japanese government, the increasing integration of research and manufacturing has narrowed the gap between innovation and mass production. The Japanese are outstanding in learning and adapting the technological innovations of other countries and applying them to the mass production of quality durable consumer goods. Administrative guidance and government assistance to key "sunrise" industries rely on new technology and advanced knowledge. At the same time, there is much less bureaucratic intervention in new product research and development in Japan than in Russia. More fundamentally, the emphasis on education and training of human resources has had many positive effects on the Japanese economy and society. The Japanese educational system is one of the most efficient in the world. The "open" nature of the information system has allowed great access to information. The commercialization of technological information has accelerated technological innovation. In contrary, governmental control of information and the low profit for innovation have obstructed technological progress in Russia.

There are compelling reasons for the Russian reformers to emphasize intensive growth. With the demise of the Soviet empire and the independence of fifteen republics, Russia's human and material resources are much more limited than that of the USSR. Although being the largest successor state, decades of brutal exploitation and mismanagement of resources under the command system left a series of environmental and ecological disasters. There is no longer unlimited natural wealth ready for continued extensive expansion. In order to upgrade the Russian economy and integrate it into the world economy, the Russians must give up extensive growth and undertake intensive growth. By learning from Japan, the Russians surely can remove many obstacles for intensive growth. This is one of the most promising areas to draw lessons that can be learned!

The Interaction of Party, State, and Business

The Soviet state was a party-state between 1918 and 1991. The CPSU dominated the state and society to a significant degree. In the traditional Soviet system, the party enjoyed political and personnel control of economic management through the party organizations and the *nomenklatura* system. Over-centralization of political and economic power in the party was a key feature of the Soviet system. The centralization of power and the lack of effective checks and balances mechanisms resulted in widespread abuse of power by party leaders. Party secretaries, particularly the first secretaries at the union, republic, and regional levels enjoyed a wide range of powers and privileges.

The Japanese LDP Policy Research Council makes policy recommendations on strategic policy, but the party does not intervene in economic management directly. There are clear-cut lines of power and authority between party organizations and state agencies. Highly professional state bureaucrats are responsible for economic planning and industrial policy. To a certain degree, Japan can be described as a country ruled by the state bureaucrats. Public economic policy making power is basically in the hands of the professional government bureaucrats rather than party politicians or the elected legislature.[15]

The LDP's role is more clearly defined than that of the CPSU because the rule of law established by the constitutional framework provides a legal demarcation between the party and the state. In addition, the existence of real opposition parties and truly independent interest groups has limited the LDP's power. Thanks to the system of competitive election, the LDP must pay attention to public opinions. The LDP depends upon the votes and financial support of others.

In contrast to the LDP's limited role in the Japanese economy, the CPSU was extremely powerful and interventionist in the Soviet Union. The *nomenklatura* system enabled the party to control all the important positions in the state and society. The lack of actual rule of law meant that party leaders were the highest arbiters for winners and losers in society. The criteria for judging performance were often political and particularistic rather than economic and universal. The growth of neo-traditionalism further consolidated the party's role in both society and the economy.[16] For instance, Soviet workers were made dependent upon the workplace for general socio-welfare. Top party leaders enjoyed great power controlling not only the administrative process but also people's daily socioeconomic life. As classic Western democratic thinkers (Montesquieu, Locke, and the Federalists) suggested, without separation of powers, corruption and abuse of power inevitably came into play.[17]

It took several years of *perestroika* to remove the CPSU's control of the economy and society. The first step was the growth of pluralism in the party system and the development of internal party democracy. The second step was the elimination of the monopoly of power by the CPSU. The abolition of the *nomenklatura* system was a prerequisite for establishing of a modern civil service system based upon rational bureaucratic principles in the Weberian tradition. Selection and promotion of officials should be based upon merit and achievement rather than personal connection with and loyalty to party leaders. The CPSU was gradually separated from the state. In 1989, the Congress of People's Deputies was elected as the supreme organ of power in the country. This was a decisive step in transforming party-state relations in the USSR.

In the socioeconomic field, legally independent economic actors should enjoy the protection of the state. It is up to the state organs, legislative and executive branches, to decide whether or not to accept the party's recommendations. In other words, the power and authority of the state organs should be superior to the party in economic affairs. Private ownership and a fully developed market are the economic foundations for the emergence of independent economic players. The growth of powerful independent socioeconomic forces will support new political forces that effectively counteract the dominant tendency of any centralized political party. In conjunction with socioeconomic development, dramatic political changes have taken place in Russia. President Yeltsin banned the activities of the Communist party in Russia after the failed coup in August 1991. The present challenge is to establish new relations between the state and the market on the basis of economic rationality rather than ideological or political consideration.

Johnson asserted that the "effectivé operation of the developmental state requires the bureaucracy implementing economic development be protected from all but the most powerful interest groups so that it can set and achieve long-range industrial priorities."[18] Japanese bureaucrats have on the whole been able to do what they think favorable to the wealth and power of the state without much regard to many special interests that might be hurt or deprived by their chosen policies. The continued economic growth has cushioned shocks for most groups, e.g., farmers still enjoy substantial government protection.

Bradley Richardson and Scott Flanagan argue that the relationships between big business and Japanese government fit the corporatist model. In some areas of broad economic policy making, such as in the formulation of national economic plans, there has been a kind of "limited" pluralism, in the sense that different ministries, the LDP, and business groups all have inputs into policy processes. The resulting pluralistic participation, however, is limited by the absence of effective participation from the opposition parties and mass interest groups including the labor unions. Weak or declining industries often have to follow administrative guidance because they need help such as special tax benefits and government loans. In such situations, relationships between business and government tend to resemble the corporatist model. Where industries are strong and economically viable, there is much greater resistance to government intervention, and therefore more pluralism.[19]

The first multi-year plan drawn up by the Japanese government following the end of the Occupation appeared in 1955. The goals of Japan's postwar economic policy, clearly enunciated in that plan, centered around the interlocking triad of "growth, investment, and exports." A rapid growth of the modern, capital-intensive sectors and a relative shrinkage of the traditional sector required massive investments and thus a high level of national savings. Much of Japanese economic policy during the postwar era was directed toward encouraging high levels of savings and investment.

The outstanding performance of the Japanese economy reflected in industries like steel and automobiles is significantly attributable to government policy. Tax incentives and other instruments required by key industry development plans helped facilitate growth by creating favorable conditions for investment in long-term capital improvements in some industries. G.C. Allen, a British expert on the Japanese economy, argued that "the strategy of industrial growth has been worked out by the large firms and the bureaucracy in conjunction, and that the allocation of investment funds and the direction of industrial development have been guided from the center."[20] Lockwood put the proposition succinctly: While the Japanese government's statutory authority to control business was less extensive than in most industrial nations, the informal, extra-statutory powers that it exercised were enormous.

> The hand of Government is everywhere in evidence. ... The Ministries engage in an extraordinary amount of consultation, advice, persuasion and threat. The industrial bureaus of the MITI proliferate sectoral targets and plans; they confer, they tinker, they exhort. This is the 'economics by admonition' to a degree inconceivable in Washington or London. Business makes few major decisions without consulting the appropriate government authority; the same is true in reverse.[21]

The Japanese bureaucracy, in pursuit of the government's economic strategy, brings its influence to bear on private firms; while the firms themselves, in return, seek to direct official policy into channels that serve their ambitions. In Japan there has been mutual trust and support between the state and industry. Private business and the government were moved by a single ambition--rapid industrial expansion--and their relations were governed by a recognition of a common interest.

In the Soviet Union, if a factory did well in fulfilling state plans, the planning committee would raise its target for next year. Managers of the plant would have difficulty in catching up with the new plan target. Thus, many managers tried to hide the real production potentials from the state planners. The Soviet practice of "planning from the achieved level" created tension between the planners and managers.[22] This tended to retard, rather than expand, production potential.

Examining the government's economic role, we should not ignore the public sector proper, that is, the part of the economy that is controlled and wholly or partly owned by public authorities. The public sector in Japan is very small compared with Great Britain or France. However, to study how the Japanese manage their public sector relatively efficiently will be instructive for the Russian reforms during the transition to the market, and for the non-market sectors even after the establishment of the market system. Even if, under the best case scenario, Russia succeeded in its transition toward a market economy, there will still be significant public sectors, e.g., education, defense, public health. It is a challenging task to efficiently manage public sectors in a market economy.

After a thorough study of how the Japanese economy works, Patrick and Rosovsky highlighted some key lessons from Japan. In their view, relations between the public and private sectors in Japan may contain the seeds of at least three alternative approaches to these relations for other countries. First, there is a high degree of cooperation between government and business--especially big business. "Major economic decisions are made only after extensive discussions, negotiations, and compromises in what is a formally and informally institutionalized, highly effective process."[23] Such cooperation has facilitated a long-term planning process to the benefit of economic performance. Second, the Japanese government has demonstrated an impressive capacity to maintain a relatively clear hierarchy of goals. In the area of industrial growth and exports, for instance, the government and the private sector have directed their efforts to solving the most serious problems facing the economy. Finally and perhaps most importantly in terms of state-market relations:

> ...the Japanese experience has also shown the value and dynamism of private enterprise when it is encouraged by government. With the risks of unbridled competition and the imperfections of markets long recognized, no society seems willing to endorse free enterprise without qualification. However, in postwar Japan private enterprise did succeed in revolutionizing the living standards of the population; and to some extent the government--especially the bureaucracy-- exercised a useful countervailing role without stifling private initiative.[24]

It is of vital importance to establish a pattern of state-market interaction which will encourage the growth of entrepreneurship on the one hand, and prevent market failures on the other hand. Postwar Japan has been relatively successful in managing its government-business relations so far. In building their new state-market relation, Russia and other newly independent states should closely examine the Japanese experience in relevant fields.

Objective Criteria for Winners and Losers

A key to the success of the Japanese economy is that there are clear-cut rules for winners and losers. Competition in the market will result in success or failure. The Japanese government, especially the MITI, intentionally encourages the prospective winning industries to grow and guides the losing industries to make transitions. The failures of the losers were not socialized in Japan. Sato points out that the Japanese government plays a critical role in picking winners and losers:

> In exercising industrial policy, MITI has to decide which industries to encourage and which to discourage, that is, to identify industries with the ability to grow in the future, encouraging prospective winning industries and discouraging prospective losing industries with various policy instruments. Thus, MITI's industrial policy is often called picking winners and losers.[25]

It is important to note that criteria for winners and losers in Japan are closely related with economic competitiveness. Economic players who are losing competition will be forced to change or even be driven to bankruptcy. In the Soviet economy, however, there were no clear-cut rules for winners and losers. There was no real incentive for people to work hard because both success and failure were socialized.[26] If there was no effective mechanism for competition, the winners were not rewarded fairly and the losers were not punished accordingly. State enterprises that were inefficient would still be protected rather than allowed to go bankrupt. Under such a situation, there was no real motivation for people to work hard and to use resources efficiently.

In order to motivate people to work hard, performance and monetary reward should be closely linked to each other. If someone works hard and gets more pay, he or she will have a wide-ranging choice of consumer goods or services in a highly developed market. Monetary motivation becomes a driving force for people to work hard. The traditional work ethic in Japan also encourages hard work. In fact, there is a strong, deeply rooted work ethic among the Japanese. The Japanese work week and school year are among the longest in the developed world.

In the Soviet Union, there was not much connection between one's performance and income. What made things worse in late 1980s was the widespread shortage of consumer goods. People must wait in line to purchase consumer goods. They would rather spend time waiting in line for purchasing the goods they need rather than working for not very valuable rubles. The argument that the Soviets did not have an ethic of hard work could not be justified. The real problem is the low-motivation system, not the ethics or morality. If there were a well developed market, if there were close connections between performance and rewards, if the rubles that people received from working were valuable and meaningful, then the majority of Soviet citizens would work hard and smart to get more rubles. In other words, they must switch from welfare-state authoritarianism and moral incentives to material incentives.[27] Changes in the basic economic system will influence even the non-market sectors. For example, the market system will stimulate competition which will encourage the work ethic.

Another lesson from Japan involves the relationship between authority and accountability. The Japanese government ministries and enterprises have clear-cut authority and accountability respectively. Such relationships did not develop well in the Soviet Union. In fact, as a result of *perestroika*, some Soviet ministries had lost formal authority over enterprises but were still held responsible for the performance of "their" enterprises. Because they were responsible for the success or failure of enterprises, different ministries found new ways or resorted to old methods to micro-manage the enterprises. The result was further confusion and deepening of the economic crisis. If the new leaders in Russia and other independent states are serious about the transition from the command economy to a market-oriented economy, they must define clear-cut lines of authority and responsibility which are compatible with market principles.

Protectionism and International Competition

Among advanced economies, the Japanese are famous because of the protectionism they practiced in guarding their infant industries against foreign competition. An industry has its infant stage, growth stage, and decline stage. At the infant stage, government protection is often considered necessary because otherwise strong and mature foreign competitors may destroy the infant industry. For example, the Japanese government protected its automobile industry in the 1950s and the early 1960s. At the growth stage, the government removed the protection policy allowing the industry to compete in the tough international market. Through competing and winning, the industry grows stronger than ever before and moves toward the front of the industry.

In comparison with the Soviet case, Japanese protectionism is very weak. Through government monopoly of foreign trade plus state ownership and administration of industries, the Soviet government put its industries in total protection against foreign competition. As a result, the links between the Soviet economy and the international market were very weak. The USSR exported fewer manufactured goods to the world market than did South Korea in the 1980s.

It took their defeat in World War II to shock the Japanese and force them to choose a trading-oriented rather than military/territorial-oriented policy. In contrast, Soviet military victory in the war restrengthened the Soviet leaders' faith in the nature of the centralized system, particularly in the significance of military power.[28] Decades of military expansion brought huge burdens to the Soviet economy and enormous suffering to the Soviet people. Although they achieved the status of a military superpower, the Soviets totally lost to the competition in the world market. The catastrophic economic failures in the USSR finally led to sociopolitical crisis by the end of the 1980s.

The Soviet Union permitted little foreign investment in the past; it had great difficulty in attracting foreign investment in the *perestroika* era because of the instability and turmoil in the country. The Soviet government did not permit its factory managers to enter the world economy independently with their exports or even give them an incentive system that encourages exports. When they finally came into direct contact with other competitors on the world market, the Soviets found themselves in a disadvantageous political and economic situation. Although a military superpower, the USSR often acted like a Third World country in the world market.

While entry of foreign goods into the Japanese market is severely restricted, local businessmen must compete with those that do enter the country. Some foreign companies have created plants inside Japan that compete with local manufacturers. In addition, domestic Japanese manufacturers are interested in exporting their goods, and sometimes the government prods them in this direction. The restriction on external entry into the Japanese market has been a matter of growing concern outside Japan. Substantial non-tariff barriers still remain. It is interesting to examine if the decline of Japanese protectionism under international pressures will have positive or negative effects on Japanese economic competitiveness.

Groupism and the Lifetime Employment System

The vitality of the Japanese market first of all is reflected in the competitiveness of Japanese products in the world market. Many Japanese products are well known in the world for their high quality and competitive prices. Besides the political system which encourages and supports Japanese exports, the high quality of the labor force, the education workers receive, their group-oriented spirit and the extra working hours they put in, as well as suggestions for technical improvement from the workers and the cooperation between managerial and technical workers, all contributed to the remarkable Japanese economic growth. One cautionary note must be made here, i.e., some of the above factors are psychological and not easy for any other society to emulate.

Many scholars maintain that the Japanese are inclined toward groupism. Japanese groupism is defined as a set of values placing the interest of the group above that of the individual and based on the belief that the two are in accord. Prime value is attached to loyalty to the group. According to scholars who support the group model:

> Relationships between superiors and inferiors are carefully cultivated and maintained, and one's status within the group is seen as being a function of the length of one's membership. Self-effacing, polite expressions serve to reinforce these values in everyday life; such language is seen as a direct expression of the Japanese psychology.[29]

If groupism plays such a important role in Japan, how about the situation in the Soviet Union? Were Soviet citizens inclined toward groupism or individualism? There are differences between Japanese groupism and Soviet collectivism. A key difference lies in the fact that individual interests and private ownership tend to be compatible with group interests in Japan in many cases. In the Soviet Union, collectivism was an ideological slogan used by political leaders to induce personal sacrifices. Collectivism supposedly should be able to bring benefits to everyone in the collective. In reality, collective interests as interpreted by the leaders were often in conflict with individual interests. As a result, many Soviet citizens lost their faith in collectivism. Collectivism could no longer motivate people to work for a better future. The "new Soviet man" with s strong collective consciousness had become nothing but an illusion.

One of the outstanding features of the Japanese economy has been the lifetime employment system. It refers to an employment pattern whereby a person, upon completing school, begins work at a specific company and is more or less guaranteed a job at the company until retirement. Moreover, the incentive structure is such that many workers do stay with the same company. This system is applied only in large companies and covers only one-quarter of the labor force. Generally speaking, the positive effects of the lifetime employment system have outweighed its negative aspects in Japan. For example, it has resulted in lower worker turnover, engendered greater worker loyalty and effort, and reduced worker resistance to technological change. The lifetime employment system has come under increasing pressure when big companies like Nissan started to lay off workers in early 1993.

"No involuntary unemployment" was a major slogan for the authoritarian Soviet welfare state. In most socialist economies, the lifetime guarantee has led to low productivity and weak incentives for hard work. Now the transition to the market-oriented economy necessarily brings serious problems of unemployment into the Russian society. For more and more workers, unemployment has become a real threat or even a fact of life. It is worth examining how the Japanese can maintain competitiveness and incentives for work under the lifetime employment system. We shall keep in mind that only one-quarter of the Japanese workers enjoy the lifetime employment system. The majority of the

Japanese workers are subject to labor market competition and often face the threat of unemployment.

Inspiring Models and the
Role of Foreign Aid

From state system to market structure, Japan has learned much from the West since the Meiji Restoration and particularly since World War II. It is widely agreed that Japan could not have reached where it is today without actively learning from advanced nations. In terms of technology, the Japanese have been working to catch up with the most advanced ones in the world. In political and constitutional aspects, Japan borrowed heavily from the Prussian system during the Meiji Restoration. Since the end of World War II, the United States has been the most influential model for Japan. Japanese experience demonstrated that the power of a model is vital for the success of the latecomer. To a large extent, the Japanese success is a story of learning from abroad. Patrick and Rosovsky suggested that:

> ...the Japanese have shown a tremendous willingness to learn from the experience of foreigners. They are quick to adopt new ideas from abroad and integrate them into the domestic economy. This procedure saves resources that would otherwise have to be devoted to original development, and permits concentration on improvement and perfection of ideas.[30]

The Japanese transition from the centralized war economy to the postwar plan-oriented market economy may provide insights about how to make a transition from a highly centralized administrative command system to a market-oriented economy. The Japanese received significant American aid during the Allied Occupation and then benefitted from American military orders for the Korean War and Vietnam War. The postwar economic recovery in most European countries was assisted by the Marshall Plan. Now, whether or not the West should help the Russians in their transition from a centrally planned to a market-oriented economy, is the subject of great controversy.

The reforms in Russia and other newly independent states are moving from planning to market, from autarky to interdependence. These states that are making the transition must join GATT, make the ruble convertible, and take part in the IMF and other institutions of world commerce. They have to overcome many self-imposed and external barriers. Because the Russian economy was not export-driven in a manner similar to Japan, there has been little imperative to export manufactured goods in return for raw materials. Foreign trade was not an engine for the Russian economy as it has been for Japan.

There are fundamental differences between the Japanese economic system and the Russian economic system. The two systems have different cultural, ideological and political backgrounds. It is impossible for the Russians to copy the Japanese system. However, in their transition from planning to market, from autarky to interdependence, the Russian people can draw important lessons from the Japanese experience. Just as the Japanese were able to learn from the West while keeping their national cultural and historical characteristics, the Russians should learn how to maintain and renew some national characteristics while learning from Japan and other countries. Japan has successfully evolved a set of internally consistent institutions favorable to long-term economic growth. Borrowing from the Japanese model piecemeal may be problematic. Systemic learning is required in order to be effective.

To what extent can Japan serve as a model for Russia? The answer largely depends upon to what extent the Russians are willing to learn, how far they are willing to go in the direction of marketization and privatization, and how much sacrifice they can afford when market transition programs come into conflict with people's short-term interests. As we have demonstrated, there are specific aspects of Japanese experience that the Russians can learn or emulate. The Japanese case showed, for instance, political leadership played a vital role in marketization and democratization. In learning from Japan, the most important thing is to establish a legal constitutional framework supporting democratization and marketization. If the fundamental political system is solid, poor leaders cannot do much harm. If the system is not good, even good-willed leaders will create disaster. The transition from charismatic authority to legal rational authority should take place as soon as possible. Charismatic leaders played only a minor role in Japanese political change and economic growth. Gorbachev and more recently Yeltsin have lost their charisma. This phenomenon can be a positive factor in establishing a legal rational framework in Russia. In sum, the most important task for Russia today is to build a legal constitutional framework for providing democratic competition and releasing and regulating the dynamism of market forces.

In order to accomplish this task, the Russian leaders must also pay close attention to improving the economy. The new constitutional framework may not survive without a solid economic foundation. Indeed, the reformers are facing a dual task, i.e., creating a democratic polity on the one hand and building a market-oriented economy on the other hand. The Japanese were able to undertake demilitarization, democratization and economic reforms simultaneously during the Occupation reforms. A thorough examination of the Japanese experience may provide inspiration for the Russian reformers.

This chapter has highlighted the strengths of Japanese state-market relations in order to propose lessons for Russia. In recent times, however, the Japanese economy and politics have come into crisis. The Japanese economy declined in 1992 and continues to be in trouble in 1993. The Tokyo stock market lost much of its value in 1992. Japan's economy is in the most difficult situation since the 1973 recession. In the world market, Japan is facing challenges from the United

States and Western Europe on the one hand, and the newly industrialized economies on the other hand. The growing Japanese trade surplus has met increasing resentment and led to greater demand to open up the Japanese market. The United States has taken a lead in asking Japan to change its policy to allow foreign companies a larger share of the Japanese market and to reduce the Japanese trade surplus. Among the Japanese population, especially the younger generations, there have been growing demands for less work stress and more leisure, and less sacrifice and more enjoyment.

More significantly, the Liberal Democratic Party (LDP)-dominated political system has finally come to an end. From its founding in 1955 to July 1993, the LDP was the only ruling party in Japan. But the LDP is no longer able to effectively meet new challenges. It has been troubled by one scandal after another to a degree that it is very difficult to find a "clean" LDP leader to form a new government that can earn the voters' trust. More and more people are demanding a *perestroika* of the Japanese political system. In June 1993, the Kiichi Miyazawa government lost a vote of confidence in the Diet. Two new parties have formed from the splintering Liberal Democrats. Mr. Miyazawa was removed from power as Japan's last ruler under the system of one-party government.

The formation of a seven-party coalition government excluding the LDP in August 1993 opened a new era in Japanese politics. Japan's new government led by Prime Minister Morihiro Hosokawa has started political reforms. A key tenet of the seven-party coalition government is that politicians must retake the policy initiative back from the bureaucracy. As his first priority, Mr. Hosokawa has promised to restructure the discredited electoral system, creating a new kind of election district and tightening laws on political contributions. The new government also wants to stimulate the flagging economy, reform the tax system, lower what are some of the world's highest consumer prices, and reduce the yawning trade surplus. The ongoing changes may eventually transform Japan's political, economic, and social systems. If the postwar system has become somewhat outdated, the search for a new pattern of state-market relations will have a significant impact on how well the Japanese can meet the challenge of the twenty-first century.

Notes

1. See James Clay Moltz, "Commonwealth Economics in Perspective: Lessons from the East Asian Model," *Soviet Economy*, Vol. 7, No. 4 (1991), pp. 342-363.
2. Chalmers Johnson, "Japan: Who Governs? An Essay on Official Bureaucracy," *Journal of Japanese Studies*, Vol. 2 (Autumn 1975), pp. 1-28.

3.   For a useful discussion of the nature and methods of indicative planning, see Kazuo Sato, "Indicative Planning in Japan," *Journal of Comparative Economics*, Vol. 14 (1990), pp. 625-647.

4.   *Ibid.*, pp. 639-640.

5.   Chalmers Johnson, *MITI and the Japanese Miracle: The Growth of Industrial Policy, 1925-1975* (Stanford: Stanford University Press, 1982), p. 18.

6.   For a significant early Soviet explanation of the growing gap between productive forces and productive relations, see "The Novosibirsk Report," *Survey*, Vol. 28, No. 1 (1983), pp. 88-108. The main author of the report is Tat'yana I. Zaslavskaya.

7.   William W. Lockwood (ed.), *The State and Economic Enterprise in Japan: Essays in the Political Economy of Growth* (Princeton: Princeton University Press, 1965); and Herman Kahn, *The Emerging Japanese Superstate: Challenge and Response* (Englewood Cliffs: Prentice-Hall, 1970).

8.   Johnson, *MITI and the Japanese Miracle*, p. 306.

9.   *Ibid.*, especially chapter 1.

10.   *Ibid.*

11.   Michele Schmiegelow and Henrik Schmiegelow, *Strategic Pragmatism: Japanese Lessons in the Use of Economic Theory* (New York and London: Praeger, 1989).

12.   Hugh Patrick and Henry Rosovsky, "Japan's Economic Performance: An Overview," in Patrick and Rosovsky (eds.), *Asia's New Giant: How the Japanese Economy Works* (Washington: Brookings Institution, 1976), p. 53.

13.   *Ibid.*

14.   On the emergence of civil society in the USSR, see S. Frederick Starr, "Soviet Union: A Civil Society," *Foreign Policy*, No. 70 (1988), pp. 26-41. Gail W. Lapidus pointed out that in the 1960s and 1970s, there was a dramatic shift in attitudes among Soviet citizens. This was reflected in "growing pessimism about the Soviet future, increasing disillusionment with official values, and an accompanying decline in civic morale." See Lapidus, "Society under Strain," in Erik P. Hoffmann and Robbin F. Laird (eds.), *The Soviet Polity in the Modern Era* (New York: Aldine de Gruyter, 1984), p.703. Such alienation from the official ideology has in fact facilitated the emergence of independent thinking among Soviet citizens.

15.   Andrew Zimbalist, Howard J. Sherman and Stuart Brown, *Comparing Economic Systems: A Political-Economic Approach* (San Diego: Harcourt Brace Jovanovich, 1989), p. 51.

16.   Kenneth Jowitt, "Soviet Neotraditionalism: The Political Corruption of a Leninist Regime," *Soviet Studies*, Vol. XXXV, No. 3 (1983), pp. 275-297; and Andrew G. Walder, *Communist Neo-traditionalism: Work and Authority in Chinese Industry* (Berkeley and London: University of California Press, 1986).

17.   See the chapters on John Locke, Montesquieu, and the Federalists in Leo Strauss and Joseph Cropsey (eds.), *History of Political Philosophy* (Chicago: University of Chicago Press, 1987), pp. 476-534, 659-679.

18.   Johnson, *MITI and the Japanese Miracle*, p. 44.

19.   Bradley M. Richardson and Scott C. Flanagan, *Politics in Japan* (Boston: Little Brown, 1984), p. 374.

20.   G.C. Allen, *The Japanese Economy* (London: Weidenfeld and Nicolson, 1981), p. 32.

21.   William W. Lockwood, "Japan's 'New Capitalism,'" in Lockwood, *The State and Economic Enterprise in Japan*, p. 503.

22.   See Igor Birman, "From the Achieved Level," *Soviet Studies*, Vol. XXX (1978), pp. 153-172.

23.   Hugh Patrick and Henry Rosovsky, "Prospects for the Future and Some Other Implications," in Patrick and Rosovsky, *Asia's New Giant*, p. 921.

24.   *Ibid.*, p. 922.

25.   Sato, "Indicative Planning in Japan," p. 633.

26.   According to Ed A. Hewett, the key to transforming the Soviet incentive system is a radical reform of the price system. "The rules for winners and losers will not work and will carry no moral force unless the price system is working well." Hewett, *Reforming the Soviet Economy: Equality versus Efficiency* (Washington: Brookings Institution, 1988), p. 350.

27.   For an analysis of the nature and characteristics of Soviet welfare-state authoritarianism, see George W. Breslauer, "On the Adaptability of Soviet Welfare-State Authoritarianism," in Hoffmann and Laird, *The Soviet Polity in the Modern Era*, pp. 219-245.

28.   It is a well-known hypothesis that lost wars trigger innovation while victories thwart it. S. Frederick Starr noted that:

>...crises of various types have been among the most important triggers to innovation throughout Russian and Soviet history . ... Conversely, many of the eras of harshest rule have come on the heels of Russian and Soviet victories, which have had the effect of confirming the existing system in all its particulars.

Starr, "The Changing Nature of Change in the USSR," in Seweryn Bialer and Michael Mandelbaum (eds.), *Gorbachev's Russia and American Foreign Policy* (Boulder & London: Westview Press, 1987), pp. 13-14. Starr also pointed out that there were exceptions to the above hypothesis.

29.   Ross Mouer and Yoshio Sugimoto, *Images of Japanese Society: A Study in the Social Construction of Reality* (London and New York: Kegan Paul International, 1990), p. 54.

30.   Patrick and Rosovsky, "Prospects for the Future and Some Other Implications," p. 922. Patrick and Rosovsky's argument here is consistent with Alexander Gerschenkron's classic thesis of "advantages of backwardness." See

Gerschenkron, *Economic Backwardness in Historical Perspective: A Book of Essays* (Cambridge: Harvard University Press, 1962). Andrew C. Janos points out that "alongside potential advantages, backward countries also faced serious disadvantages, especially with respect to capital formation." Another disadvantage is the "adverse political consequences of cultural strain created by the borrowing of alien technologies and institutional arrangements." See Janos, *Politics and Paradigms: Changing Theories of Change in Social Science* (Stanford: Stanford University Press, 1986), p. 32.

6

Conclusion

The state and the market are two of the most important institutions in modern society. The relationship between them has been and will continue to be vital in deciding how people live and work. Traditionally, the market was seen as a domain of economics. As there are close links between politics and economics, however, the state and the market have been coexisting and interacting with each other for a long time. Recently more political scientists have realized the significance of studying the patterns of interaction between the state and the market.[1] Political scientists often refer to "state intervention" when describing the use of legal and/or administrative mechanisms to influence or decide the rules of the market, the prices of key merchandise, the size of the market, and sociopolitical conditions in which market exchange takes place. Differences in the level and degree of state intervention have decisive effects on state-market relations. The market is an institution for the exchange of goods, capital, credits and services. Even a classic free market must have legal and political protection and regulation. At a minimum, the state should play a role similar to that of an umpire in a baseball game. The state should help to define impersonal rules for winners and losers in market competition, and provide legal and political protection for the market system.

In analyzing the role of the state in the economy, a challenging issue is the operationalization of state-market relations. There are qualitative and quantitative factors in deciding the state's capacities for intervention in the economy. Quantitatively, we can look at how many bills are passed by the legislature, how many executive orders are given by the administration, and how many of these bills and orders have been carried out. However, looking only at the numbers can be deceiving. What is more critical in deciding state-market relations is the qualitative aspect. A strong state is not necessarily an effective state. If a state intervenes too much in the details of the market, it will reduce or even stifle the dynamism of the market. If the market loses its dynamism, how can the state build its strength on a weak economic basis? Logically, it is hard to argue that the more the state intervenes in the market, the more autonomy the state enjoys over the market. On the other hand, it will be troublesome if the state does not have the capacity to intervene in the market when intervention is necessary. The key for solving this problem is to decide what is "necessary intervention" and how such intervention can be effectively carried out by the state.

Contending Theoretical Perspectives

Political economics has come a long way from the days of Adam Smith. Characteristics of both the state and market have changed dramatically since Smith's time. Nevertheless, some basic principles revealed by his study are still valid and strengthened by recent developments in Russia. The worldwide rediscovery of the market and newly strengthened interests in studying Smith are not coincidental.

Smith's argument for a free market economy should be modified to reflect the experiences of Japan and Russia/USSR. The "invisible hand" was prohibited from full play in both countries, though the degree of state control differed sharply. In Japan, the state consciously used legal and administrative mechanisms to regulate the economy and manipulate market activities. In the Soviet Union, the state tried to eliminate the market. When the Soviet leaders realized that it was impossible to eliminate completely the market, they attempted to create an artificial market to replace the real market.

In the Soviet Union, the official formal economy was designed to work according to plan. The informal economy, i.e., the second economy and the shadow economy, tended to follow market principles. However, the informal economy was not able to function normally like it should under a free market economy because of strict political and ideological restraints on the informal sector. The informal economy which was inclined to follow market principles was not able to work according to free market principles.

If state intervention has become a necessary part of contemporary life in both the West and the East, then it is important to learn what are the differences in the actual operations under the two systems. In the market economy, the legal and constitutional framework bounds both the political and economic players, yet the economic players have an independent power base. As a result, they can have direct or indirect access to political power. Consequently, state interventions in the market often act in the interests of the rich and powerful. State bureaucrats are under legal constraints in self-serving activities. In contrast, there are no legally independent large economic actors in the centrally planned economy. Top political leaders are the ultimate arbiters of both political and economic policies. The party-state leaders were under only nominal legal restraint from self-serving activities. Thus, they often intervened in the economy on behalf of the state. State interests perceived by the top political leaders often deviated from the real interests of the majority of people in society.

Lenin and Stalin found that Marxism had to be adjusted to Russian conditions. Each revised Marxism in ways that he considered appropriate for his own political needs. Stalinism has been discredited since Khrushchev's de-Stalinization campaign of 1956. Leninism has come under attack in the age of *glasnost*. The popular vote in Leningrad favoring the return of the city's name to "St. Petersburg" reflected the profound shifts in people's thinking.

Max Weber's conception of the state and his ideas about legitimacy are relevant to contemporary study. According to Weber, "a state is a human community that (successfully) claims the monopoly of the legitimate use of physical force within a given territory."[2] There are three inner justifications, hence basic legitimations of domination. First, the authority of the "eternal yesterday," i.e., of the mores sanctified through the ancient recognition and habitual orientation to conform. This is "traditional" domination. Second, there is the authority of the extraordinary and personal gift of grace (charisma), the absolutely personal devotion and personal leadership. This is charismatic domination. Finally, there is domination by virtue of legality, by virtue of the belief in the validity of legal statutes and functional competence based on rationally created rules. This is domination as exercised by the modern "servants of the state" and by all those bearers of power who in this respect resemble them.[3]

Legal-rational legitimacy is the foundation for building a modern democratic state. Japan has been moving toward legal-rational authority and legitimacy since the Meiji Restoration. Before the defeat in World War II, however, the Japanese claimed that the emperor was the source of all legitimacy, authority and power. Only through constitutional reforms during the Allied Occupation did legal-rational authority achieve primacy over any other authority. The Soviet system was never close to the legal-rational model. As Kenneth Jowitt pointed out, it was more accurate to describe the Soviet system as "neotraditional."[4] *Perestroika* was an effort at replacing revolutionary charisma and ideological legitimation with legal-rational legitimacy. The Soviet state collapsed when it totally lost its legitimacy by the end of 1991. The Russian government is facing the challenge of legitimacy building. Boris Yeltsin abandoned constitutionality or legitimacy on the old basis by using military force against the Russian Parliament. He claimed that his actions in October 1993 were legitimate because he had the support of the public opinion. Following the fall of the Parliament, Yeltsin took a series of strong measures against the opposition. Some officials in the Yeltsin government argue that extraordinary times require undemocratic methods to reach a democratic end. Many Russian citizens are concerned with the growth of unrestrained presidential power and the rise of authoritarian trends. The full implications of Yeltsin's use of force and oppression remain to be seen.

In Japan, the claim by the state to use force domestically is not in question. But for many years, Japan's lack of such basic democratic traditions as regular transfer of power between political parties has crippled its ability to cope with many challenges. The Liberal Democratic Party (LDP) dominance of Japanese politics finally ended in summer 1993. The seven-party coalition government led by Prime Minister Morihiro Hosokawa considers political reform a top priority. The coalition's reform proposals would end the present system in which candidates, even of the same party, compete for several seats in one district. The system has helped breed corruptive pork-barrel politics and fosters little debate over issues. The new government is also exploring an American-style idea of allowing taxpayers to give 1 percent of their income tax to a party. This system would force politicians to devise policies for voters rather than big business, as the LDP often did. Hosokawa agrees that Japan's unique culture has failed to fully adopt democracy. His reform intends to break the traditional domination of society by LDP-bureaucracy-big business. The reform is likely to reduce popular discontent and strengthen legitimacy.

The State's Role in Modernization

What are the links between the degree of state intervention and the stage of economic development? Japan's experience argued for direct state management and ownership at the initial stage of industrialization. The critical question is at what point the state should withdraw from direct involvement in economic management. One view is that when the economy becomes advanced and more complicated, the state can no longer manage it. It is better to let individual initiatives have full play. The opposite view is that production becomes socialized as the economy achieves more advanced development. At the advanced level of socialized mass production, over-competition in the market may lead to chaos. Therefore, the state must play an unprecedented role in economic planning and development. According to Warren J. Samuels, the most influential view regarding state-market relations is the "market-plus-framework" approach.[5] This approach emphasizes the interdependence of the state and the market. Effective cooperation between the two institutions is the key for economic growth and political development.

Both Japan and Russia are latecomers to modernization. Compared with earlier modernizers like Britain and France, the state tends to play a larger role in the industrialization of latecomers. The lessons from the Japanese and Russian modernization drives are instructive to other countries that are struggling for modernization. For latecomers, the state generally played a more significant role in creating the market and managing or limiting the negative effects of the market. A classic market-creating case is the Customs Union formed by the Prussian government.

The need for state intervention is rooted in the nature of the market. As a mechanism with double edges, the market can promote economic development by stimulating competition, facilitating distribution, and realizing values and making profits. On the other hand, the "invisible hand" may lead to over-production, over-competition, inflation, and to the social ills of unemployment and exploitation. The market does not automatically solve many emergent social welfare problems. Therefore, the state must assume its political and economic roles.

Japan and Russia/USSR provide two distinctive patterns of industrialization. Both were profoundly influenced by historical, cultural and natural conditions, yet political factors and external military pressure also have played a vital role in determining the path of industrialization that is chosen. Ultimately, sharply different political structures and ideologies dictated the widely divergent roads taken by the two countries.

In its industrialization process, the Russian state emphasized extensive growth while the Japanese state stressed intensive growth strategy. Extensive growth is compatible with early industrialization but not with advanced industrialization. Countries like Japan that began the modernization process with more emphasis on intensive rather than extensive approaches enjoy an obvious advantage in making the adaptation to domestic and international changes in the patterns of economic growth in the age of advanced industrial revolution.

According to the Weberian conception, coercion is a core characteristic of the state. One big difference between the modernization of Japan and Russia is the varying degree of coercion employed by the state. Russian/Soviet rulers used much more coercive power to enforce their policy and to keep people's compliance than did the Japanese leaders.

At the early stage of modernization, the Japanese state employed a significant amount of coercion. Only after the defeat in World War II and the Allied Occupation did Japan begin to build a democratic state system which allowed people to make key decisions directly or through their representatives. In order to understand how the state manipulates and facilitates the market, it is important to study how the state uses its coercive power to change the rules of the game.

The notion of a compulsory service state is central for understanding the continuity between tsarist Russia and the Soviet Union. It is a deeply rooted political tradition.[6] When political control is significantly reduced, the system can no longer function in the old way. If the Soviet state relinquished its control of the means of production, the state could not continue to coerce people to work for the state goals. The authoritarian welfare-state was a central feature of the Soviet system.[7] The state was supposed to give people a job, which gave them economic security, in exchange for their political compliance or even support. By making people dependent on the government for education and employment, the Soviet state deprived people of economic independence. Many Soviet citizens lost incentives to work hard because of the lack of control over their own destiny.

Reflections on the Contrasting Cases

This research started by examining the two ideal types of state-market relations, i.e., the purely market and the purely state.[8] Though no system perfectly fits either type, the ideal types do provide a useful analytical tool for exploring the logic and dynamics of state-market relations in Japan and Russia. Neither Japan nor Russia/USSR has been a purely state system or a purely market system. Both countries have experienced periods of fluctuation in the role of the state in the market. Both states have tried to control or even to eliminate the market, e.g., in the case of "war communism." In spite of the similarities, it is the differences between the Japanese and the Soviet system that attracted more attention.

What is more interesting are the patterns of postwar changes in state-market relations in the two countries. In the postwar era, the Japanese system has been moving toward the plan-oriented market economy while the state remains a powerful regulator and mediator among the market players. The role of the Japanese state as a direct market player has been declining. When the economy grows stronger, the market tends to gain more autonomy from the state. However, market forces are still regulated by indicative planning and administrative guidance. As Chalmers Johnson has demonstrated, the Japanese state plays a developmental role by formulating and implementing industrial policy.[9] Although mainly relying upon economic means to carry out government policies that emphasize state preferences, the elite bureaucrats do not hesitate to use administrative mechanisms in conjunction with market mechanisms whenever they consider them necessary.

The USSR in the postwar period provided a contrasting model of state-market relations. The victory in the Second World War strengthened the military and territorial orientations of the Soviet state. The needs of the military and political elites further consolidated the centrally planned system. In other words, the military and political victory disguised the weaknesses in the administrative command economy. The apparent abundance of natural resources in the USSR reduced the necessity of and desires for trading with other countries. The emergence of the Cold War between the East and the West further encouraged the tendency for autarky. As a result, the centrally planned economy went on its course of extensive expansion in spite of the ostentatious discussion among some Soviet elites about the coming of the Scientific Technological Revolution (STR) and the need for a transition to intensive growth. The bureaucratic party state grew to an unprecedented size and became increasingly incompatible with the diverse needs of a developing economy. The Soviet state which started with developmental goals became a true obstacle to economic growth.

When the market was de-legalized and pushed out of the formal system in the USSR, new channels of resource allocations and distributions developed through the black market, second economy, and other anti-system or extra-system ways of exchange. Various elements of the informal system lacked the legitimacy and power to function in a way similar to a market economy. Thus, despite some superficial similarities of the informal system with the market mechanisms in an advanced economy, the informal system in the Soviet Union was not rational in terms of modern Weberian norms. Although providing a lubricant for the formal system, the informal system did not change the nature of the administrative command system. Without fundamental changes in the formal system, mere legalization of the black market could not help the Soviet Union to move into a market economy.

Although the state can and should play a significant role in socioeconomic life, the Soviet and Japanese cases showed that the state should not replace the marketplace. The Soviet efforts at eliminating the market have been a total failure. "War communism" attempted replacing the market with political mechanisms of distribution. It created a profound crisis which forced Lenin to change his basic idea about state-market relations and to announce the New Economic Policy (NEP) in order to save the Soviet regime from collapse. The essence of the NEP was to let market mechanisms play a legitimate role in the Soviet economy.

Stalin's revolution from above ended the NEP and created a centrally planned economy. Serious problems of distribution and production of goods were often ignored or resolved by political means. Since Khrushchev, there have been many efforts at fine tuning and reforming the Stalinist system. However, there was no overhaul of the command system before Gorbachev. The stagnation and particularly Brezhnev's policy of "trust in cadres" deepened the socioeconomic and political crises. The crisis situation finally led to a general push to marketization in the late 1980s and early 1990s.

Comparative analysis of state-market relations involves the questions of the correlation between the centrally planned economy and political authoritarianism, and of the relationship between private ownership and the market economy. It is risky to draw a general conclusion of such profound issues based upon a comparative study of two cases. More research needs to be done in this field. Nevertheless, it is both fitting and proper to generate some propositions based on the Japanese and Soviet cases.

The emergence of the centrally planned economy in the Soviet Union was closely linked to the centralization of power. The administrative command economy relied heavily upon the support of the coercive forces of the state and particularly the exclusive control of the party-state in the allocation of main resources. On the other hand, the centralized political power was reinforced by its monopoly of the economy. There was an intrinsic connection between politics and economics in the centralized state. A strong economy and a powerful military were among the top priorities of the Soviet state; the main mechanisms for realizing the goals were administrative commands. In fact, there were very few independent economic players. As Max Weber predicted, without the market, the state rules.

Without private ownership of the means of production, the market does not have real autonomy. A market without private ownership tends to be either a black market or an artificial market based upon artificial prices fixed by the state or decided by chance in illegal or extra-legal transactions. At a deeper level, private ownership is the basis of economic freedom which in turn closely connécts with political freedom.

Soviet experience demonstrated that public ownership in the form of state ownership did not give people a sense of being masters of their own destiny. On the contrary, state ownership created a whole special class of party-state bureaucrats who controlled resource allocations and income distribution. Those people who belonged to the *nomenklatura* cared much more about how to operate the system in their personal interests or in the state's interests as perceived by them rather than in the real interests of the majority of the people. At the same time, being prohibited from owning any significant amount of private property or initiating private business, most Soviet citizens only had the chance to work for the government as state employees. Despite the initial enthusiasm about being free of exploitation, as the official propaganda proclaimed, the Soviet people soon found that they did not have much say about how to govern the country or how to run the economy. There was a growing sense of alienation among the populace. The lack of real incentives led to the necessity of strong working discipline imposed from above. When the militaristic working culture declined as the revolutionary fever receded, the economy naturally lost its dynamism.

In order to control people, the Soviet state imposed restrictions on people's access to information. The built-in secrecy system severely limited information flow while the bureaucratic tardiness further complicated the issue. At the same time, the expanded economy and complex society were creating more and more demand for information. The central planning agencies were overloaded by an increasing amount of information. The problems of information overload and the lack of information became more and more serious when the economy became increasingly complex. The insulation of the Soviet economy from the world market had very negative effects on the competitiveness of Soviet industry and trade.

What are the proper relations between the state and market? The answer to this question should be different from country to country according to specific conditions. The history of Japan and Russia/USSR has shown that too much state domination of the market will stifle the vitality of the market and finally lead to the stagnation of the economy and the weakening of the state. On the other hand, it is unrealistic to eliminate all economic functions of the state. Therefore, a middle ground must be found between state-domination and market-freedom.

Transition to the Market

Since the late 1980s there have been growing demands in the former USSR and now Russia for the transition to a market economy. We have identified several sources of pressure for marketization. First, with prolonged low productivity and a poor consumer market, more and more Soviet citizens became discontented and disenchanted with the old system. When the people found that the government was unable to deliver what it kept promising people for several decades, many people finally lost their faith in the old system and started to look for alternatives.

Second, with more knowledge about the outside world, particularly about advanced market economies, the Russians realized the growing gap between their living standard and that of the West. In the 1970s, former defeated powers in the Second World War such as Japan and Germany overtook the USSR in living standards and productivity. What was particularly painful for the Soviets to accept was that some small neighbors, e.g., Hungary and South Korea, had been doing much better than them in the 1970s and the 1980s. Such unfavorable comparison stimulated a psychological push for changes in the Soviet system.

Third, generational changes in Soviet elites brought new blood into the decision-making system. The post-revolution young generations have a different orientation than their older counterparts. Generally speaking, the young leaders are better educated and more open-minded. They are less burdened with tradition and better prepared to make necessary changes.

Fourth, dramatic shifts in the international system have not been in favor of the USSR. In Andrew C. Janos' words, the international demonstration effect has shown that "the Stalinist regimes may have accomplished breakthroughs in other aspects, but they have not changed the relative backwardness of their societies within the larger picture of the world community."[10] This was largely related to the Soviet Union's single-minded pursuit of military power regardless of socioeconomic costs. The end of the Cold War enabled the Soviet leaders to make strategic adjustments in resource allocation from putting emphasis on military and heavy industry to civilian industry and consumer goods. In order to realize such transformation, especially to build organic links with the world market, the Russians must create a competitive market system. The centrally planned economy was not compatible with the world economy. The transition to the market was a necessary condition for integrating Russia into the mainstream world civilization.

A transition from the command economy to a market economy is necessary and desirable though it involves many painful problems. The Soviet government announced in June 1991 that it would pay unemployment benefits to workers who lose their jobs. It is agonizing but necessary to remove the veil and reveal real socioeconomic problems in Russia. In the past, the Soviet Union was proud to claim that there was no involuntary unemployment in the country. Public ownership and "free" input of labor and capital created an artificial shortage of labor. In other words, economic losses were socialized. In the transition to the market, enterprises that cannot produce quality goods, make profits or at least avoid financial losses must be restructured or go bankrupt. Advanced market economies have not thoroughly solved all their social problems and economic difficulties. An emerging market economy in Russia and other republics will have many unpredictable crises and problems. When making a revolutionary transition to the market, a task that took the West and Japan a long time to accomplish, people in the Commonwealth of Independent States must be prepared to suffer many of the difficulties the West and Japan encountered in their evolution toward the market system. The intensification of marketization will have traumatic effects when many side effects of the emerging market economy appear in Russia and other newly independent states.

There are qualitative differences both between a primitive market and an emerging market and between these two and a mature market. The mature market systems in Japan and Western countries have developed a series of adjustment mechanisms facilitating market operations. However, it is impossible to build a mature market in a short period of time. A mature market is not only an economic institution; it also consists of legal, political, social, and cultural aspects. The market system cannot work without these essential organic parts. Prior to the 1917 Revolution, Russia had some basic conditions for a market economy at the early stage of capitalist development. The revolution destroyed the tsarist political system and the primitive Russian market. It also destroyed the attempt made at representative democracy in the February Revolution. It is much easier to destroy an old system than to build a new one. The formation of the Stalinist administrative command system took more than a decade.[11] As soon as the system was formed, those social groups that benefitted from the system tried to protect it by all available means. Before Gorbachev came to power, there was only fine-tuning but no radical transformation of the centrally planned economy. Thus, it is no exaggeration to argue that the Soviet system lags at least fifty years behind the advanced economies in building market mechanisms.

While there is no logical or theoretical argument for the impossibility of transition to the market, neither are there any historical precedents from which to learn. Poland and Hungary are only now experiencing the transition from the command economy to the market economy. Hence, the transition of the Japanese war economy to the postwar market-oriented economy may provide some insights into the issue. Russia and other newly independent states should learn valuable lessons from them.

The Soviet economic system had many particularistic rather than universalistic features. Jerry Hough argued that the Soviet system worked not in spite of the rampant particularism but because of it.[12] Now it seems the system described by Hough worked well only until the 1960s. Since the 1970s, the Soviet state had been increasingly losing its control of economic growth. In fact, the system created in the 1930s has become an obstacle for advanced modernization. If the basis for the particularism is removed, can the system still work? The answer is obviously not.

There is both change and continuity in state-market relations in Russia and the USSR. Lenin once said, there will be no revolutionary movement without revolutionary theory. Now it is fitting to say that without theoretical guidance, there can be no successful transition to the market. For an economy on the scale of the former Soviet Union, only systemic domestic changes could save it from total collapse in a crisis situation. Western aid might have some positive effects during the Russian transition to the market. However, foreign assistance will be wasted if the administrative command system remains entrenched. Foreign assistance will be used to sustain the system rather than to transform it. The most valuable assistance the advanced market economies may provide is to teach the Russians how to build and run a market economy.

Interaction of Internal and External Factors

Defensive modernization had a deep impact on the patterns of state-market relations in Japan and the Soviet Union. The Cold War also had repercussions on the economic development of Japan and the USSR. The rise of Japan as a trading state was made possible, or at least was greatly facilitated, by the Cold War.

Without the Allied Occupation reforms, Article 9 of the constitution, the distaste of war and delegitimation of the war mongers, Japan could not just focus upon "enrich the country" while ignoring "strengthen the army." Taking economic construction as the first national goal contributed much to the emergence of Japan as an economic superpower.

Partly by decision of the Kremlin, and in part by external pressure, the USSR chose to build a strong military machine. The high level of military spending in the last several decades became a huge burden for the Soviet economy. The end of the Cold War should have a positive effect on economic and political transition in Russia. Lacking the kind of outside guidance and tutelage as the Americans gave the Japanese during the Occupation, the Russians have to act on their own to adjust to the new situation. The challenging task of reforming the command system provides both opportunities and constraints on the scale and speed of reforms. It provides opportunities because the Russians have more control over decision making and they can listen to or not listen to advice from various sources. On the other hand, many necessary reforms cannot be carried out in the absence of outside pressure for change and without absolute authority from the top. For example, Gorbachev and Yeltsin issued many administrative orders and decrees for reforming the economy. Few of them were carried out thoroughly. One lesson from the Occupation reforms of Japan is that outside pressure and high authority might facilitate the implementation of tough measures of radical reform.

Examining the international context, we must keep in mind two different kinds of factors. One is objective and the other is subjective. Objective factors include the geographical and natural environment which cannot be changed at people's wish easily. Subjective factors include the perception of the country's power/status in the world by its people and leaders. Such factors also will have strong influences on policy making. "New Political Thinking" changed Soviet perceptions of the position of the USSR and its relations with the outside world. New thinking has facilitated the formulation of policies leading to the easing of tension and building a better environment for trading.

The trading state has characteristics different from those of the military-territorial or garrison state. Economic growth and foreign trade are top priorities of the trading state. With light defense spending and a weak military orientation, the state is able to utilize most human and material resources in civilian production. On the one hand, the trading state is international because its very survival depends upon global economic interdependence which consists of necessary regimes for world trade. On the other hand, the trading state is highly nationalistic because it conducts policies protecting domestic industries against foreign competition and promoting national exports to the world market. A trading state can be very effective in regulating its relations with the domestic and international market due to its special concern of trading and its sophisticated skills in economic affairs. Compared with a military-territorial state, the market in a trading state is usually more dynamic and competitive.[13]

In the present age of growing global economic interdependence, the traditional policy of autarky or "nationalistic economic policy" no longer works. The countries that succeed in the new era are those that can make necessary changes in time. What are the links between political democratization and the emergence of civil society? After its defeat in World War II, Japan went through a dramatic process of democratization which established a solid foundation for a democratic political system and a civil society.[14] The essence of a civil society is freedom of association. Without economic freedom, there is no material basis for independent economic organizations. Therefore, it seems that the emergence of a market economy is a prerequisite for the emergence of civil society.

Many scholars, including Gail Lapidus and S. Frederick Starr, took the growth of black markets and the second economy as signs of the emergence of civil society in the Soviet Union.[15] However, as long as the second economy and black market remained illegal or extra-legal as part of the informal system rather than the formal system, civil society in the Soviet Union did not have a legal and solid economic foundation. Freedom and liberty are preconditions for political democracy. Political democracy is the guarantee for freedom and liberty. Economic freedom and political democracy cannot survive and thrive without each other.

Re-examining Key Lessons from Japan

Historically, both Japan and Russia/USSR have experiences of extensive cultural borrowing from relatively advanced nations. In the twentieth century, the Japanese have been more successful than the Soviets in learning from others. Now the Russians must learn from other people about how to make the transition to a market economy. "Lessons from Japan," as analyzed in Chapter 5, merit examination. It is fitting and appropriate to highlight some key lessons from Japan.

The Japanese government has successfully practiced indicative planning rather than administrative command planning. Administrative command planning is the core of the centrally planned system. Indicative planning relies on market mechanisms for plan implementation. Administrative planning is only of limited utility for the extensive growth at the early stage of industrialization. Indicative planning is appropriate for the intensive growth in a market-oriented economy.

Postwar Japan has followed a stronger trading orientation and a less military-territorial orientation. With the changing nature of power, economic power and technological edge are more important than military power itself in deciding the comprehensive power of nations. Postwar history has shown that countries with strong trading orientations have benefitted more from the world economy than those with weak trading orientations. States like the USSR with a strong military orientation sacrificed many other interests to create gigantic military machines. Without comparable economic growth and technological advancement, the level of Soviet military technology lagged behind the advanced economies. Furthermore, the military industrial complex became not a locomotive for growth but a big burden on the national economy. Without the substantial transfer of human and natural resources from the military to civilian sectors, restructuring of the Russian economy cannot achieve the expected results.

Market forces should have a significant role in resource allocations and price determination. Although we do not argue for a minimal state as some classic thinkers did, we believe that the Russian state should remove its domination of the market. Because of the nature of the party state, the first task of reducing the state control of the economy was de-partification. The collapse of the CPSU in late 1991 provided an opportunity for a transition to a pluralist state and a market-oriented economy. But more difficult and concrete work is still ahead for the reformers. In Stephen F. Cohen's view, Yeltsin is relying on the tsarist and Soviet tradition of centralizing authority.[16] The violent events in October 1993 provide a strong case for such an argument.

In building a market-oriented system, it is necessary to carry out the de-politicization of the economic bureaucracy. The Japanese economic ministries, particularly MITI, are famous for their professional efficiency. The Soviet central economic ministries were highly politicized and directly controlled by cadres appointed by the *nomenklatura* system. The main criteria for *nomenklatura* system were political. Even in the technical aspect, the main demand was knowledge about and loyalty to the administrative command system that counted for the recruitment and promotion of individual cadres. Such a practice is obviously outdated and inappropriate for a state bureaucracy in a market-oriented economy. Establishing a professional bureaucracy that is compatible with a market economy is a gigantic task for Russian reformers. They must build a system of bureaucratic institutions based on merit rather than personal connections, and act on the economic welfare of the nation rather than on political demands of the leaders.

In order to provide a predictable, stable but dynamic environment for state-market interaction, it is absolutely vital to establish the rule of law based upon legal-rational authority. Postwar Japan has a system based on the rule of law which provides a solid legal foundation for the plan-oriented market economy. Predictability and stability are two basic conditions for the development of a modern market economy. These conditions can only be established under the rule of law, not the will of individual leaders. William Butler pointed out that law and the legal system were at the heart of *perestroika* in two aspects: as objects of reform themselves, and as vehicles of reform in all realms of political, socioeconomic, and cultural life.[17] According to Lapidus, the thrust of Gorbachev's strategy was to alter the basic premise of the Stalinist system from "all that is not permitted is prohibited" to the principle that "all that is not prohibited is permitted."[18] This reform strategy involved a significant redefinition of the role of the state.

The state should promote private ownership and develop new forms of ownership which will facilitate the growth of the market economy. As the basis of the market economy, private ownership must be protected by law. The world has not witnessed any large scale successful market economies based mainly upon public ownership. De-statization and privatization are keys to marketization.

The reformers must get rid of ideological rigidity and embrace pragmatism. The Japanese are very pragmatic while the Soviets were ideological. But the situation in the Soviet Union changed dramatically in the age of *perestroika*.

Fundamental shifts have taken place in Russian thinking regarding the relationship of market economics to socialism. Stalin predicted that the movement toward full communism would be marked by the steady reduction of the sphere of commodity-money relations, and even as late as the Brezhnev period the possibility of market socialism was scorned by Soviet sources. Yet by 1987 Gorbachev was setting the theme that the advantages of planning would be increasingly combined with stimulating factors of the socialist market. Soviet leaders traditionally described the market as a setting of dog-eat-dog competition in capitalist societies, and praised the alternative of the more comradely "socialist emulation" among workers in their economy. The desire to introduce more vigorous competition in the Soviet economy led Soviet reformers to conclude that the market has features pertinent to any system based on a developed division of labor and a commodity form of economic ties. In other words, no highly developed economy can operate efficiently without large elements of market relations.[19] Such debates paved the way to thought- provoking and path-breaking statements in the several market transition plans about the role of the state and the market.

Russia must make the painful but necessary transition from extensive growth to intensive growth. The contrasting patterns of resource allocations in Japan and Russia/USSR have sufficiently demonstrated that intensive growth is the key to success in the age of advanced industrialization. As Seweryn Bialer argued, the Soviet economy must switch to:

> ...an intensive strategy of growth, where the following elements necessarily would play a decisive role: (i) increased productivity of labor and capital through technological progress and better incentives; (ii) declining relative costs of production; (iii) conservation of raw materials and energy; and (iv) improved quality of products and a buildup of the infrastructure.[20]

Limited by time and resources, each government can only do certain things. Therefore, it is crucial to set national priorities. Up to 1945, the Japanese state concentrated on building a strong army and a rich country. Japan was forced to give up the first goal; however, this very factor has turned out to be a plus for building a competitive economy. The newly independent republics in the former USSR, facing grave economic and political crises today, must make some hard choices. These new states should set their national priorities following the majority of the people's desires. If so, their national priorities will most likely to be fundamentally different from that of the Soviet state which was a one-dimensional superpower based upon military strength. In the field of distribution, the new republics can also learn some lessons from Japan. Japan has achieved one of the most equitable distributions in advanced market economies.

Learning from Comparative Analysis

What lessons in comparative analysis can be drawn from this study? Japan and Russia are two very different cases. Does the current study reveal the value of comparative historical analysis? The two contrasting cases, Japan and Russia, each represent a type of state-market relations. According to Mattei Dogan and Dominique Pelassy, binary comparison can be used not only for increasing, through contrast, our knowledge of two different systems. In the best cases, the two countries considered are thought of as contrasted illustrations for a broad, encompassing theoretical reflection. A comparison between contrasting countries implies (1) that attention is fixed on situations presenting a maximum of contrasts, and (2) that these contrasts are of broad significance and delineate political areas defined by systemic features. "Contrast," in this perspective, is not synonymous with trivial difference. It is of a general character; that is, it implies that the situations under consideration have been chosen for their exemplarity.[21] We consider the comparison between Japan and the Soviet Union as such a contrasting comparison.

"Structural factors" and "contextual factors" are both important in deciding the patterns of state-market relations. A successful reformer should take full advantage of the contextual factors and make necessary changes in the structural factors so that the structure will fit the environment better.

There are similarities between the current Russian opening to the outside world and the Japanese systematic learning from the West. The common background is that reform leaders in both countries publicly acknowledged that the West has more advanced socioeconomic systems, that their home countries were/are backward and facing a crisis situation which will lead to further deterioration if reform measures were not taken decisively and immediately. Reformers in both countries are prepared to accept not only the more advanced economic system, but also some essential elements of democratic social political values.

While talking about similarities, we should not omit differences between the two cases. The most obvious variance is the different starting points. Japan was an imperial system facing military challenges from the West. The Soviet Union was a communist-ruled system facing economic crisis rather than military crisis. Even in economic chaos, the Soviet military machine was able to defend the huge country against outside invasion. For the Japanese in the late nineteenth century, the dual task was to enrich the country and strengthen the army. For Soviet reformers, the main task was to vitalize the economy through the transition to the market. Logically, a critical step in the transition has been demilitarization of the Soviet state and society.

The economic basis of neo-traditionalism was the domination or replacement of the market by the state. In other words, non-market relations of the Soviet economic system have been the economic foundation of neo-traditionalism which was considered by Andrew Walder as the core of the Leninist system.[22] Neo-traditionalism was thought to have consolidated the system in such a way that it could hardly be brought back to the normal economy. How to define the term "normal" is still in question. But one thing is certain, i.e., the particularistic nature of the Soviet economy has been weakened since *perestroika* and will be further reduced if the reforms continue to move toward the market. With radical reforms, the market will gain its rightful and legitimate place and re-shape its relations with the state. When a market economy is fully established, neo-traditionalism will become an antique that belongs to the museum of history.

The political basis of neo-traditionalism was the monopoly of power by the Communist party. As a result of *glasnost* and *perestroika*, the CPSU's monopoly of power was ended. The party also lost its ideological unity. Both the radicals and the conservatives in the party voiced their conflicting orientations to an unprecedented degree. After the failed coup in August 1991, the once powerful CPSU rapidly disintegrated. The monolithic party has become history.

The social basis of neo-traditionalism was a social tradition of dependency of the populace on the officialdom. In the age of *glasnost* and *perestroika*, an increasing number of Soviet citizens have become more and more independent and outspoken. These independent-minded people may not yet know exactly what they want, but they have no doubt about their rejection of the Stalinist social system which nurtured the dependence of people on the state and which was marked by extensive coercion of the people by it without rule of law. A nostalgic sentiment does exist among some Russians about the days that the state "took care of" everyone. However, such feeling represents the shadow of the past rather than the wave of the future.

One significant development is the decline of the informal system and rampant particularism. The informal system and particularism were considered the lubricant which helped to make the gigantic Stalinist economic machine workable. The informal system was based upon economic rationality rather than ideological and political rationality. Extensive political control by the party-state and the minimal role of the market were necessary conditions for the existence of both the formal and informal systems. Following the transition to the market and political democratization, particularly the privatization of the ownership of means of production and disintegration of the CPSU, the political and economic bases of the old system have substantially eroded. Legalization of many parts of the former informal system and the growth of market mechanisms have made or are making the informal system into the formal system based on universalism rather than particularism.

There is no ready answer for questions regarding the relationship between the market economy and political democracy, and the centrally planned economy and political authoritarianism. We cannot over-generalize that the market economy will necessarily lead to political democratization. The world has witnessed political authoritarianism based on market-oriented economic systems. By comparative analysis of the cases of Japan and Russia/USSR, we have learned the following: (1) Changes in market relations lead to changes in the political arena; on the other hand, changes in the state structure lead to changes in market relations. (2) The growth of market forces shapes and re-shapes a new political balance of power by creating new socioeconomic groups or forming group coalitions. (3) The centrally planned economy and highly centralized bureaucratic party state are mutually supportive. The administrative command economy cannot function without an extremely powerful centralized state supported by force. (4) A new market system cannot emerge in Russia without reducing political control over the economy. (5) During the period of military and territorial expansion, the Japanese state tried to establish centralized control over the economy; market relations were strongly controlled and regulated by the state. The growing market forces have supported the growth of pluralism in postwar Japan and consolidated the democratic constitutional system established during the Allied Occupation. The Japanese case has demonstrated that a dynamic market economy can be a solid basis for a democratic political system transformed from a system once dominated by authoritarianism and militarism.

By comparative analysis of state-market relations, we have gained a better understanding of the theoretical and sociopolitical bases of the various Soviet/Russian market transition programs, and the major problems and possible solutions during the transition. The grave legacy of the administrative command system, the inconsistency and half-heartedness of the implemented economic reform measures, including errors in the leadership of the economy, and the lack of respect for the law, have caused a profound economic crisis in Russia.

Some Russian reformers had a romantic view of the market. They tended to see only the advantages of the market system while ignoring the potential tension and crisis of the market mechanisms. They overlooked the fact that it took the advanced market economies many decades or even centuries to develop and improve their market systems. Trying to develop a market system in a country like the USSR in 500 days was a dream that could not come true.

The centrally planned economy in the USSR was incompatible with the market economy. It was impossible to build a market economy on the old foundation. Therefore, the first step in the transition to the market was dismantling of the old system. It was true that Gorbachev was not able to build a market system. However, no one should underestimate the amount of work that Gorbachev did in dismantling the Stalinist system, particularly in its political and military aspects. Such "destruction" has laid out a new foundation for construction. In fact, *perestroika* (restructuring) includes both destruction and construction. The deepening of economic crisis in the USSR was mainly a result of the breaking-down of the old system and the birth-pain of the new system. It is hard to believe that Gorbachev was such a calculating politician that he deliberately created the economic crisis to augment popular pressure for radical restructuring of the state-dominated system. Nevertheless, the crises do reveal the ills of the old system. Many radical reformers have realized that marketization is a viable alternative to the centrally planned economy. As the Presidential plan declared: "There is no alternative to switching to a market. All world experience has shown the viability and effectiveness of the market economy."[23]

It is difficult to draw conclusions regarding state market relations in Japan and Russia partly because such relations are still evolving in both countries. Revolutionary changes have taken place in Russia. The centrally planned economy in the Soviet Union was a failed experiment. The transition of the Russian economy from a unique system that deviated from the market system for more than half a century and which was only partly into it prior to the revolution to a normal market economy is "revolutionary" in the very sense of the word. We shall draw some tentative conclusions from historical and theoretical perspectives.

First, both Japan and Russia have distinctive patterns of state-market relations. Political and economic decisions influenced by conflicting ideas had deep impacts on the evolution of the two systems. Between the 1860s and 1917, Japan and Russia followed the road of state-led capitalist development. In terms of state-market relations, there were more similarities between the two countries in that period of time than in more recent times. The Soviet system established under Stalin was in sharp contrast with the Japanese system.

In the postwar era, revolutionary changes took place in Japanese state-market relations. In the USSR, the Stalinist system was sustained until the late 1980s. Although the gap between the Soviet model and the Japanese model has been narrowed since the radical reforms, enormous differences between the Russian system and the Japanese system are going to exist for a long time. If the current market reforms in Russia succeed, however, there will be more similarities and fewer differences between Japan and Russia. Thus, lessons from Japan can be valuable for the Russians.

Second, although it may be too soon to claim the seventy years of Soviet centrally planned system as a total failure, it is safe to say that Soviet efforts to eliminate the market were a complete failure and should not be repeated again. Without the market, state bureaucrats rule. Life is miserable under the mercy of the bureaucrats who put so-called "state interests" ahead of individual rights, civil liberties, and decent levels of consumption. In spite of the tendencies toward over-competition, inflation, unemployment and other market failures, the opportunities and advantages provided by the market far outweigh the possible dangers accompanying the market system. In short, people can be better off in a more market-oriented system than in a heavily state-dominated system. A society with a market has a much better chance for the development of economic competitiveness and political democracy than a society totally controlled by the state.

Third, the monopoly of power by the party-state in the USSR or by the military in Japan was devastating to the market. A healthy market needs the protection of the state. The "market" without legal protection for private ownership and real prices for goods is nothing but an "artificial market." The artificial market cannot perform many functions of the normal market. Thus, legalization of the black market itself is not enough to bring about marketization of a command economy.

Fourth, both the state and the market are institutions evolving with time and space. Therefore, it is impossible to design a single pattern of interaction between the market and the state that is acceptable for all countries at all times. On the other hand, differences among nations do not exclude the possibility for one country to learn from others. While keeping some of its national and cultural traditions, Japan has successfully learned from the West in many aspects.

Fifth, the relations between market freedom and political democracy are similar to that of chickens and eggs. Because of the long historical interactions between the state and the market, it is impossible to separate the two completely. The distinction between the state and the market is more meaningful in analytical than in empirical terms. Just as a biologist can study eggs and chickens separately, a social scientist can examine the state independent from the market. To find out the dynamics of the real life, however, the social scientist had better examine the interaction of the state and the market.

Sixth, transformation of state-market relations also involves a cultural revolution, especially a transition from the command culture to the exchange culture. Charles Lindblom argued that authority is as "fundamental to government as exchange is to the market system."[24] In administrative command systems, centralized power and authority were often supported by the command culture which emphasized the state's right to rule and intervene in socioeconomic life. In contrast, the exchange culture underlies the market-oriented systems in which equal and free exchange of goods and services is the norm rather than the exception.

Questions and Prospects

There are many questions worth further inquiry in future research. For instance, how can some of the conclusions drawn from comparative analysis of Japan and Russia/USSR be further generalized by extending to more case studies? How can state-market relations be operationalized in such a way that will enable theoretical studies based upon empirical data to be carried out on a larger scale? What are the lessons for other societies that are undergoing transitions from centrally planned economies and authoritarian politics to market-oriented economies and political democracy? How can the strength of the state or autonomy of the state versus civil society in general and the market in particular be operationalized? The strength of the state cannot be accurately measured without reasonable operationalization of key variables.

Based upon our study of the patterns of change and continuity in state-market relations in Japan and Russia/USSR, can we predict the future trends of state-market interactions in two countries? What is the best sequence or combination of marketization and democratization? As events have shown, economic reform could not succeed without really epochal political reform, involving a remaking of Soviet/Russian political institutions handed down since Stalin's time. But in most cases, reformers have to take steps first in one field and then in the other. If the reformers are forced to chose their priority, should they first go to marketization or first engage in democratization? Which approach is more realistic? Theoretically, the two should not be separated from each other. In reality, more work needs be done in one field than the other at a particular juncture. How can a wise decision be made when facing two almost equally important and difficult tasks?

An urgent issue for Soviet and post-Soviet studies today is what is going on after the end of the party-state. The popularly elected Russian President Yeltsin officially banned the CPSU from the workplace and the government. Dramatic changes removed the party's ideological and political foundations. By the end of 1991, the CPSU collapsed as a centralized political party. What are and what should be the essential features of the new independent states in the absence of a monolithic communist party? Furthermore, how is the emerging multiparty system going to be institutionalized?

Since the end of World War II, Japan has done remarkably well in building and maintaining dynamic state-market relations that promote quality, productivity, and trade. The Japanese are good at the game of catching up with advanced nations. Having come to the forefront of wealth creation and technological innovation, the new challenge to the Japanese people is whether they can find the vision, and political leadership that will allow them to operate successfully in the global society of today and tomorrow.

The ability to catch up and the credentials to lead are different. Japan lacks some commonly accepted elements of leading powers of the world. Although with a rapidly growing military budget, Japan still does not have the ability and the will to project its military power far beyond its border. In fact, the security of Japan still heavily depends on the U.S.-Japanese security system. With very limited domestic natural resources, Japan totally relies on foreign supply for vital energy and raw materials. If such supply is interrupted by a serious international crisis, Japan will have great difficulties in overcoming shortages. The homogeneity of the Japanese culture, though perceived positively by some Japan experts, will inhibit transmitting Japanese influence in the global community. Internationalization, the catchword for many Japanese in the 1980s, remains a challenging task that cannot be accomplished easily. In spite of many existing and potential problems, many analysts believe that Japan is well prepared to meet the challenges of the next century.[25]

The Cold War confrontation and the economic competition between the centrally planned and market-oriented economies are over, but another competition between two different forms of capitalism is already under way. The individualistic and more market-oriented British-American form of capitalism is competing with the communitarian and more state-directed German and Japanese variants of capitalism. As Lester Thurow points out, "The essential difference between the two forms of capitalism is their stress on communitarian versus individualistic values as the route to economic success."[26]

The industrial technologies critical for success in the twenty-first century include microelectronics, biotechnology, the new materials-science industries, telecommunications, civilian aviation, robotics plus machine tools, and computers plus software. Thurow suggests that Japan, Western Europe, and the United States are the key players in the head-to-head competition for winning these strategic industries.

Considering the current economic crisis in Russia, many analysts tend to count Russia out of the head-to-head competition. For instance, Thurow only pointed out Russia's dilemma without providing any hope for significant progress. "Just letting the market work may take too long, yet active government involvement to speed up the transition is resisted, given everyone's memory of communism."[27]

Does Russia have a chance to win in head-to-head competition in the twenty-first century? There are still reasons for a more optimistic assessment for Russia's future. Like Germany and Japan, Russia trumpets communitarian values rather than individualistic values. Russian culture has strong communitarian roots. Americans believe in "consumer economics"; Japanese believe in "producer economics." Russians have a strong preference for producer economics over consumer economics. Both Japan and Germany believe that government has a vital role to play in economic growth. In Russian history, the state played a significant role in economic development.

Both Germany and Japan were defeated in World War Two. The failure in the war became a great catalyst for change that allowed the two nations to build new state-market relations for postwar economic growth and political development. The USSR was totally defeated in the Cold War. Political and economic failures in the Cold War have had a deep impact on the Russian people. If the Russians learn their lessons well, losing the Cold War can help them prepare themselves better for the political and economic cooperation and competition in the next century.

The collapse of the Soviet empire relieved Russia of some substantial economic, military and political burdens. Empire building and empire maintenance are always expensive. An independent Russia can be much more competitive in the world market than the huge Soviet empire which had unbalanced development and was costly to maintain. In fact, both Russia and Japan have learned through bitter experience that the imperial overextension was both expensive and dangerous.[28]

A relatively well-educated population gives Russia a competitive edge over many other countries entering the new game of head-to-head competition. Russia has one of the largest scientific and technological manpower bases in the world. If fully mobilized by a rational and effective incentive system, human talents and skills can play a decisive role in future Russian economic growth. However, the transformation from basic sciences to applied sciences and productive technology takes time. An enormous amount of training and retraining is necessary for the Russian people to acquire new information and new skills compatible to a market-oriented economy.

Russia is undergoing the unprecedented transition from authoritarian/totalitarian politics to democratic politics, and from a centrally planned to a market-oriented economy. Lessons from postwar reforms in Japan and West Germany can be instructive. Russia is in deep economic and political crisis. However, the Russians have experienced more difficult times. The Germans and the Japanese in the late 1940s were in no better situations. Historical experience suggests that it will be a big mistake if one tries to write off Russia from the future competition of nations. The stake for Russia is extremely high: without making a fundamental shift from the military-territorial state to the trading state, Russia will further lag behind advanced industrial trading nations and possibly will be pushed out of the game in head-to-head competition.

Economic competition is much less dangerous than military confrontation. Thus, the West and Japan have an interest in helping Russia become a responsible and competitive player in the head-to-head economic battle. A Russia isolated from the world economy may go back to the dangerous old game. That is obviously not in the interest of the civilized world.

This is indeed a time for great changes as reforms are going on in both Russia and Japan. For Russia, the main task is to build a new system because the administrative command system has totally collapsed. The task of making a market may turn out to be more difficult than building democracy. As Michael Mandelbaum argues, "Making markets where none existed before is an enterprise of daunting scale. It is far greater in parallel shift from communist to democratic governance."[29] Japan is facing a different type of problem. The key is adapting the existing institutions to new changes in the internal and external environment. To some that means to open up the Japanese market for fair competition. In politics, the main task is to clean the scandal-plagued Liberal Democratic Party and build a truly competitive multiparty democracy. The on-going battles for power, authority, and economic resources will shape and be shaped by the state-market relations.

It is the responsibility of social scientists to study past experience, analyze the current situation and provide guidance for future actions. Social scientists cannot describe the picture of Russia in the year 2000 as accurately as the biologist can anticipate the growth of a particular plant. What we can and should do is to meet the challenges, examine the opportunities and dangers, study alternatives and choices, inform people and help decision-makers to make the best choices. Multi-disciplinary research is necessary and beneficial for understanding the dynamics of state-market relations. Political scientists should pay particular attention to key political variables while not ignoring socioeconomic and cultural factors.

The state and the market are institutions created by human beings for serving people's interests. However, the two institutions seem to have gained a life of their own and tend to go beyond people's control. Market-oriented systems have experienced great depression and economic crises. The state-centered systems have resulted in authoritarianism and totalitarianism which violated or even annihilated basic human rights and political freedom. Obviously, the interaction of the state and the market has a profound impact on people's lives. The more we learn about state-market relations, the better we understand the past events, the current trends, and future directions of human society. More knowledge about state-market relations will lead to greater opportunity for resolving conflicts between the state and the market.

With the end of the Cold War, many factors facilitated the formation and evolution of postwar state-market relations have been removed or lost their initial rationale. As a result of the collapse of the Soviet empire, nationalism and ethnic conflicts have surged to the forefront in the former Soviet Union and Eastern Europe. In contrast, West European countries are accelerating their political and economic integration process. There also is a paradoxical economic situation: the rise of global interdependence and the formation of regional trading blocs have led to conflicting trends of increased trade volume and growing protectionist sentiments. It seems the traditional state-market relations are losing effectiveness in managing new problems. But before human beings build more effective and popular institutions, the state and the market are likely to remain the most important mechanisms dealing with authority and exchange. Therefore, the changing patterns of state-market relations will demand more attention from scholars, policy-makers, and responsible citizens.

Notes

1.   Charles E. Lindblom, *Politics and Markets: The World's Political-Economic Systems* (New York: Basic Books, 1977); John Zysman, *Government, Markets, and Growth: Financial Systems and the Politics of Industrial Change*

(Ithaca: Cornell University Press, 1983); and Susan Strange, *States and Markets* (New York: Basil Blackwell, 1988).

2.   Max Weber, "Politics as a Vocation," in David Held, et al., (eds.), *States and Societies* (New York: Open University Press, 1983), p. 111.

3.   *Ibid.*, p. 112.

4.   Kenneth Jowitt, "Soviet Neotraditionalism: The Political Corruption of a Leninist Regime," *Soviet Studies*, Vol. XXXV, No. 3 (1983), pp. 275-297.

5.   Warren J. Samuels (ed.), *Fundamentals of the Economic Role of Government* (New York: Greenwood Press, 1989).

6.   Robert C. Tucker, "Swollen State, Spent Society: Stalin's Legacy to Brezhnev's Russia," in Erik P. Hoffmann and Robbin F. Laird (eds.), *The Soviet Polity in the Modern Era* (New York: Aldine de Gruyter, 1984), p. 44.

7.   George W. Breslauer, "On the Adaptability of Soviet Welfare-State Authoritarianism," in Hoffmann and Laird, *The Soviet Polity in the Modern Era*, pp. 219-245.

8.   Robert Gilpin, *The Political Economy of International Relations* (Princeton: Princeton University Press, 1987), especially chapter 1.

9.   Chalmers Johnson, *MITI and the Japanese Miracle: The Growth of Industrial Policy, 1925-1975* (Stanford: Stanford University Press, 1982).

10.   Andrew C. Janos, *Politics and Paradigms: Changing Theories of Change in Social Science* (Stanford: Stanford University Press, 1986), p. 123.

11.   Robert C. Tucker, *Stalin in Power: The Revolution from Above, 1928-1941* (New York: W. W. Norton, 1990).

12.   Jerry Hough, *The Soviet Prefect: The Local Party Organs in Industrial Decision-making* (Cambridge: Harvard University Press, 1969).

13.   Richard Rosecrance, *The Rise of the Trading State: Commerce and Conquest in the Modern World* (New York: Basic Books, 1986); Paul Kennedy, *The Rise and Fall of the Great Powers: Economics Change and Military Conflict from 1500 to 2000* (New York: Vintage Books, 1987); and Andrew C. Janos, "Social Science, Communism, and the Dynamics of Political Change," *World Politics*, Vol. 44, No. 1 (1991), pp. 81-112.

14.   Robert E. Ward, "Conclusion," in Ward and Sakamoto Yoshikazu (eds), *Democratizing Japan: The Allied Occupation* (Honolulu: University of Hawaii Press, 1987), pp. 392-433.

15.   Gail W. Lapidus, "State and Society: Toward the Emergence of Civil Society in the Soviet Union," in Seweryn Bialer (ed.), *Politics, Society, and Nationality Inside Gorbachev's Russia* (Boulder: Westview Press, 1989), pp. 121-147; and S. Frederick Starr, "Soviet Union: A Civil Society," Foreign Policy, No. 70 (1988), pp. 26-41.

16.   Stephen F. Cohen, "What's Really Happening in Russia," *The Nation*, March 2, 1991, p. 263.

17.   William E. Butler, "The Role of Law and the Legal System," in Stephen White, Alex Pravda and Zvi Gitelman (eds.), *Developments in Soviet Politics* (Durham: Duke University Press, 1990), pp. 104-119.

18.   Lapidus, "State and Society: Toward the Emergence of Civil Society in the Soviet Union," p. 123.

19.   Alfred B. Evans, Jr., "Rethinking Soviet Socialism," in White, Pravda and Gitelman, *Developments in Soviet Politics*, p. 37.

20.   Seweryn Bialer, "Domestic and International Factors in the Formation of Gorbachev's Reforms," *Journal of International Affairs*, Vol. 42, No. 2 (1989), p. 286.

21.   Mattei Dogan and Dominique Pelassy, *How to Compare Nations: Strategies in Comparative Politics* (Chatham: Chatham House, 1990), pp. 126-130, 144-149.

22.   Andrew G. Walder, *Communist Neo-Traditionalism: Work and Authority in Chinese Industry* (Berkeley: University of California Press, 1986).

23.   "Basic Guideline for the Stabilization of the National Economy and the Transition to a Market Economy," in Foreign Broadcast Information Service, *Daily Report on the Soviet Union*, October 22, 1990, p. 45.

24.   Lindblom, *Politics and Markets*, p. 13.

25.   See Paul Kennedy, *Preparing for the Twenty-First Century* (New York: Random House, 1993), especially chapter 8; and Jeffrey T. Bergner, *The New Superpowers: Germany, Japan and the U.S. and the New World Order*. (New York: St. Martin's Press, 1991).

26.   Lester Thurow, *Head to Head: The Coming Economic Battle Among Japan, Europe, and America* (New York: William Morrow, 1992), p. 32.

27.   *Ibid.*, p. 88.

28.   Jack Snyder, *Myths of Empire: Domestic Politics and International Ambition* (Ithaca: Cornell University Press, 1991), chapters 2 & 6.

29.   Michael Mandelbaum's introduction to Shafiqul Islam and Michael Mandelbaum (eds.), *Making Markets: Economic Transformation in Eastern Europe and the Post-Soviet States* (New York: Council on Foreign Relations Press, 1993), p. 1.

Bibliography

I. Theory and Methodology

Alford, Robert R., and Roger Friedland. 1985. *Powers of Theory: Capitalism, the State, and Democracy*. Cambridge: Cambridge University Press.

Apter, David A. 1965. *The Politics of Modernization*. Chicago: University of Chicago Press.

Bates, Robert H. 1981. *Markets and States in Tropical Africa: The Political Basis of Agricultural Policies*. Berkeley and Los Angeles: University of California Press.

Bendix, Reinhard et al., eds. 1973. *State and Society*. 2d ed. Berkeley: University of California Press.

Bergner, Jeffrey T. 1991. *The New Superpowers: Germany, Japan, the U.S. and the New World Order*. New York: St. Martin's Press.

Bergson, Abram. 1978. *Productivity and the Social System--The USSR and the West*. Cambridge: Harvard University Press.

_____. 1989. *Planning and Performance in Socialist Economies: The USSR and Eastern Europe*. Boston: Unwin Hyman.

Black, Cyril E. 1966. *The Dynamics of Modernization: A Study of Comparative History*. New York: Harper & Row.

Black, Cyril E., et al. 1975. *The Modernization of Japan and Russia: A Comparative Study*. New York: Free Press.

Bornstein, Morris ed. 1979. *Comparative Economic Systems: Models and Cases*. Fourth edition. Homewood, Illinois: Richard D. Irwin.

Brown, Archie and Jack Gray, eds. 1977. *Political Culture and Political Change in Communist States*. New York: Holmes & Meier.

Brus, Wlodzimierz and Kazimierz Laski. 1989. *From Marx to the Market: Socialism in Search of an Economic System*. Oxford: Clarendon Press.

Buchanan, James M. 1986. *Liberty, Market and State: Political Economy in the 1980s*. Brighton, Sussex: Wheatsheaf Books.

148

_____. 1989. *Essays on the Political Economy*. Honolulu: University of Hawaii Press.

Carnoy, Martin. 1984. *The State and Political Theory*. Princeton: Princeton University Press.

Crouch, Colin ed. 1979. *State and Economy in Contemporary Capitalism*. London: Croom Helm.

Dahl, Robert A. 1956. *A Preface to Democratic Theory*. Chicago: University of Chicago Press.

Dahl, Robert, and Charles E. Lindblom. 1953. *Politics, Economics, and Welfare*. New York: Harper.

De Jasay, Anthony. 1985. *The State*. Oxford: Basil Blackwell.

Deutsch, Karl W. 1961. "Social Mobilization and Political Development," *American Political Science Review* 55: 493-502.

Dogan, Mattei, and Dominique Pelassy. 1990. *How to Compare Nations: Strategies in Comparative Politics*. Chatham: Chatham House.

Downs, Anthony. 1957. *An Economic Theory of Democracy*. New York: Harper & Row.

Easton, David. 1981. "*The Political System Besieged by the State*." Political Theory 9: 303-325.

Eckstein, Harry. 1975. "Case Study and Theory in Political Science." In *Handbook of Political Science*, vol.7, ed. Fred I. Greenstein and Nelson W. Polsby. Reading, Mass.: Addison-Wesley.

Elkin, Stephen L. 1985. "Between Liberalism and Capitalism: An Introduction to the Democratic State." In *The Democratic State*, ed. Roger Benjamin and author. Lawrence: University Press of Kansas.

Etzioni, Amitai and Fredric L. Dubow. eds. 1970. *Comparative Perspectives: Theories and Methods*. Boston: Little, Brown.

Evans, Peter B., Dietrich Rueschemeyer, and Theda Skocpol, eds. 1985. *Bringing the State Back In*. New York: Cambridge University Press.

Evans, Peter, D. Rueschemeyer, and E.H. Stephens. eds. 1985. *States versus Markets in the World-System*. Beverly Hills: Sage Publications.

Fagen, Richard R. 1969. *The Transformation of Political Culture in Cuba*. Stanford: Stanford University Press.

Fleron, Frederic J. Jr. ed. 1969. *Communist Studies and the Social Sciences: Essays on Methodology and Empirical Theory*. Chicago: Rand McNally.

Fleron, Frederic J. Jr. and Erik P. Hoffmann. 1991. "Sovietology and Perestroika: Methodology and Lessons from the Past," *The Harriman Institute Forum*, 5, 1: 1-12.

_____. eds. 1993. *Post-Communist Studies & Political Science: Methodology and Empirical Theory in Sovietology*. Boulder: Westview Press.

Fried, Morton H. 1968. "State (The Institution)." In *International Encyclopedia of the Social Sciences*, ed. David L. Sills. New York: Macmillan.

Friedman, Milton. 1982. *Capitalism and Freedom*. Chicago: University of Chicago Press.

Fukuyama, Francis. 1989. "The End of History?" *National Interest* 16: 3-18.

Gerschenkron, Alexander. 1962. *Economic Backwardness in Historical Perspective, A Book of Essays*. Cambridge: Belknap Press of Harvard University Press.

Gilpin, Robert. 1987. *The Political Economy of International Relations*. Princeton: Princeton University Press.

Hall, Peter. 1986. *Governing the Economy: The Politics of State Intervention in Britain and France*. New York: Oxford University Press.

Heibroner, Robert L. 1985. *The Nature and Logic of Capitalism*. New York: W.W. Norton.

Herz, John H. 1957. "Rise and Demise of the Territorial State." *World Politics* 9: 473-493.

Holt, Robert and John Turner. 1966. *The Political Basis of Economic Development*. Princeton: Van Nostrand.

Holt, Robert and John Turner, eds. 1970. *The Methodology of Comparative Research*. New York: Free Press.

Huntington, Samuel P. 1968. *Political Order in Changing Societies*. New Haven: Yale University Press.

Islam, Shafiqul and Michael Mandelbaum. eds. 1993. *Making Markets: Economic Transformation in Eastern Europe and the Post-Soviet States*. New York: Council of Foreign Relations Press.

Janos, Andrew C. 1986. *Politics and Paradigms: Changing Theories of Change in Social Science*. Stanford: Stanford University Press.

_____. 1991. "Social Science, Communism, and the Dynamics of Political Change," *World Politics* 44: 81-112.

Jenkins, Arthur Hugh. 1969. *Adam Smith Today: An Inquiry into the Nature and Causes of the Wealth of Nations*. Port Washington, N.Y.: Kennikat Press.

Johnson, Chalmers. 1974. "Political Science and East Asian Area Studies," *World Politics* 26 (July): 560-575.

Kalleberg, Arthur L. 1966. "The Logic of Comparison: A Methodological Note on the Comparative Study of Political Systems." *World Politics* 19: 69-82.

Katzenstein, Peter J. ed. 1978. *Between Power and Plenty: Foreign Economic Policies of Advanced Industrial States*. Madison: University of Wisconsin Press.

_____. 1985. *Small States in World Markets: Industrial Policy in Europe*. Ithaca: Cornell University Press.

Kennedy, Paul. 1987. *The Rise and Fall of the Great Powers: Economic Change and Military Conflict from 1500 to 2000*. New York: Vintage Books.

_____. 1993. *Preparing for the Twenty-first Century*. New York: Random House.

Keohane, Robert O. 1984. *After Hegemony: Cooperation and Discord in the World Political Economy*. Princeton: Princeton University Press.

Kernell, Samuel ed. 1991. *Parallel Politics: Economic Policymaking in the United States and Japan*. Washington: Brookings Institution.

Kindleberger, Charles P. 1970. *Power and Money: The Economics of International Politics and the Politics of International Economics*. New York: Basic Books.

Krasner, Stephen D. 1976. "State Power and the Structure of International Trade." *World Politics* 28: 317-347.

_____. 1984. "Approaches to the State: Alternative Conceptions and Historical Dynamics." *Comparative Politics* 16: 223-246.

Kuhn, Thomas S. 1970. *The Structure of Scientific Revolutions*. 2nd ed., enlarged. Chicago: University of Chicago Press.

150

Lane, Jan-Erik ed. 1985. *State and Market: The Politics of the Public and the Private*. Beverly Hills: Sage Publications.

Lane, Robert E. 1991. *The Market Experience*. Cambridge: Cambridge University Press.

Lasswell, Harold D., and Abraham Kaplan. 1950. *Power and Society: A Framework for Political Inquiry*. New Haven: Yale University Press.

Lentner, Howard H. 1984. "The Concept of the State: A Response to Stephen Krasner." *Comparative Politics* 16, no.3.

Lijphart, Arend. 1971. "Comparative Politics and the Comparative Method." *American Political Science Review* 65: 682-693.

_____. 1975. "The Comparable-Cases Strategy in Comparative Research." *Comparative Political Studies* 8: 158-177.

Lindblom, Charles E. 1977. *Politics and Markets: The World's Political-Economic Systems*. New York: Basic Books.

_____. 1988. *Democracy and Market System*. London and New York: Norwegian University Press.

Maddison, Angus. 1969. *Economic Growth in Japan and the USSR*. New York: W.W. Norton.

March, James G., and Johan P. Olsen. 1984. "The New Institutionalism: Organizational Factors in Political Life." *American Political Science Review* 78:734 749.

Meckstroth, Theodore W. 1975. "'Most Different System' and 'Most Similar System': A Study in the Logic of Comparative Inquiry," *Comparative Political Studies* 8: 132-157.

Melossi, Dario. 1990. *The State of Social Control: A Sociological Study of Concepts of State and Social Control in the Making of Democracy*. Cambridge: Polity Press.

Moltze, James Clay. 1991. "Commonwealth Economics in Perspectives: Lessons from the East Asian Model." *Soviet Economy* 7: 342-363.

Moore, Barrington, Jr. 1966. *Social Origins of Dictatorship and Democracy: Land and Peasant in the Making of the Modern World*. Cambridge: Harvard University Press.

Nee, Victor, and David Mozingo. eds. 1983. *State and Society in Contemporary China*. Ithaca: Cornell University Press.

Nettl, J.P. 1968. "The State as a Conceptual Variable." *World Politics* 20: 559-592.

Neuberger, Egon, and William J. Fuffy. 1976. *Comparative Economic Systems: A Decision-Making Approach*. Boston: Allyn and Bacon.

Nordlinger, Eric A. 1981. *On the Autonomy of the Democratic State*. Cambridge: Harvard University Press.

Nordlinger, Eric A., Theodore J. Lowi, and Sergio Fabbrini. 1988. "The Return to the State: Critiques." *American Political Science Review* 82: 875-901.

Nye, Joseph S. 1990. "The Changing Nature of World Power." *Political Science Quarterly* 105: 177-192.

Poggi, Gianfranco. 1978. *The Development of the Modern State*. Stanford: Stanford University Press.

Prybyla, Jan S. 1990. *Reform in China and Other Socialist Economies*. Washington: The AEI Press.

Przeworski, Adam, and Henry Teune. 1970. *The Logic of Comparative Social Inquiry*. New York: Wiley-Interscience.

Przeworski, Adam. 1991. *Democracy and the Market: Political and Economic Reforms in Eastern Europe and Latin America*. New York: Cambridge University Press.

Pye, Lucian W. and Sidney Verba. eds. 1965. *Political Culture and Political Development*. Princeton: Princeton University Press.

Rogowski, Ronald. 1983. "Stucture, Growth, and Power: Three Rationalist Accounts," *International Organization*, 37: 713-739.

Rosecrance, Richard. 1986. *The Rise of the Trading State: Commerce and Conquest in the Modern World*. New York: Basic Books.

Rostow, Walt. W. 1971. *Politics and the Stages of Growth*. New York: Cambridge University Press.

Rustow, Dankwart. 1970. "Transition to Democracy: Toward a Dynamic Model." *Comparative Politics* 2, no.3.

Samuels, Warren J., ed. 1989. *Fundamentals of the Economic Role of Government*. New York: Greenwood Press.

Schumpeter, Joseph A. 1950. *Capitalism, Socialism, and Democracy*. 3d ed. New York: Harper and Row.

Shand, Alexander H. 1990. *Free Market Moraltity: The Political Economy of the Austrian School*. London and New York: Routledge.

Skocpol, Theda. 1979. *States and Social Revolutions: A Comparative Analysis of France, Russia, and China*. Cambridge: Cambridge University Press.

Smith, Adam. 1776 (1937). *An Inquiry into the Nature and Causes of the Wealth of Nations*. New York: The Modern Library.

Snyder, Jack. 1991. *Myths of Empire: Domestic Politics and International Ambition*. Ithaca: Cornell University Press.

Stepan, Alfred. 1978. *The State and Society: Peru in Comparative Perspective*. Princeton: Princeton University Press.

Stiglitz, Joseph E. et al. 1989. *The Economic Role of the State*. Oxford: Basil Blackwell.

Strange, Susan. 1988. *States and Markets*. New York: Basil Blackwell.

Strauss, Leo, and Joseph Cropsey. eds. 1987. *History of Political Philosophy*. Chicago: University of Chicago Press.

Wade, Robert. 1990. *Governing the Market: Economic Theory and the Role of Government in East Asian Industrialization*. Princeton: Princeton University Press.

Walder, Andrew G. 1985. "The Political Dimension of Social Mobility in Communist States: Reflections on the Soviet Union and China." In *Research in Political Sociology*, Vol.1, ed. by Richard Braungart, pp. 101-7. Greenwich, Conn.: JAI Press.

_____. 1986. *Communist Neo-Traditionalism: Work and Authority in Chinese Industry*. Berkeley: University of California Press.

Waltz, Kenneth. 1979. *Theory of International Politics*. New York: Random House.

Weber, Max. 1922 (1978). *Economy and Society: An Outline of Interpretative Sociology*, 2 vols. Ed. by Guenther Roth and Claus Wittich. Berkeley and Los Angeles: University of California Press.

_____. 1947. *The Theory of Social and Economic Organization*. New York: Free Press.

_____. 1983. "Politics as a Vocation." In *States and Societies*. eds. David Held, et al. New York: New York University Press.

Weiner, Myron and Samuel Huntington. eds. 1987. *Understanding Political Development*. Boston: Little, Brown.

Welch, Claude E., Jr. 1967. "The Challenge of Change: Japan and Africa," in *Patterns of African Development* ed. Herbert J. Spiro. Englewood Cliffs: Prentice Hall.

_____. ed. 1971. *Political Modernization: A Reader in Comparative Political Change*. 2nd ed. Belmont, CA: Wedsworth.

Whynes, David K. 1983. *Comparative Economic Development*. London and Boston: Butterworths.

Zimbalist, Andrew, H.J. Sherman and S. Brown. 1989. *Comparing Economic Systems: A Political-Economic Approach*. 2nd ed. San Diego: Harcourt Brace Jovanovich.

Zysman, John. 1983. *Government, Markets, and Growth: Financial Systems and the Politics of Industrial Change*. Ithaca: Cornell University Press.

II. Japan

Allen, G.C. 1981. *The Japanese Economy*. London: Weidenfeld and Nicolson.

Balassa, Bela, and Marcus Noland. 1988. *Japan in the World Economy*. Washington, DC: Institute for International Economics.

Barnhart, Michael A. 1987. *Japan Prepares for Total War: The Search for Economic Security, 1919-1941*. Ithaca: Cornell University Press.

Beasley, W.G. 1972. *The Meiji Restoration*. Stanford: Stanford University Press.

Berger, Gordon Mark. *Parties Out of Power in Japan*. Princeton: Princeton University Press.

Berger, Peter L., and Hsin-Huang Michael Hsiao. eds. 1988. *In Search of an East Asian Development Model*. New Brunswick and Oxford: Transaction Books.

Bibney, Frank. 1982. *Miracle by Design: The Real Reasons Behind Japan's economic Success*. New York: Times Books.

The Constitution of Japan. 1947. Published by U.S. Department of State.

Curtis, Gerald L. 1988. *The Japanese Way of Politics*. New York: Columbia University Press.

Dore, Ronald. 1965. *Education in Tokugawa Japan*. Berkeley: University of California Press.

_____. 1987. *Taking Japan Seriously: A Confucian Perspective on Leading Economic Issues*. London: Athlone Press.

Eccleston, Bernard. 1989. *State and Society in Post-War Japan*. Oxford: Polity Press.

Fairbank, John K., Edwin O. Reischauer, and Albert M. Craig. 1973. *East Asia: Tradition and Transformation*. Boston: Houghton Mifflin Company.

Hane, Mikiso. 1986. *Modern Japan: A Historical Survey*. Boulder: Westview Press.

Hollerman, Leon. 1988. *Japan, Disincorporated: The Economic Liberalization Process*. Stanford: Hoover Institution Press.

Inoue, Kyoko. 1991. *MacArthur's Japanese Constitution: A Linguistic and Cultural Study of Its Making*. Chicago: University of Chicago Press.

Ishida, Takeshi, and Ellis S. Krauss. eds. 1989. *Democracy in Japan*. Pittsburgh: University of Pittsburgh Press.

Jansen, Marius B., and Lawrence Stone. 1967. "Education and Modernization in Japan and England," *Comparative Studies in Society and History* 9: 208-232.

Johnson, Chalmers. 1975. "Japan: Who Governs? An Essay on Official Bureaucracy."
Journal of Japanese Studies 2: 1-28.

_____. 1982. *MITI and the Japanese Miracle: The Growth of Industrial Policy,
1925-1975*. Stanford: Stanford University Press.

Kahn, Herman. 1970. *The Emerging Japanese Superstate: Challenge and Response*.
Englewood Cliffs: Prentice-Hall.

Kataoka, Tetsuya ed. 1992. *Creating Singe-Party Democracy: Japan's Postwar
Political System*. Stanford: Hoover Institution Press.

Lockwood, William W. 1954. *The Economic Development of Japan: Growth and
Structural Change: 1868-1938*. Princeton: Princeton University Press.

_____. 1969. "Japan's Response to the West: The Contrast with China." *World
Politics* 1: 366-381.

Lockwood, William W. ed. 1965. *The State and Economic Enterprise in Japan*.
Princeton: Princeton University Press.

Maruyama, Masao. 1963. *Thought and Behavior in Modern Japanese Politics*. New
York: Oxford University Press.

Michio, Morishima. 1982. *Why has Japan "Succeeded"? Western Technology and the
Japanese Ethos*. Cambridge: Cambridge University Press.

Molony, Barbara. 1990. *Technology and Investment: The Prewar Japanese Chemical
Industry*. Cambridge: Harvard University Press.

Mouer, Ross and Yoshio Sugimoto. 1990. *Images of Japanese Society: A Study in the
Social Construction of Reality*. London and New York: Kegan Paul International.

Nakane, Chie. 1970. *Japanese Society*. Berkeley: University of California Press.

Okimoto, Daniel I. 1989. *Between MITI and the Market: Japanese Industrial Policy
for High Technology*. Stanford: Stanford University Press.

Ozaki, Robert S. 1970. "Japanese Views on Industrial Organization." *Asian Survey*,
X, 10: 872-889.

Patrick, Hugh and H. Rosovsky. eds. 1976. *Asia's New Giant: How the Japanese
Economy Works*. Washington, D.C.: The Brookings Institution.

Pempel, T. J. 1982. *Policy and Politics in Japan: Creative Conservatism*.
Philadelphia: Temple University Press.

Reischauer, Edwin, and Albert M. Craig. 1978. *Japan: Tradition & Transformation*.
Boston: Houghton Mifflin.

Reischauer, Edwin. 1981. *The Japanese*. Cambridge: Harvard University Press.

Richardson, Bradley M. 1974. *Political Culture of Japan*. Berkeley: University of
California Press.

Richardson, Bradley M., and Scott C. Flanagan, 1984. *Politics in Japan*. Boston:
Little Brown.

Rosecrance, Richard and Jennifer Taw. 1990. "Japan and the Theory of International
Leadership." *World Politics* 42: 184-209.

Saburo, Okita. 1980. *The Developing Economics and Japan: Lessons in Growth*.
Tokyo: University of Tokyo Press.

Sato, Kazuo. 1990. "Indicative Planning in Japan." *Journal of Comparative Economics*
14: 625-647.

Scalapino, Robert. 1976. "The American Occupation of Japan--Perspectives after Three
Decades," *Annals of American Academy of Political & Social Sciences* 428: 104-113.

Schmiegelow, Michele and Henrik Schmiegelow. 1989. *Strategic Pragmatism: Japanese Lessons in the Use of Economic Theory*. New York and London: Praeger.

Scott, Bruce R., John Rosenblum, and Audrey Sproat. 1980. *Case Studies in Political Economy: Japan 1954-1977*. Boston: Harvard Business School.

Stockwin, J.A. 1984. "Japan as a Political Model?" in *East Asia: International Review of Economic, Political, and Social Development*. vol. 2., pp.3-17. Frankfurt: Campus Verlag.

Vogel, Ezra. ed. 1975. *Modern Japanese Organizations and Decision-making*. Berkeley: University of California Press.

_____. 1979. *Japan as Number One: Lessons for America*. Cambridge: Harvard University Press.

_____. 1985. *Comeback America*. New York: Simon and Schuster.

Ward, Robert E. ed. 1968. *Political Development in Modern Japan*. Princeton: Princeton University Press.

Ward, Robert E., and D. Rustow. eds. 1964. *Political Modernization in Japan and Turkey*. Princeton: Princeton University Press.

Ward, Robert E., and Sakamoto Yoshikazu. eds. 1987. *Democratizing Japan: The Allied Occupation*. Honolulu: University of Hawaii Press. Whitehill, Arthur M. 1991. Japanese Management: Tradition and Transition. London and New York: Routledge.

III. Russia/USSR

Aganbegyan, Abel. 1988. ed. by M.B. Brown. Translated by Pauline Tiffen. *The Challenge: Economics of Perestroika*. London: Hutchinson.

_____. 1989. *Moving the Mountain: Inside the Perestroika Revolution*. Translated by Helen Szamuely. New York: Bantam Press.

Aslund, Anders. 1991. *Gorbachev's Stuggle for Economic Reform*. Ithaca: Cornell University Press.

Bailes, Kendall E. 1978. *Technology and Society under Lenin and Stalin: Origins of the Soviet Technical Intelligentsia, 1917-1941*. Princeton: Princeton University Press.

"Basic Guidelines for the Stabilization of the National Economy and the Transition to a Market Economy," Pravda, October 18, 1990, in Foreign Broadcast Information Service (FBIS), *Daily Report on the Soviet Union*, October 22, 1990.

Battle, John M. 1988. "Uskorenie, Glasnost' and Perestroika: The Pattern of Reform under Gorbachev," *Soviet Studies* XL, 3: 367-384.

Balzer, Harley D. ed. 1991. *Five Years That Shook the World: Gorbachev's Unfinished Revolution*. Boulder: Westview Press.

Bergson, Abram. 1962. *The Real National Income of Soviet Russia Since 1928*. Cambridge: Harvard University Press.

Berliner, Joseph. 1957. *Factory and Manager in the USSR*. Cambridge: Harvard University Press.

Bialer, Seweryn. 1986. *Soviet Paradox: External Expansion, Internal Decline*. New York: Knopf.

_____. 1989. "The Domestic and International Sources of Gorbachev's Reforms." *Journal of International Affairs*. 42: 267-297.

_____. ed. 1989. *Politics, Society, and Nationality Inside Gorbachev's Russia*. Boulder: Westview Press.

Bialer, Seweryn and Michael Mandelbaum. eds. 1988. *Gorbachev's Russia and American Foreign Policy*. Boulder: Westview Press.

Billington, James H. 1966. *The Icon and the Axe: An Interpretive History of Russian Culture*. New York: Knopf.

Birman, Igor. 1978. "From the Achieved Level." *Soviet Studies* XXX: 153-172.

Black, Cyril E. ed. 1960. *The Transformation of Russian Society: Aspects of Social Change Since 1861*. Cambridge: Harvard University Press.

Blackwell, William. 1968. *The Beginnings of Russian Industrialization: 1800-1860*. Princeton: Princeton University Press.

_____. 1970. *The Industrialization of Russia: An Historical Perspective*. New York: Crowell.

Blum, Jerome. 1961. *Lord and Peasant in Russia: From the Ninth to the Nineteenth Century*. Princeton: Princeton University Press.

Bornstein, Morris. ed. 1981. *The Soviet Economy: Continuity and Change*. Boulder: Westview Press.

_____. 1991. "Soviet Assessment of Economic Reforms in Other Socialist Countries." *Soviet Economy* 7: 14-45.

Bova, Russell. 1988. "The Soviet Military and Economic Reform," *Soviet Studies* XL, 3: 385-405.

_____. 1991. "Political Dynamics of the Post-Communist Transition: A Comparative Perspective." *World Politics* 44: 113-138.

Breslauer, George W. 1982. *Khrushchev and Brezhnev as Leaders: Building Authority in Soviet Politics*. Boston: George Allen & Unwin.

_____. 1990. "Soviet Economic Reform Since Stalin: Ideology, Politics, and Learning." *Soviet Economy* 6, 3: 252-280.

Burant, Stephen R. 1987. "The Influence of Russian Tradition on the Political Style of the Soviet Elite." *Political Science Quarterly* 102: 273-29.

Claudin-Urondo, Carmen. 1977. *Lenin and the Cultural Revolution*. Translated from French by Brian Pearce. Atlantic Highlands, N.J.: Humanities Press.

Cohen, Stephen F. 1985. *Rethinking the Soviet Experience: Politics and History Since 1917*. New York: Oxford University Press.

_____. 1992. "What's Really Happening in Russia?" *The Nation*. (March 2), 259-268.

Cohen, Stephen F., and Katrina vanden Heuvel. 1989. *Voices of Glasnost: Interviews with Gorbachev's Reformers*. New York: W.W. Norton & Company.

Colton, Timothy J. 1986. *The Dilemma of Reform in the Soviet Union*, 2nd ed. New York: Council on Foreign Relations.

Conquest, Robert. 1986. *The Harvest of Sorrow: Soviet Collectivization and the Terror-Famine*. New York: Oxford University Press.

Davies, R.W. 1980. The Socialist Offensive: *The Collectivisation of Soviet Agriculture, 1929-1930*. Cambridge: Harvard University Press.

Eklof, Ben. 1989. *Soviet Briefing: Gorbachev and the Reform Period*. Boulder: Westview Press.

Fitzpatrick, Sheila ed. 1978. *Cultural Revolution in Russia, 1928-1931*. Bloomington: Indiana University Press.

Fitzpatrick, Sheila, Alexander Robinowitch, and Richard Stites eds. 1991. *Russia in the Era of Nep: Explorations in Soviet Society and Culture*. Bloomington: Indiana University Press.

Flaherty, Patrick. 1990. "The State and the Dominant Class in the Soviet Perestoika." In *Research in Political Economy*. Vol. 12. ed. Paul Zarembka. Greenwich and London: JAI Press.

Fleron, Frederic J., Jr. and Lou Jean Fleron. 1972. "Administration Theory as Repressive Political Theory: The Communist Experience," *Telos* 12: 63-92.

Fleron, Frederic J., Jr. ed. 1977. *Technology and Communist Culture: The Socio-Cultural Impact of Technology under Socialism*. New York: Praeger.

Friedrich, Carl J., and Zbigniew K. Brzezinski. 1966. *Totalitarian Dictatorship and Autocracy*. 2nd ed. rev. New York: Praeger.

Gardner, H. Stephen. 1983. *Soviet Foreign Trade: The Decision Process*. Boston: Kluwer-Nijhoff Publishing.

Gelman, Harry. 1990. *Gorbachev's First Five Years in the Soviet Leadership: The Clash of Personalities and the Remaking of Institutions*. Santa Monica: RAND.

Gershenkron, Alexander. 1970. "Problems and Patterns of Russian Economic Development." In *The Structure of Russian History*. ed. Michael Cherniavsky. New York: Random House.

Goldman, Marshall. 1987. *Gorbachev's Challenge. Economic Reform in the Age of High Technology*. New York: W.W. Norton.

_____. 1991. *What Went Wrong with Perestroika*. New York: W.W. Norton.

Gorbachev, Mikhail. 1988. *Perestroika: New Thinking for Our Country and the World*. Updated ed. New York: Harper & Row.

Graham, Loren. 1990. *Science and Social Order in the Soviet Union*. Cambridge: Harvard University Press.

Green, Donald W. 1991. "The Soviet Economy Through Nine Months of 1991: Country Falling Apart, Economy Collapsing," *PlanEcon Report* 7: 43-44.

Gregory, Paul R. and Robert Stuart. 1981. *Soviet Economic Structure and Performance*. 2nd ed. New York: Harper & Row.

Hewett, Ed A. 1988. *Reforming the Soviet Economy: Equality versus Efficiency*. Washington, D.C.: The Brookings Institution.

_____. 1990/91. "The New Soviet Plan." *Foreign Affairs* 69, 5: 146-166.

Hewett, Ed A., and Victor H. Winston. eds. 1991. *Milestones in Glasnost and Perestroika: The Economy*. Washington: The Brookings Institution.

_____. eds. 1991. *Milestones in Glasnost and Perestroika: Politics and People*. Washington: The Brookings Institution.

Hoffmann, Erik P., and Frederic J. Fleron, Jr. eds. 1980. *The Conduct of Foreign Policy*. 2nd edition. Hawthorne: Aldine Publishing Company.

Hoffmann, Erik P. and Robbin Laird. 1982. *The Politics of Modernization in the Soviet Union*. Ithaca: Cornell University Press.

_____. eds. 1984. *The Soviet Polity in the Modern Era*. New York: Aldine de Gruyter.

_____. 1985. *Technocratic Socialism: The Soviet Union in the Advanced Industrial Era*. Durham: Duke University Press.

Hosking, Geoffrey. 1985. *The First Socialist Society: A History of the Soviet Union from Within*. Cambridge: Harvard University Press.

_____. 1990. *The Awakening of the Soviet Union.* Cambridge: Harvard University Press.

Hough, Jerry F. 1969. *The Soviet Prefect: The Local Party Organs in Industrial Decision-making.* Cambridge: Harvard University Press.

_____. 1983. "Pluralism, Corporatism and the Soviet Union." In *Pluralism in the Soviet Union*, ed. by Susan G. Soloman. London: Macmillan.

_____. 1988a. *Opening Up the Soviet Economy.* Washington, DC: The Brookings Institution.

_____. 1988b. *Russia and the West: Gorbachev and the Politics of Reform.* New York: Simon and Schuster.

IMF, International Monetary Fund, The World Bank, Organization for Economic Cooperation and Development, European Bank for Reconstruction and Development. 1990. *A Study of the Soviet Economy.* Paris: OECD.

Ioffe, Olimpiad S. 1989. ed. by David Rome. *Gorbachev's Economic Dilemma: An Insider's View.* St. Paul: Merrill/Magnus.

Jowitt, Kenneth. 1983. "Soviet Neotraditionalism: The Political Corruption of a Leninist Regime." *Soviet Studies* 35, no.3 (July): 275-297.

Joyce, John M. 1984. "The Old Russian Legacy." *Foreign Policy* 55: 132-153.

Juviler, Peter, and Miroshi Kimura. eds. 1988. *Gorbachev's Reform.* New York: A de Gruyter.

Katsenelinboigen, Aron. 1977. "Coloured Markets in the Soviet Union." *Soviet Studies* 29: 62-85.

Keenan, Edward L. 1986. "Muscovite Political Folkways." The *Russian Review* 45: 115-181.

Kushnirsky, Fyodor I. 1982. *Soviet Economic Planning, 1965-1980.* Boulder: Westview Press.

Lavigne, Marie. 1990. *Financing the Transition in the USSR: The Shatalin Plan and the Soviet Economy.* New York: Institute for East-West Security Studies.

Lewin, Moshe. 1978. "Society, State, and Ideology during the First Five Year Plan." In *Cultural Revolution in Russia, 1928-1931*, ed. by Sheila Fitzpatrick, pp. 41-77. Bloomington: Indiana University Press.

Lukacs, John. 1986. "The Soviet State at 65." *Foreign Affairs* 65: 1 (Fall), pp.21-37.

Lynch, Allen. 1989. *The Soviet Study of International Relations.* Cambridge and New York: Cambridge University Press.

McKay, John P. 1970. *Pioneers for Profits: Foreign Entrepreneurship and Russian Industrialization, 1885-1913.* Chicago: University of Chicago Press.

Motyl, Alexander J. 1990. *Sovietology, Rationality, Nationality: Coming to Grips with Nationalism in the USSR.* New York: Columbia University Press.

_____. 1980. *The Soviet Economic System.* 2nd ed. London: Allen & Unwin.

_____. 1989. *Glasnost' in Action: Cultural Renaissance in Russia.* Boston: Unwin Hyman.

"The Novosibirsk Report." 1983. *Survey* 28, 1: 88-108.

Ofer, Gur. 1990. "Revolution in the Socialist System: The Convergence Hypothesis Revisited." Paper presented to the Conference on "The Economic Contest Between Communism and Capitalism: What's Ahead?" Institute for the Study of Free Enterprise Systems, State University of New York at Buffalo.

Parrott, Bruce. 1983. *Politics and Technology in the Soviet Union.* Cambridge: MIT Press.

Robertson, Myles L. 1988. *Soviet Policy towards Japan: An Analysis of Trends in the 1970s and 1980s.* New York: Cambridge University Press.

Rutland, Peter. 1985. *The Myth of the Plan: Lessons of Soviet Planning Experience.* London: Hutchinson.

Schapiro, Leonard. 1971. *The Communist Party of the Soviet Union.* New York: Vintage Books.

The Shatalin Working Group formed by a joint decision of M.S. Gorbachev and B.N. Yeltsin. 1990. *Transition to the Market: Part I (The Concept and Program).* Translated and printed by the Cultural Initiative Foundation, Moscow.

Smith, Gordon. 1987. *Soviet Politics: Continuity and Contradiction.* New York: St. Martin's Press.

Soviet Foreign Policy Today: Reports from the Soviet Press. 1989. Selections from the *Current Digest of Soviet Press.* 3rd ed.

Starr, S. Frederick. 1988. "Soviet Union: A Civil Society." *Foreign Policy* 70: 26-41.

Sutton, Antony C. 1968. *Western Technology and Soviet Economic Development, 1917 to 1930.* Stanford: Hoover Institution Press.

_____. 1976. *Western Technology and Soviet Economic Development, 1930-1945.* Stanford: Hoover Institution Press.

Treadgold, Donald W. 1987. *Twentieth Century Russia.* Boulder: Westview Press.

Tucker, Robert C. 1987. *Political Culture and Leadership in Soviet Russia: From Lenin to Gorbachev.* New York: W.W. Norton & Company.

_____. 1990. *Stalin in Power: The Revolution from Above, 1928-1941.* New York: W.W. Norton & Company.

Van Atta, Don. 1989. "The USSR as a 'Weak State': Agrarian Origins of Resistance to Perestroika." *World Politics* 42: 129-149.

Viola, Lynne. 1987. *The Best Sons of the Fatherland: Workers in the Vanguard of Soviet Collectivization.* New York: Oxford University Press.

Von Lau, Theodore H. 1963. *Sergei Witte and the Industrialization of Russia.* New York: Columbia University Press.

_____. 1964. *Why Lenin? Why Stalin? A Reappraisal of the Russian Revolution, 1900-1930.* Philadelphia and New York: Lippincott.

White, Stephen, Alex Pravda, and Zvi Gitelman. eds. 1990. *Developments in Soviet Politics.* Durham: Duke University Press.

Zaleski, Eugene. 1971. *Planning for Economic Growth in the Soviet Union, 1918-1932.* Chapel Hill: University of North Carolina Press.

_____. 1980. *Stalinist Planning for Economic Growth, 1933-1952.* Chapel Hill: University of North Carolina Press.

Index

About the Book and Author

This pathbreaking study provides the first comprehensive comparative analysis of states and markets in Japan and Russia/USSR. Utilizing a strong theoretical foundation, Guoli Liu examines the interaction of the state and market in general and the transition from one type of state-market relationship to another. In an ambitious attempt to discover macro trends and changing patterns of state-market relations, the author compares six leading cases in Japanese and Russian/Soviet history from the 1860s to the early 1990s, with an emphasis on post–World War II development.

By bridging the gap between political and economic analysis and by integrating two significant but isolated bodies of area studies literature on Japan and Russia, this book will advance understanding of democratization and marketization in societies with markedly different political and socioeconomic backgrounds. Moving smoothly from the theoretical to the pragmatic, the author also draws on the Japanese experience to suggest policy options for Russia as the country moves simultaneously from a totalitarian/authoritarian to a democratic state and from a planned to a market-oriented economy.

Guoli Liu is assistant professor of political science at the College of Charleston. He received his Ph.D. in political science from the State University of New York–Buffalo and was visiting assistant professor at the State University of New York–Brockport.